Praise for *Index, A History of the*

"Engaging. . . . [Dennis] Duncan draws rich parallels to anxieties surrounding our own 'age of search' and makes an impassioned case for the continued relevance of the human-crafted index." —*The New Yorker*

"Entertaining and erudite. . . . In an unexpectedly high-spirited book on indexes, the fun continues to the very last page." —Barbara Spindel, *Christian Science Monitor*

"A decidedly fun history . . . Dennis Duncan's enthusiasm for the subject matter shines through." —Erica Ezeifedi, *Book Riot*

"A learned and playful study, by British academic Dennis Duncan, of a textual machinery so successful it's become almost invisible." —Brian Dillon, *4Columns*

"Duncan . . . mixes humor and scholarship to brilliant effect in this accessible deep dive. . . . [E]nlightening and entertaining." —*Publishers Weekly*, starred review

"Sparkles with geeky wit . . . and shines with an infectious enthusiasm. . . . Always erudite, frequently funny, and often surprising—a treat for lovers of the book qua book." —*Kirkus Reviews*, starred review

"Backmatter has never enjoyed such a spotlight; sure to amuse bibliophiles and casual readers alike." —*Library Journal*, starred review

"[A] witty and wide-ranging study. . . . [Duncan] is adventurous as well, often writing as if academic research were as revved-up as a Formula One race."

—Peter Conrad, *Guardian*

"To me, a truly great history book is one that changes something in the way in which I see the world. Dennis Duncan's *Index, A History of the* certainly achieved that."

—Katja Hoyer, *History Today* (UK)

"As Dennis Duncan's charming book shows, though today they suggest fusty libraries, indexes were once a novelty."

—*Economist*

"Duncan proves an amiable companion on what his subtitle aptly refers to as a 'bookish adventure.'"

—James Waddell, *Times Literary Supplement*

"Dennis Duncan's fascinating study of the origins of the index offers subversion, whimsy—and hope."

—Houman Barekat, *Financial Times*

"[A] puckish eulogy to an often overlooked appendage. . . . [W]ittily engaging [and] wide-ranging."

—Adam Douglas, *Literary Review* (UK)

"Masterful. . . . [B]oth an entertaining and edifying journey through index-history and a spirited defense of the index (and indexers) in the technological age."

—Michael Delgado, *Prospect*

"I learned a huge amount from this wry, clever, diverting book. . . . [E]xceptionally good."
—Stuart Kelly, *Scotsman*

"An exemplar of contemporary scholarship, *Index, A History of the* will change how people think about indexes, and may well change how people think about books."
—Stuart Kells, *Sydney Morning Herald*

Index, A History of the

A Bookish Adventure from Medieval
Manuscripts to the Digital Age

DENNIS DUNCAN

W. W. NORTON & COMPANY
Celebrating a Century of Independent Publishing

For Mia and Molly

For information about permission to reproduce selections from this book, write to
Permissions, W. W. Norton & Company, Inc., 500 Fifth Avenue, New York, NY 10110

For information about special discounts for bulk purchases, please contact
W. W. Norton Special Sales at specialsales@wwnorton.com or 800-233-4830

Manufacturing by Lakeside Book Company

Library of Congress Cataloging-in-Publication Data

Names: Duncan, Dennis (Dennis J. B.), author.
Title: Index, a history of the : a bookish adventure from medieval manuscripts to the
digital age / Dennis Duncan.
Description: First American edition. | New York, NY : W. W. Norton & Company, 2022. |
First published in Great Britain under the title Index, a history of the : a bookish adventure. |
Includes bibliographical references and index.
Identifiers: LCCN 2021050496 | ISBN 9781324002543 (hardcover) |
ISBN 9781324002550 (epub)
Subjects: LCSH: Indexing—History. | Indexes—History.
Classification: LCC Z695.9 D86 2022 | DDC 025.3—dc23/eng/20211123
LC record available at https://lccn.loc.gov/2021050496

ISBN 978-1-324-05051-3 pbk.

W. W. Norton & Company, Inc., 500 Fifth Avenue, New York, N.Y. 10110
www.wwnorton.com

W. W. Norton & Company Ltd., 15 Carlisle Street, London W1D 3BS

1 2 3 4 5 6 7 8 9 0

Contents

Introduction

'I for my part venerate the inventor of Indexes . . .
that unknown labourer in literature who first laid
open the nerves and arteries of a book.'

Isaac D'Israeli, *Literary Miscellanies*

It is hard to imagine working with books – writing an essay, a lecture, a report, a sermon – without the ability to find what you're looking for, quickly and easily: without, that is, the convenience of a good index. This convenience, of course, is not confined to people who write for a living. It spills over into other disciplines, into everyday life, and some of the earliest indexes appear in legal statutes, medical texts, recipe books. The humble back-of-book index is one of those inventions that are so successful, so integrated into our daily practices, that they can often become invisible. But, like any piece of tecÙology, the index has its history, one that, for nearly 800 years, was intimately entwined with a particular form of the book – the codex: the sheaf of pages, folded and bound together at the spine. Now, however, it has entered the digital era as the key tecÙology underpinning our online reading. The very first webpage, after all, was a subject index.[1] As for the search engine, the port of embarkation for so much of our internet navigation, Google engineer Matt Cutts explains that 'The first thing to understand is that when you do a Google search, you aren't actually searching the web. You're

[handwritten marginal annotations:] occurs throughout the book ? · is this meaningful ? · ??

I

searching Google's index of the web.'[2] Today, the index organizes our lives, and this book will chart its curious path from the monasteries and universities of Europe in the thirteenth century to the glass-and-steel HQs of Silicon Valley in the twenty-first.

A history of the index is really a story about time and knowledge and the relationship between the two. It's the story of our accelerating need to access information at speed, and of a parallel need for the contents of books to be divisible, discrete, extractable units of knowledge. This is information science, and the index is a fundamental element of that discipline's architecture. But the evolution of the index also offers us a history of reading in microcosm. It is bound up with the rise of the universities and the arrival of printing, with Enlightenment philology and punchcard computing, the emergence of the page number and of the hashtag. It is more than simply a data structure. Even today, faced with the incursions of Artificial Intelligence, the book index remains primarily the work of flesh-and-blood indexers, professionals whose job is to mediate between author and audience. The product of human labour, indexes have produced human consequences, saving heretics from the stake and keeping politicians from high office. They have also, naturally, attracted people with a special interest in books, and our roster of literary indexers will include Lewis Carroll, Virginia Woolf, Alexander Pope and Vladimir Nabokov. The compiling of indexes has not, historically, been either the most glamorous or the most lucrative of professions. We might think of Thomas Macaulay's lament that Samuel JoÙson, the most eminent writer of his age, nevertheless spent his days surrounded by 'starving pamphleteers and indexmakers'.[3] Had he but known it, JoÙson might at least have consoled himself with the thought that in this company of indexers he would be surrounded by the most eminent writers of other ages too, and that, though undersung, the tecÙology they were tinkering with would be central to the reading experience at the dawn of the next millennium.

What do we mean by an index? At its most general, it is a system adopted as a timesaver, telling us where to look for things. The name suggests a spatial relationship, a map of sorts: something here will point you to – will *indicate* – something there. The map need not exist in the world; it is enough for it to exist in our minds. Writing in the middle of the last century, Robert Collison proposed that, whenever we organize the world around us so that we know where to find things, we are in fact indexing. He offers a pair of illustrations that could hardly be more 1950s if they came wearing brothel creepers: !!

> When a housewife makes a separate place for everything in the kitchen she is in fact creating a living index, for not only she, but all her household, will gradually get used to the system she has created and be able to discover things for themselves . . . A man will get into the habit of always putting change in one pocket, keys in another, cigarette-case in a third – an elementary indexing habit which stands him in good stead when he checks up in his hurry to the station to see whether he has remembered his season-ticket.[4]

A mental index: that's how women find the sugar and men find their cigarette-cases. In fact, glibness aside, Collison makes an important point here. The mapping of the kitchen works not just for the housewife but for 'all her household': it exists in multiple minds. What if someone were to write it down: 'flour: top cupboard on the right; spoons: drawer by the fridge', and so on? Then we would have a system that could be used instantly, on the fly, even by someone who was unfamiliar with the kitchen. Now we are getting closer to something more like what we, surely, think of as an index, something that doesn't exist solely in the mind; a kind of list or table telling us where things are. We expect some abbreviation, presumably. A map that's as big as the territory is an absurdity; so too with an index. A library catalogue – library catalogues, as we will see in Chapter 1, have played a major role in information science – will boil books down to their salient details: title, author, genre. In the same way, a back-of-book index will distil its source work into a collection of keywords: names, places, concepts. Abstraction, then: reducing the material, summarizing it, to create something new and separate. The index is not a copy of the thing itself.

What else? As Collison says, most of us can carry around the layout of a kitchen in our heads. If you had to write it down, how long would your kitchen inventory be? Not, perhaps, unmanageable. But what about a longer inventory? All the objects in your house? All the books in a library? When the list approaches a certain length it becomes unwieldy: it becomes no more convenient to search through the list than to search the shelves themselves. What we need is arrangement. The index needs to be ordered in a way that its users will recognize, that makes it easy to navigate. This is where the index and the table of contents diverge.

Samuel JoÙson's *Dictionary*, rather unhelpfully, defines *index* as 'the table of contents to a book', and on the face of it the two have much in common. Both are lists of labels with locators, i.e. page numbers (but, as we'll see, the page number too has its own history, and other types of locator – Bible chapters, for instance – predate it). Both point to places in, or sections of, the main text, and in the late Middle Ages the two even go by the same array of names – *register*, *table*, *rubric* – making them indistinguishable without closer inspection. When Chaucer's Knight briskly refuses to speculate on what happens to one of the characters in his tale after their death – 'I nam no divynistre: / "Of soules" find I nought in this registre' (in other words, 'I have no special insight: my register has no entry for "Souls"') – it is hard to know precisely which type of list he has in mind. Nevertheless, the two are quite distinct book parts – bookends straddling the main text, one before, one after – each with its own function and history.

Even without locators, the table of contents provides an overview of a work's structure: it follows the ordering of the text, revealing its architecture. We can glance at a table and reasonably conjecture what the overall argument is. To a degree, therefore, a table of contents is platform independent. It offers broad-brush navigation even in a work that exists as a series of scrolls – and indeed it has a history that stretches back into antiquity, before the arrival of the codex. We know of at least four Latin writers, and one Greek, from the classical period who attached a table of contents to their works.[5] Here, for example, is Pliny the Elder, the great Roman naturalist, dedicating his magnum opus the *Natural History* to the Emperor Titus:

> As it was my duty in the public interest to have consideration for claims upon your time, I have appended to this letter a table of contents of the several books, and have taken very careful precautions to prevent your having to read them. You by these means will secure for others that they will not need to read right through them either, but

only look for the particular point that each of them wants, and will know where to find it.[6]

Or, to paraphrase, 'Because you're so busy and important, I know you won't be able to read the whole thing. Therefore, I've attached a handy table so you can browse what's on offer and pick the chapters that interest you.'

A lengthy work like the *Natural History* would be spread over many scrolls, maybe even dozens. Locating a portion of the work would be a matter first of finding the right one, then laying it on the table and unfurling it carefully to the desired section. Not an unimaginably tedious process, as long as one *does* end up at the desired section. The chapter, after all, is a large enough division of text to make the effort worthwhile. But let us for a moment allow ourselves an anachronistic fantasy: let us imagine that, along with the table of contents, Pliny also supplies a new device with his work, an innovation beamed in from another age a thousand years hence, an instrument that Pliny, without knowing quite why, decides to call an 'index'. And let us imagine that Titus, late one night, is moved to see what the *Natural History* has to say about one of his predecessors on the throne, the Emperor Nero, murderer of Titus' childhood best friend. (In modern webspeak we have a name for this type of late-night reading: doomscrolling.) By candlelight our imperial reader unrolls Pliny's index. The *Natural History* makes six references to Nero: three in Book VIII, one in Book X, a couple more in Book XI. Titus notes them all down and, after locating the scroll containing Book VIII, spends an age finding the first mention, a passing reference to a minor architectural alteration to the Circus Maximus carried out at Nero's command. Another frenzy of rolling and unrolling, but the second reference is even more glancingly related to the topic in hand. It concerns the faithful howling of a dog distraught at its master's execution under Nero. Titus groans. By now he is getting frustrated. The balance of labour and reward, of time spent scrolling versus time spent reading, is not, he reasons, a favourable one. He checks the third locator, but several minutes later all he has learned is that his predecessor once spent 4 million sesterses on woollen bedspreads. The Emperor allows himself a brief smile then retires, unsatisfied, to bed. It is not hard to see why the index is an invention of the codex era, and not the age of the scroll. It is a truly random-access tecÙology, and as such it relies on a form of the book that can be opened with as much ease in the middle, or at the end, as at the beginning. The codex is the medium in which the index first makes sense.

Furthermore, unlike a table of contents, an index without locators is about as much use as a bicycle without wheels. It doesn't enable us to gauge roughly where to open the book, and it doesn't present us with the argument in summary. This is because the chief mechanism of the index is arbitrariness. Its principal innovation is in severing the relationship between the structure of the work and the structure of the table. The ordering of an index is reader-oriented, rather than text-oriented: if you know what you're looking for, the letters of the alphabet provide a universal, text-independent system in which to look it up. (We might even say that most indexes are doubly arbitrary, since the commonest locator – the page number – bears no intrinsic relationship to the work or its subject matter, but only to its medium, the book.)

So, while the odd table of contents may creep in from time to time, this is a book about the index, about the alphabetical table that breaks down a book into its constituents, its characters, its subjects, or even its individual words; a piece of tecÙology – an add-on – designed to speed up a certain mode of reading, what academics have taken to calling 'extract reading', for those of us who, like the Emperor Titus, are too time-poor to start at the beginning.

As for the vexed issue of the plural – whether we should use the Anglicized *indexes* or the Latinate *indices* – the great Victorian bibliographer Henry Wheatley, in his book *What is an Index?* (1878), points to Shakespeare's *Troilus and Cressida*, where the word is *indexes*. If the Anglicized form is good enough for Shakespeare, reasons Wheatley, it should be good enough for us, and this book will follow him in this. Indices are for mathematicians and economists; indexes are what you find at the back of a book.

When I first began to teach English Literature at university, here is how a lesson would typically begin:

> Me: Can everyone please turn to page one hundred and twenty-eight of *Mrs Dalloway*?
> Student A: What page is it in the Wordsworth edition?
> Student B: What page is it in the Penguin edition?
> Student C (*holding up a book: mid-century; hardback; no jacket*): I don't know what edition I've got – it's my mum's. What chapter is it?

After a minute or so, homing in via chapters and paragraphs, we would all be ready to analyse the same passage, only to go through the same process a couple of times more each class. About seven years ago, however, I noticed that something different was beginning to happen. I would still ask everyone to look at a particular extract from the novel; I would still, more in hope than expectation, give the page reference from the prescribed edition; a sea of hands would still go up immediately. But this time the question would be different: 'What does the passage start with?' Many of the students now were reading on digital devices – on Kindles, on iPads, sometimes on their phones – devices which did not use page numbers, but which came equipped with a search function. Historically, a special type of index, known as a concordance, would present an alphabetical list of every word in a given text – the works of Shakespeare, say, or the Bible – and all the places they appear. In my classroom I began to notice how the power of the concordance had been extended infinitely. Digitization had meant that the ability to search for a particular word or phrase was no longer tied to an individual work; now it was part of the eReader's software platform. Whatever you're reading, you can always hit Ctrl+F if you know what you're looking for: 'One of the triumphs of civilisation, Peter Walsh thought.'

At the same time, the ubiquity of the search engine has given rise to a widespread anxiety that search has become a mentality, a mode of reading and learning that is supplanting the old modes, bringing with it a host of cataclysmic ills. It is, we are told, changing our brains, shortening our attention spans and eroding our capacity for memory. In literature, the novelist Will Self has declared that the serious novel is dead: we no longer have the patience for it.[7] This is the Age of Distraction, and it is the search engine's fault. A few years ago, an influential article in the *Atlantic* asked the question, 'Is Google Making Us Stupid?' and answered, strongly, in the affirmative.[8]

But if we take the long view, this is nothing more than a recent outbreak of an old fever. The history of the index is full of such fears – that nobody will read properly any more,

that extract reading will take the place of lengthier engage-
ments with books, that we will ask new questions, perform
new types of scholarship, forget the old ways of close reading, become deplorably, incurably inattentive – and all because
of that infernal tool, the book index. In the Restoration
period, the pejorative *index-raker* was coined for writers who
pad out their works with unnecessary quotations, while on
the Continent Galileo grumbled at the armchair philosophers
who, 'in order to acquire a knowledge of natural effects, do
not betake themselves to ships or crossbows or cannons, but
retire into their studies and glance through an index or a table
of contents to see whether Aristotle has said anything about
them'.[9] The book index: killing off experimental curiosity
since the seventeenth century.

And yet, four centuries later, the sky has not fallen down.
The index has endured, but so, alongside it, have readers,
scholars, inventors. The way we read (the *ways* that we read,
we should say, since everyone, every day, reads in many different modes: novels, newspapers, menus, street signs all require
a different type of attention of us) might not be the same as
twenty years ago. But neither were the ways we read then the
same as those of, say, Virginia Woolf's generation, or a family
in the eighteenth century, or during the first flush of the printing press. Reading does not have a Platonic ideal (and, for
Plato, as we will find out, it was far from ideal). What we consider to be normal practice has always been a response to a
complex of historical circumstances, with every shift in the
social and tecÙological environment producing an evol-
utionary effect in what 'reading' means. Not to evolve as
readers – to wish that, as a society, we still read habitually with
the same profound absorption as, say, the inhabitants of an
eleventh-century monastery, isolated from society with a

library of half a dozen volumes – is as absurd as complaining that a butterfly is not beautiful enough. It is how it is because it has adapted perfectly to its environment.

This history of the book index, then, will do more than recount simply the successive refinements of this seemingly innocuous piece of text tecÙology. It will show how the index responded to other shifts in the reading ecosystem – the rise of the novel, of the coffee-house periodical, of the scientific journal – and how readers, and reading, changed at these points. And it will show how the index often shouldered the blame for the anxieties of those invested in the modes of reading that went before. It will chart the relative fortunes of two types of index, the word index (also known as a *concordance*) and the subject index, the first unfailingly faithful to the text it serves, the second balancing its allegiances between the work and the community of readers who will come to it. Both emerged at the same moment in the Middle Ages, with the subject index rising steadily in stature so that, by the mid nineteenth century, Lord Campbell could boast of having tried to make indexes mandatory by law in new books.[10] The concordance, by contrast, remained a specialist tool for much of the last millennium before roaring to prominence after the emergence of modern computing. But, for all our recent reliance on digital search tools, on search bars and Ctrl+F, I hope that this book will show that there is still life – exactly that: *life* – in the old back-of-book subject index, compiled by indexers who are very much alive. With this in mind, and before we start in earnest, two examples will illustrate the distinction I have been attempting to draw.

In March 1543, Henry VIII's religious authorities raided the home of JoÙ Marbeck, a chorister at St George's Chapel in

Windsor. Marbeck was accused of having copied out a religious tract by the French theologian JoÙ Calvin. In doing so, he had broken a recent law against heresy. The penalty was death by burning. A search of Marbeck's house turned up evidence of further questionable activity, handwritten sheets that testified to an immense and unusual literary endeavour. Marbeck had been compiling a concordance to the English Bible. He was about halfway through. Only half a decade previously, the Bible in English had been contraband, its translators sent to the stake. Marbeck's concordance looked suspicious, precisely the kind of unauthorized reading that had made the translation of the scriptures such a contentious matter. The banned tract had been his original crime, but now the concordance was, as Marbeck put it, 'not one of the least matters . . . to aggrauate the cause of my trouble'.[11] He was taken to Marshalsea prison. It was likely that he would be executed.

In Marshalsea, Marbeck came under interrogation. The authorities were aware of a Calvinist sect in Windsor and saw Marbeck as a minor player, someone who might, under pressure, implicate others. For Marbeck this was a chance to acquit himself. With regard to the Calvinist tract, the statute forbidding it had only come into law four years earlier in 1539. But, protested Marbeck, he had made his copy before that. A simple defence. The concordance posed a more serious problem. While ardently religious and industriously literate, Marbeck was also an autodidact. He had not been schooled deeply in Latin, but had learned just enough to navigate a Latin concordance, plundering it for its locators – the instances of each word – then looking these up in an English Bible and thereby building his English concordance. To Marbeck's interrogators it seemed unthinkable that he could be working between two languages without being fluent in both. Surely a theological project like this could not be undertaken by a single amateur, devoted but untutored. Surely Marbeck was merely the copyist, taking direction from others, an underling in a broader faction. Surely there must be some coded intent in the concordance, some heretical selection or retranslation of its terms, rather than the guileless, procedural conversion Marbeck claimed.

An account of the inquisition, probably taken first hand from Marbeck, appears in JoÙ Foxe's *Actes and Monuments* (1570). The accuser here is Stephen Gardiner, Bishop of Winchester:

> What helpers hadest thou in settyng forth thy boke?
> Forsoth my lord, quoth he, none.
> None, quoth the Bishop how can that be? It is not possible that thou shouldest do it without helpe.
> Truly my lord, quoth he, I can not tell in what part your Lordshyp doth take it, but how soever it be, I wil not deny but I dyd it without the helpe of any man saue God alone.[12]

The questioning continues in this vein, with others joining in the attack:

> Then said the Bishop of Salisbury, whose help hadst thou in setting forth this booke?
> Truly my Lord, quoth he, no helpe at all.
> How couldest thou, quoth the bishop, inuent such a booke, or know what a Concordance ment, without an instructer.

Amidst the disbelief there is also a curious type of admiration. When the Bishop of Salisbury produces some sheets from the suspect concordance, one of the other inquisitors examines them and remarks, 'This man has been better occupied than a great many of our priests.'

Now Marbeck plays his trump card. He asks the assembled bishops to set him a challenge. As they are all aware, the concordance had only got as far as the letter L before Marbeck was arrested and his papers confiscated. Therefore, if the inquisitors were to choose a series of words from later in the alphabet and Marbeck were to compile entries for them – alone in prison – he would thereby demonstrate that he was perfectly capable of working unabetted. The panel accept. Marbeck is given a list of terms to index, along with an English Bible, a Latin concordance, and materials to write with. By the next day, the task has been triumphantly completed.[13]

Marbeck was pardoned, but the drafts of his concordance were destroyed. Still, innocent and undeterred, he began again, and seven years after his arrest he was able to bring the work uncontroversially into print. Nevertheless, Marbeck's preface sounds a cautious note. He states that he has used 'the moste allowed translation' so that no heretical doctrine might have slipped in that way. Furthermore, he declares that he has not 'altered or added any Worde in the moste holy Bible'. Nothing added, altered, or retranslated. Marbeck would live for another four decades, an organist and composer whose life had been spared because his concordance was only, scrupulously, that: a complete list of words and their instances, with no interpretation and therefore no heresy.

By contrast, let us glance briefly at the back pages of a history book from the late nineteenth century. The work is by J. Horace Round, and its title is *Feudal England*. Much of Round's study sets out to correct what he sees as scholarly errors made by Edward Augustus Freeman, Regius Professor of Modern History at Oxford. Freeman emerges as Round's *bête noire*, responsible, Round feels, for a significant wrong turn in the study of the medieval period. Over the course of 600 pages, however, this animosity is diffuse. Feudal England, after all, and not Edward Freeman, is the principal subject of the book. In the index, however, the gloves come off:

Freeman, Professor: unacquainted with the Inq. Com. Cant. 4; ignores the Northamptonshire geld-roll 149; confuses the Inquisitio geldi 149; his contemptuous criticism 150, 337, 385, 434, 454; when himself in error 151; his charge against the Conqueror 152, 573; on Hugh d'Envermeu 159; on Hereward 160–4; his 'certain' history 323, 433; his 'undoubted history' 162, 476; his 'facts' 436; on Hemings' cartulary 169; on Mr. Waters 190; on the introduction of feudal tenures 227–31, 260, 267–72, 301, 306; on the knight's fee 234; on Ranulf Flambard 228; on the evidence of Domesday 229–31; underrates feudal influence 247, 536–8; on scutage 268; overlooks the Worcester relief 308; influenced by words and names 317, 338; on Normans under Edward 318 sqq.; his bias 319, 394–7; on Richard's castle 320 sqq.; confuses individuals 323–4, 386, 473; his assumptions 323; on the name Alfred 327; on the Sheriff Thorold 328–9; on the battle of Hastings 332 sqq.; his pedantry 334–9; his 'palisade' 340 sqq., 354, 370, 372, 387, 391, 401; misconstrues his Latin 343, 436; his use of Wace 344–7, 348, 352, 355, 375; on William of Malmesbury 346, 410–14, 440; his words suppressed 347, 393; on the Bayeux Tapestry 348–51; imagines facts 352, 370, 387, 432; his supposed accuracy 353, 354, 384, 436–7, 440, 446, 448; right as to the shield-wall 354–8; his guesses 359, 362, 366, 375, 378–9, 380, 387, 433–6, 456, 462; his theory of Harold's defeat 360, 380–1; his confused views 364–5, 403,

hilarious !

439, 446, 448; his dramatic tendency 365–6; evades difficulties 373, 454; his treatment of authorities 376–7, 449–51; on the relief of Arques 384; misunderstands tactics 381–3, 387; on Walter Giffard 385–6; his failure 388; his special weakness 388, 391; his splendid narrative 389, 393; his Homeric power 391; on Harold and his Standard 403–4; on Wace 404–6, 409; on Regenbald 425; on Earl Ralk 428; on William Malet 430; on the Conqueror's earldoms 439; his Domesday errors and confusion 151, 425, 436–7, 438, 445–8, 463; on 'the Civic League' 433–5; his wild dream 438; his special interest in Exeter 431; on legends 441; on Thierry 451, 458; his method 454–5; on Lisois 460; on Stigand 461; on Walter Tirel 476–7; on St. Hugh's action [1197] 528; on the Winchester Assembly 535–8; distorts feudalism 537; on the king's court 538; on Richard's change of seal 540; necessity of criticising his work, xi., 353.[14]

One could hardly imagine a more comprehensive or devastating attack, and yet it is hard not to be amused by it – by its relentlessness, its obsessional intensity. It is difficult to see its scare quotes – 'his "certain" history . . . his "undoubted" history . . . his "facts"' – without imagining Round speaking, delivering the index out loud, a livid sarcasm in his voice. This is the subject index in its most extreme form, as far from the concordance as it can get. Where Marbeck's method was meticulously neutral, Round's is the polar opposite, *all* personality, all interpretation. Where Marbeck's concordance was thorough, Round's index is partial. It would be fair to say that JoÙ Marbeck owed his life to the difference between a concordance and a subject index.

But Round's index is a curio, a wild outlier. The good subject index, though inevitably imbued with the personality of its compiler – their insights and decisions – is far more discreet. As with acting, it is rarely a positive sign if the general viewer starts to notice the workings that have gone into the performance. The ideal index anticipates how a book will be read, how it will be *used*, and quietly, expertly provides a map for these purposes. Part of what will emerge from this story, I hope, will be a defence of the humble subject index, assailed by the concordance's digital avatar, the search bar. The concordance and the subject index, as it happens, came into being at the same moment, perhaps even the same year. They have both been with us for nearly eight centuries. Both are vital still.

I

Point of Order
On Alphabetical Arrangement

'(Stoop) if you are abcedminded, to this claybook,
what curios of sings (please stoop), in this allaphbed!'
James Joyce, *Finnegans Wake*

In the summer of 1977, the literary magazine *Bananas* ran a
short story entitled 'The Index' by the British science-fiction
writer J. G. Ballard. The story begins with a brief Editor's Note:

the text printed below is the index to the unpublished and
perhaps suppressed autobiography of a man who may
well have been one of the most remarkable figures of the
twentieth century ... Incarcerated within an unspecified
government institution, he presumably spent his last years
writing his autobiography of which this index is the only
surviving fragment.[1]

The rest of the story – the rise and fall of one Henry Rhodes
Hamilton – comes in the form of an alphabetical index, from
which the reader must piece together a narrative using only
keywords, brief subheadings, and the sense of chronology
that the page numbers provide. This oblique approach to
storytelling offers plenty of opportunities for wry euphemism.
We are left to guess, for instance, at Hamilton's true ancestry
from the following non-consecutive entries:

Avignon, birthplace of HRH, 9–13.

George V, secret visits to Chatsworth, 3, 4–6; rumoured liaison with Mrs. Alexander Hamilton, 7; suppresses court circular, 9.

Hamilton, Alexander, British Consul, Marseilles ... depression after birth of HRH, 6; surprise recall to London, 12; first nervous breakdown, 16; transfer to Tsingtao, 43.

Further entries reveal Hamilton to have been foremost among the twentieth century's alpha males:

D-Day, HRH ashore on Juno Beach, 223; decorated, 242.

Hamilton, Marcelline (formerly Marcelline Renault), abandons industrialist husband, 177; accompanies HRH to Angkor, 189; marries HRH, 191.

Hemingway, Ernest ... portrays HRH in *The Old Man and the Sea*, 453.

Inchon, Korea, HRH observes landings with Gen. MacArthur, 348.

Jesus Christ, HRH compared to by Malraux, 476.

Nobel Prize, HRH nominated for, 220, 267, 342, 375, 459, 611.

Meanwhile, the pattern of entries relating to statesmen and religious figures – initial friendships followed by denouncements – suggests the story's clearest plot line, concerning Hamilton's world-conquering megalomania:

Churchill, Winston, conversations with HRH, 221; at Chequers with HRH, 235; spinal tap performed by HRH, 247; at Yalta with HRH, 298; 'iron curtain' speech, Fulton, Missouri, suggested by HRH, 312; attacks HRH in Commons debate, 367.

Dalai Lama, grants audience to HRH, 321; supports HRH's initiatives with Mao Tse-tung, 325; refuses to receive HRH, 381.

Gandhi, Mahatma, visited in prison by HRH, 251; discusses *Bhagavadgita* with HRH, 253; has dhoti washed by HRH, 254; denounces HRH, 256.

Paul VI, Pope, praises Perfect Light Movement, 462; receives HRH, 464; attacked by HRH, 471; deplores messianic pretentions of HRH, 487; criticises Avignon counter-papacy established by HRH, 498; excommunicates HRH, 533.

For the story of Hamilton's downfall, Ballard picks up the pace of the action by clustering the events sequentially around the last letters of the alphabet. HRH forms a cult, the Perfect Light Movement, which proclaims his divinity and seizes the UN Assembly, calling for a world war on the US and the USSR; he is arrested and incarcerated, but then disappears, with the Lord Chancellor raising questions about his true identity. The final entry concerns the mysterious indexer himself: 'Zielinski, Bronislaw, suggests autobiography to HRH, 742; commissioned to prepare index, 748; warns of suppression threats, 752; disappears, 761'.

Ballard's conceit with 'The Index' is a rather brilliant one. Nevertheless, on one key level, 'The Index' doesn't quite *get* indexes, and perhaps no readable narrative really can. Ballard knows we'll read his index from start to finish – from A to Z – and so he pegs the chronology of his story, albeit loosely, to the order of the alphabet, the index's primary ordering system. Keywords to the front of the alphabet tell of HRH's early years; his hubris becomes pathological in the Ts through Vs; his comeuppance is told among the Ws and Ys. Two discrete ordering systems, alphabetical and chronological, are actually largely congruent here: the form and the content of the index are in a rough alignment. This is not what indexes are about at all.

If we are going to understand the index, we will need to delve into its prehistory to get a sense of what a strange, miraculous thing alphabetical order really is: something we take for granted, but something which appeared, almost out of nowhere, 2,000 years ago; something we use every day, but which a civilization as vast as the Roman Empire could choose to ignore completely in its administrative apparatus. With that curious hiatus fresh in our minds, let us start not in Greece or Rome but in New York, and not in antiquity but rather closer to our own time.

On 10 April 1917, at the Grand Central Palace on Lexington and 46th Street, the Society of Independent Artists opened the doors on its first annual exhibition. Modelled on the Salon des Indépendents in France, itself a response to the rigid traditionalism of the French Academy, the Independents' Show in New York invited work by all-comers, with no selection jury and no prizes. Its guiding light was Marcel Duchamp, who had exhibited (and controversially removed) his *Nude Descending a Staircase, No. 2* from the Parisian Indépendents five years earlier.

In its hanging, the New York exhibition introduced an innovation that had been absent from its European predecessor – an approach that, as Duchamp's friend Henri-Pierre Roché put it, was being tried out 'for the first time in any exhibition': the works would be displayed in alphabetical order, by the artists' surnames.[2] The exhibition catalogue spells out the reasoning for this approach:

The arrangement of all the exhibits in alphabetical order, regardless of manner or medium, is followed with a view to freeing the individual exhibit from the control of the merely personal judgements which are inevitably the basis of any system of grouping.[3]

Beatrice Wood, whose job it was to hang the exhibition, describes a slightly chaotic practice, the day before the exhibition was due to open, with paintings turning up out of order and needing to be shuffled into their rightful place:

> And the mess of trying to remember the alphabet correctly four hundred times! It was fairly simple till we came to the Schmidts – about eight in all. But we no sooner decided they belonged one place than someone placed them in another, and for an hour every time we moved a picture it turned into a Schmidt. With a sigh I would drag heavy framed canvases along the floor.[4]

An alphabetical exhibition. It is not hard to understand the logic at work: each exhibitor has the right to buy ('on the payment of nominal dues') a space to exhibit without being judged – promoted, grouped, buried – by the show's organizers. The alphabet is a great leveller: nothing is implied by its ordering. But what about the viewer? What about *us* as potential visitors to the show? What about curation, the idea that some intrinsic organization – by style, subject, size – will make the viewing experience a coherent one and therefore more satisfying to the punter perusing several hundred works?

A hundred years later, it's fair to say that the alphabetical exhibition has not exactly caught on. Why not? How does the idea strike us now? As lazy? Wilfully zany? Perhaps – and this is my own gut response, I think – as interesting but naive, an

Figure 1: The catalogue to the Independents' Show, boasting on its title page its three unique features: 'No Jury. No Prizes. Exhibits Hung in Alphabetical Order'.

approach that overlooks too readily the fact that a collection of artworks will have threads to it, clusters whose members bring meaning to each other; that sensitive arrangement can reveal things about the collection on a level larger than the individual unit. That, after all, is why galleries have curators.

If any of that rings true, then it may give us a sense of why alphabetical order, though not unknown, was extremely rare during the early part of the Middle Ages. As the medieval historians Mary and Richard Rouse put it, 'The Middle Ages did not like alphabetical order, which it considered to be the antithesis of reason.'[5] That same repugnance we feel at an exhibition whose hanging is arbitrary, outsourced to an unrelated ordering, was felt too by medieval scholars considering the way that ideas were organized in their books:

> God had created a harmonious universe, its parts all linked to each other; it lay with the scholar to discern these rational connections – those of hierarchy, of chronology, of similarity and difference, etc. – and to reflect these in the structure of their writing. Alphabetical order implied the abdication of this responsibility.

The Rouses suggest there may even have been a deeper anxiety at work, that to opt out of the quest for intrinsic order was to imply that no such order really existed: 'To deliberately employ alphabetical order amounted to a tacit recognition that each person who used a work could rearrange it in a personal order, different from others and from the author himself.'

For us today, while we might not warm to an alphabetical art show, it's not as if we won't happily use alphabetical order in other contexts. As schoolchildren, our names are read out from an alphabetical register every morning; when we are older, we will scroll without a pang through the contacts lists on our mobile phones. What could be more convenient? And when we see the names of the dead listed on a memorial, we do not, surely, worry that their sacrifices are diminished for being commemorated alphabetically. With barely a thought we know how to use a table where alpha order is the sole organizing system (as in the old residential phone books), or where it works in tandem with another specialized or context-specific categorization (as in the old Yellow Pages, where entries were grouped first by trade, then alphabetically within these). It's a system with which we are completely familiar, something so deeply ingrained, something we acquire so early, that it might seem self-evident. Can you remember being taught, for the first time, how to look something up in a dictionary? I can't; I'm not sure it happened that way, that I didn't just figure it out. And yet, somehow, we must all have learned that lesson, one that has not always been considered intuitive.

In 1604, Robert Cawdrey published what is generally considered the first English dictionary. As with many books of the time, the full title of Cawdrey's work, as it appears on the first page, might strike us today as extraordinarily long and detailed:

> A Table Alphabeticall conteyning and teaching the true writing, and vnderstanding of hard vsuall English wordes, borrowed from the Hebrew, Greeke, Latine, or French, &c. With the interpretation thereof by plaine English wordes, gathered for the benefit & helpe of ladies, gentlewomen, or any other vnskilfull persons. Whereby they may the more easilie and better vnderstand many hard English wordes, vvhich they shall heare or read in scriptures, sermons, or elswhere, and also be made able to vse the same aptly themselues.

There is much to take in here, not least that charmless phrase, 'ladies, gentlewomen, or any other vnskilfull persons'. But at least we can glean the gist of Cawdrey's intention: that this is a book intended to provide the definitions of loan words, words that are used in English but that are 'borrowed from the Hebrew, Greeke, Latine, or French, &c.'. It is for readers who have not had the benefit of having been schooled in these languages, so that they might understand these words when they crop up in English books. Although most scholars now speak of Cawdrey's *Table Alphabeticall*, abbreviating the title like this has the rather odd effect of telling us how the book is arranged, but not what it contains.

Given that the work announces itself, first and foremost, as an alphabetical table, it comes as some surprise to see this lengthy explanation, in the opening pages, of how the book should be used:

> If thou be desirous (gentle Reader) rightly and readily to vnderstand, and to profit by this Table, and such like, then thou must learne the Alphabet, to wit, the order of the Letters as they stand, perfectly without booke, and where euery Letter standeth: as (b) neere the beginning, (n) about the middest, and (t) toward the end. Nowe if the word, which thou art desirous to finde, begin with (a) then looke in the beginning of this Table, but if with (v) looke towards the end. Againe, if thy word beginne with (ca) looke in the beginning of the letter (c) but if with (cu) then looke toward the end of that letter. And so of all the rest. &c.[6]

What we have here is a lesson in how to use an alphabetical list, one that goes back to first principles: first, gentle reader, you will have to learn the order of the alphabet – *really* learn it – so that you can recall it 'without booke'. It is quite a shock to see just how 'vnskilfull' Cawdrey imagines his audience to be! He is spelling out something that modern readers will take for granted: that there will be a spatial relationship between the alphabet and the book, such that entries beginning with letters near the front of the alphabet can be found near the front of the book. What's more, this alphabetical arrangement is *nested*, that is, *capable* will appear before *culpable* because both words start with *c* but *a* comes before *u*, and so on.

In fact, Cawdrey's alphabetical arrangement was not a new invention in 1604. Nor was his How To guide, with similar, though slightly less patronizing, sets of instructions prefaced to the Latin dictionaries of Papias the Lombard (*c.* 1050) and

Giovanni Balbi (1286).[7] What these all demonstrate, however, is that alphabetical ordering is *not* intuitive. To take the sequence of the letters with which we spell our words, and to use that sequencing for something entirely different – books in a library; pictures in an exhibition; plumbers in your area – requires an imaginative leap that is nothing short of extraordinary. It is a leap into arbitrariness, leaving behind the intrinsic qualities of the material being arranged, turning from content to form, from meaning to spelling.

The sequencing of the letters of the alphabet was around for a long time before it was pressed into administrative service. Clay tablets discovered in northern Syria have shown that the order of the letters in the alphabet used in the city of Ugarit was established by the middle of the second millennium BCE.[8] The tablets are *abecedaria*, that is, simply, rows of letters written in order, probably as an aid for people learning to read and write, much as British and American children today learn the letters of the alphabet by singing them, in order, to the tune of 'Twinkle Twinkle Little Star'.

Ugaritic was a cuneiform script, its letters formed by pressing a wedge-shaped reed into wet clay. The ordering of its

Figure 2: Tablet dating from the fourteenth century BCE showing the characters, in order, of the Ugaritic alphabet.

sounds, however, is mirrored in another related alphabet, that of the Phoenicians, which uses the linear style of lettering that is more familiar to us. And this same ordering carries through to the Hebrew, Greek, and ultimately Latin alphabets.

In Hebrew, the earliest known abecedarium is an inscription found at Lachish in central Israel. Carved into a limestone stairway at around the beginning of the ninth century BCE, it shows the first five letters of the alphabet beside a drawing of a rather fierce-looking lion.[9] As with the Ugaritic abecedaria, the likelihood is that this was the work of a learner. Announcing the discovery at a lecture in London immediately after the dig, the archaeologist Charles Inge proposed that it was 'the work of a schoolboy airing his knowledge writing the equivalent of ABCDE until he reached the top of the step'.[10] Alphabetical order in the ninth century BCE, it seems, was still nothing more than a memory aid.

A few centuries later, however, alphabetical order began to be used for something altogether more surprising. Parts of the Hebrew Bible, among them Proverbs 31:10–31 as well as Psalms 25, 34, 37, 111, 112, 119 and 145, are written in the form of alphabetic acrostics, that is, the sequence of the alphabet determines the first letter of each verse. Most notable of all is the Book of Lamentations, in which four out of the five chapters follow this arrangement, each composed of twenty-two verses, the first of which begins with the letter *aleph*, the second *beth*, the third *gimmel*, and so on through to *tav*, the twenty-second and final letter of the Hebrew alphabet. (Chapter 3, at sixty-six verses long, triples the constraint: *aleph*, *aleph*, *aleph*, *beth*, *beth*, *beth*, etc.) The sequence of the letters, then, is being used as a kind of poetical scaffolding, with the alphabet – like rhyme or metre in modern verse – determining what the poet is allowed to do.

There is sometimes a tendency to dismiss acrostics, along with anagrams, lipograms (the avoidance of certain letters) and other types of verbal constraint, as intrinsically whimsical, affectations that are somehow beneath the serious poet. Joseph Addison, in the early eighteenth century, exemplifies this line when he thunders that acrostics were a way for 'the most arrant undisputed Blockheads . . . to set up for polite Authors'.[11] And yet, the Lamentations are among the bleakest sections of the Hebrew Bible. Written during the sixth century BCE in the wake of the destruction of Jerusalem, they constitute a sustained howl of despair at the fate of the city: 'How doth the city sit solitary, that was full of people! How is she become as a widow!' To quibble at its acrostic form would be as absurd as to bemoan the fact that Shakespeare limited himself with pentameter, or to wonder how much better the *Canterbury Tales* might have been if Chaucer had not constrained himself with rhyme. Better by far to look in wonder at the mind that could see the order of the alphabet as more than an aid for schoolchildren, that could pick it up and experiment with it as a way of harnessing the tumultuous pain of exile, a catalyst for literary creativity.

We are still, however, not at the point where alphabetical order is being used as a finding aid, where its special property – that anyone who has learned their *aleph beth gimmel* or their *alpha beta gamma* will be able to translate position in this scale to position somewhere else, a list or a book or a shelf – has been exploited. For this we need to fast forward three centuries from the horrors of the Lamentations, and travel 300 miles west from Jerusalem.

The death of Alexander the Great in 323 BCE had brought about a series of civil wars in which the empire he had built was divided between his successors. Egypt came under the control of one of Alexander's generals, Ptolemy I Soter, who began a dynasty that would last until Cleopatra's defeat by the Romans nearly 300 years later. Ptolemy's capital was the newly founded city of Alexandria, and it was here, around the beginning of the third century, that he built an institution in which the greatest scholars of the age would live, study and teach. It would be rather like a modern university – this is not the last time that the development of the university will prove pivotal for our story – and it would be dedicated to the muses, hence the name *Mouseion*, or in Latin *Musaeum*, which gives us our modern word *museum*. Its centrepiece would be the largest library in the ancient world, the Library of Alexandria. The library flourished during the reign of Ptolemy's successor, Ptolemy II, with conservative estimates suggesting that it housed 40,000 scrolls (other sources put the figure at half a million).[12] A collection on this scale would need to be brought into order to be useful. It would be a man named Callimachus, armed with the twenty-four letters of the alphabet, who would bring the sprawling library to heel.

Callimachus is best known today for his verse. He is the author of the elegy to a fellow poet, Heraclitus of Halicarnassus, often anthologized in its translation by William JoUson Cory: 'They told me, Heraclitus, they told me you were dead.' A proponent of shorter forms – hymns, elegies, epigrams – he is said to have coined the witticism *mega biblion, mega kakon* ('big book, big evil') to express his disdain for epic poetry. Nevertheless, it is his work not as a poet but as a scholar which will concern us, and here Callimachus was responsible for a very big book indeed, the *Pínakes*, said to have run to 120 papyrus scrolls. For many centuries it was thought that Callimachus produced the *Pínakes* while serving as *bibliophylax*, or Keeper of the Library. However, at the beginning of the last century, a papyrus fragment was discovered in the waste piles of Oxyrhynchus that appears to list the head librarians in order. Callimachus' name is not on it.[13] Instead, there is the name of one of his former pupils, Apollonius of Rhodes, a man with whom Callimachus had a bitter literary spat, a man who – coincidentally or not – wrote epic poetry.[14]

Callimachus may have been passed over for the role of Chief Librarian, but, in compiling the *Pínakes*, it was he who did most of all to preserve the library's memory. *Pínakes* simply means 'Tables', as in writing boards or 'tablets', and the full title of Callimachus' work was the *Tables of Men Illustrious in Every Field of Learning and of Their Writing*. It was a catalogue of all the works housed in the great library. To be useful, these tables would need to be organized in such a way that a reader consulting them could find what they were looking for among the many thousands of entries. Although nothing of the *Pínakes* itself survives, we can derive a sense of its arrangement from the couple of dozen fragmentary references to it in other works by later classical writers who had seen copies of it. From these we can deduce that the work was organized firstly by genre: rhetoric, law, epic, tragedy, etc. And we know that the last of these classes – the catch-all 'miscellaneous' group – had subdivisions including *deipna* and *plakuntopoiïka*, i.e. banquets and cakemaking, as when Athenaeus of Naucratis, at the end of the second century CE, writes, 'I am aware that Callimachus in his *Tablet of Miscellaneous Treatises* recorded treatises on the art of cakemaking by Aegimus, Hegesippus, and Metrobius, as well as by Phaestus.'[15] There is something important to notice about this list. Besides revealing how seriously the Greeks took their cakes, it tells us that, within each of his classes, Callimachus had arranged authors in alphabetical order according to their names.[16] Having provided this two-tiered ordering – by genre and alphabetically by name – so that readers could locate an author, Callimachus went on to provide further information. There was biographical data: father's name, for example, birthplace, nickname (helpful for authors who had common names), profession, whether they had studied with a famous teacher; and then bibliographical data: a list of the author's works, along with their *incipits* or opening words (since works in this period would not necessarily have a title as such), and the length of the work in lines. This last detail was important in the days before print, as it would allow librarians to determine whether they had a full copy of the work in question, as well as meaning that bookdealers could estimate the cost of having a copy made.

There's a strong argument that the title of Callimachus' catalogue referred to tablets that might have hung over the cases in which the scrolls were stored – shelfmarks, essentially, indicating what was there. If this is true, then 'pínakes' nicely expresses something important about the way that future indexes would work: the spatial relationship between reference and referent. Something *here* locates something *there*: a heading in the catalogue points to its equivalent on the shelves.

A brief digression on how scrolls were stored: a tablet hung above the shelves is one method of locating what you're looking for in an ancient library, but the Greeks had another, one that would identify an individual scroll. (Remember that dust-jackets, printed spines, and even title pages – the methods we use to quickly single out a particular book – are all relative newcomers, no more than a few centuries old, and all fundamentally reliant on the *codex*, that is, the book as we know it today, with flippable leaves, gathered together and bound at the spine.) In order to identify a scroll without having to unroll it, a small parchment tag – essentially a name label – would be glued to the roll so that it stuck out, displaying the author and title of the work. It was known as a *sittybos*, or more commonly *sillybos* (whence our word *syllabus*, which we use to describe the contents of a course, just as a *sillybos* indicates the contents of a scroll).

When Cicero, the great Roman statesman and orator, decided to tidy up his personal library, one of the jobs that needed doing was the fixing of these labels to each roll. He writes to his friend Atticus:

> It will be delightful of you to pay us a visit. You will find that Tyrannio has made a wonderful job of arranging my books. What is left of them is much better than I expected. And I should be grateful if you would send me a couple of your library clerks to help Tyrannio with the gluing and other operations, and tell them to bring a bit of parchment for the labels, *sittybae* as I believe you Greeks call them.[17]

Figure 3: Now in the British Library, this papyrus fragment from the second century CE still has its *sillybos* identifying the roll as the Dithyrambs of Bacchylides.

Because Atticus spoke Greek, Cicero drops in the Greek term, *sittybae*, for the scroll labels. In his next letter, however, Cicero reports being delighted with the work that the librarians have done. The image he draws here, of the orderly bookshelves bringing the whole house to life, is a rather wonderful one, but let us pay attention to the word Cicero uses for the labels. This time he doesn't switch to Greek:

> And now that Tyrannio has put my books straight, my house seems to have woken to life. Your Dionysius and Menophilus have worked wonders over that. Those shelves of yours are the last word in elegance, now that the labels [*indices*] have brightened up the volumes.

There we have it: to a Roman, an *index* meant a label, a name tag for a scroll. These are not indexes in our modern sense. Not quite. But we're getting somewhere: indicating the contents; helping us to find what we're looking for among the vastness of a library. Meanwhile, we may quibble over whether the Latin *indices* or the Anglicized *indexes* is the correct plural in English, but at least history has not plumped for the Greek: *sillyboi*. ꙮ

Looking back to the Library of Alexandria, it cannot be said for certain that the principle of alphabetical organization was the invention of Callimachus or his colleagues at the Mouseion. Nevertheless, given the lack of earlier evidence, and the appreciable requirements imposed by the accumulation of information on an unprecedented scale, it seems, in Lloyd Daly's measured phrase, 'a reasonable and attractive hypothesis'.[18] The vastness of the Library – ancient Greek Big Data – necessitated a major tecÙological shift: from abecedarium to alphabetical list, from *knowing* alphabetical order to *using* it. The use of alphabetical order represents a huge intellectual leap: the rejection of the intrinsic characteristics of the materials being organized in favour of something off-the-peg, something arbitrary. The payoff is a system that is universal, one that relies on information that any literate person will know already and that can be applied to anything, breaking it up into more manageable chunks. At its loosest, where ordering is only applied to the initial letter, the Greek alphabet provided for twenty-four separate buckets into which to divide the total, a significant improvement in the searchability of information. (This doesn't only work for discrete information like lists. Another innovation at the Mouseion was to divide Homer's epics, the *Iliad* and the *Odyssey*, into the twenty-four books in which we read them today. A work dating from slightly later states that this number was significant: the poems were divided 'into the number of the letters of the alphabet, not by the poet himself but by the grammarians associated with Aristarchus'. Aristarchus was Keeper of the Library about a century after Callimachus.[19])

In the Greek world, this use of alphabetical order spread beyond the scholarly sphere and its booklists, passing into civic administration, cultic practices, market trading. An octagonal column, found on the island of Cos and dating from the late third century BCE, lists members in the cult of Apollo and Heracles, with instructions that the list should be kept 'according to letter in order from alpha'.[20] At Akraiphia on the Greek mainland, two stones dating from the beginning of the second century list the names of dozens of species of fish along with prices for them. The fish are in alpha order.[21] And the accounts of ancient Greek tax collectors have been found among the Oxyrhynchus waste piles with payees grouped alphabetically by name.[22] Meanwhile, a statuette of the dramatist Euripides, discovered in Rome and now in the Louvre, depicts the dramatist seated in front of an alphabetical list of his plays.

Ancient Rome, by contrast, though familiar with alphabeticization, was not hugely impressed with it. It is used in

Figure 4: This statuette of Euripides dates from the second century CE. Behind the playwright is a list of his works in alphabetical order.

some scholarly works, though not with the gusto we find in the Greek world. A sense of the pejorative – that this is an order that will have to do when no better arrangement can be readily found – often attaches to it. Take Pliny, for example. Sighting the finish line of the section on gemstones in his vast *Natural History*, he declares how the remaining items will be arranged: 'I have now discussed the principal gemstones, classifying them according to their colour, and shall proceed to describe the rest in alphabetical order.'[23] The alphabet will do for the leftovers, the dregs, now that the important items have been classified more appropriately. Furthermore, alphabetical order did not spill over beyond the academic world into the administrative as it had in the Greek-speaking world. In a society as large and highly organized as the Roman empire, one might have suspected that alpha order would be indispensable. This, however, was not the case.[24]

The first appearance of alphabetical order in Latin comes not in a scholarly work, but in a bawdy comedy. Written around the beginning of the second century BC, Plautus' *Comedy of Asses* concerns an old man, Demaenetus, and his attempts to cheat his wife out of enough money to buy the freedom of a certain prostitute so that she can marry his son. At the play's climax, Artemona, Demaenetus' wife, bursts into the brothel to find both father and son cavorting with the lady in question. Outraged, Artemona exclaims, 'That explains why he has to go to dinner every day. He says he's going to Archidemus, Chaerea, Chaerestratus, Clinia, Chremes, Cratinus, Dinias, Demosthenes.'[25] What alphabetical order gives us here, of course, is the possibility of a joke about abbreviation: we have eight alibis in Artemona's list, eight times Demaenetus has lied to his wife, claiming to be dining with friends, and we have only got up to the Ds. The audience is left to scale up the offence. No earlier examples exist in Latin, and yet we must assume that the audience were familiar enough with the principle to get the joke. Later, in Book VII of Virgil's *Aeneid*, when the warriors of Italy are amassing to drive the newly arrived Trojans from their shores, the order in which the local chieftains are described is a familiar one: Aventinus, Catillus, Coras, Caeculus . . .[26]

As an aside, then, we might note that there is a small but curious literary genre – what we might call alphabetical literature – that runs from the Book of Lamentations, through Plautus and Virgil, and down to modern works like Ballard's 'The Index' or Walter Abish's *Alphabetical Africa*. Not everything in this category is as it seems, however. In Agatha Christie's *The ABC Murders*, after the killings of Alice Ascher of Andover, Betty Barnard on the beach at Bexhill, and Carmichael Clarke at his home in Churston, the police hurry to Doncaster to prevent the next crime. Here, however, the victim is a barber named George Earlsfield: the series has been broken. Not only that, but, as Poirot deduces, the killer is not the prime suspect, Alexander Bonaparte Cust – Mr A. B. C. – but rather one Franklin Clarke, brother to the third victim, whose only motive was greed, and who concocted the alphabetical killings as a way of implicating the other man.

Back in ancient Rome, the Romans may not have welcomed alphabetical order into their hearts, but for one type of work it had a usefulness that meant that it persisted. In the writings of the grammarians, in glossaries, lexicons and treatises explaining the workings of language, alphabetical order – to the first letter at least – endured through the classical period and beyond. That is, where the subject is language itself, where words are considered *as words* – in tables of nouns that decline a certain way, for example, or abbreviations that readers might encounter in certain types of literature – alphabetical lists can be found throughout the first millennium of the Common Era. Alphabetical order is used for Photius' *Lexicon* (ninth century), for the Suda – the great tenth-century encyclopedia of the classical world – and for Papias' dictionary, mentioned earlier, which ramps up the precision of the ordering by nesting it to the third letter of each headword. In England, Anglo-Saxon glosses that list their terms in alpha order can be found as early as the ninth century.[27] It would be a stretch, then, to say that when the first great book index arrives, in the middle of the thirteenth century, its arrangement is unheard of; more that it is a rehabilitation of something that had lapsed – for a millennium – into obscurity.

But if an index is to list its terms in alphabetical order, there still remains the question: which alphabet? Figure 5 shows the opening pages of a book index from the mid sixteenth century, by which point it would have been a familiar feature to readers. Ignoring the squiggles and nonsense words and looking just at the ordering – *a, e, i* – it is clear that there is *an* alphabetical order here, but it is certainly an idiosyncratic one. Why start with the vowels? What order are the consonants in? What are those unfamiliar letters?

The book is called *An Orthographie, conteyning the due order and reason, howe to write or paint thimage of mannes voice, most like to the life of nature*, and its author is JoÙ Hart. Hart's *Orthographie* is a call for spelling reform that would bring writing into line with

A Table.

/ a tabl direkting tu d'spesiaul mâterz ov dis buk ~ / de first paz marked 1, and de sekund, 2.

/ a

Aunsient iuz or voëlz.   fôlio 33.pag.2.
  d' / autor armeth himself agenst hiz kalumniators.   fol.23.
an / alegori of an undiskryt painter, kompard tu-our dkustumd wreiting.   fol.27.
/ dfinite ov sevn perz of konsonants from de.36, tu de.43.leaf.
  d' / akiut or sarp tiun.   fol.40 pag.2.
/ abrizments lesi, and de rezon.   der.
  d' / aksidents untu-our voises.   fol.43.44
  d' / asking point.   fol.45.pa.2
  d' / author enkourazed tu put dis treatiz in print upon de knolez dat / sir Thomas Smith iz aulso dezirus ov de reformasion ov our abiurd/inglis wreiting.   fol.6.pa.1
/ abrizment ov wreiting ouht tu bi huen de spiG duts iuz it.   fol.62.pa.1
  d' / autor taketh exampl ov weiz & lerned men for traveling in so smaul a mâter az sum du tink hier-of.   fol.62.pa.2

/ envi

A Table

/ e.

/ envi ov de living invensions.   fol.3.pa.1
/ experiens mistres ov aul arts.   pa.2
/ element { ov spiG, de vois.   fol.9.pa.1
    ov wreiting de leter.   der
/ enemiez ov perseksion ar enimies tu bod / god and man.   fol.13.pa.2
for / etimolozi no diferens saul nid.   fol.19.20.
/ ei diphthong sounded for buer i, iz writn alon.   fol.31.pa.1
/ e, final for teim me bi lesi.   fol.33.pa.1
/ exampls ov diphthongs and triphthongs.   fol.43.pa.2
/ an experiens hou-an / inglis man me pronouns de / frens bei d'order observd in dis niu maner, dob hi-understand not de / frens, muG nerer der kómon spiG den bei der oun maner ov wreiting.   fol.65.66.

/ i

  d' / invensions of de living envied.   fol.3.pa.1
  d' / inventors first ov leters ar unserten.   fo.8.pa.2
/ inventerz ov leters konsidred de spiG.   der.
/ inglis de best huat it iz.   fol.21.pa.1
S.1.   d' / in-

Figure 5: The opening pages of the index to JoÙ Hart's *Orthographie* show a revised alphabetical order which puts the vowels first.

pronunciation. Because Hart is at pains to transcribe how people spoke in the sixteenth century, his book is a key text for the modern Shakespeare in Original Pronunciation movement. Fittingly, Hart seems to find an echo – albeit not a very sympathetic one – in *Love's Labour's Lost*, when the ludicrous Holofernes complains that people should pronounce words exactly as they're spelled:

> such rackers of orthography, as to speak 'dout' sine b, when he should say 'doubt'; 'det', when he should pronounce 'debt', – d,

e, b, t, not d, e, t: he clepeth a calf 'cauf'; half, 'hauf'; neighbour vocatur 'nebor'; neigh abbreviated 'ne'. This is abhominable – which he would call abominable. (Act 5, Scene 1)

Hart, by contrast, wants us to write the way we talk, and, to show what he means, his small book contains an analysis of spoken English establishing the sounds people actually use. Many of these, of course, are already represented by letter forms in the roman alphabet, but Hart notes that some letters are surplus to requirements: good-bye *j*, *w*, *y*, *c* and *q*. More significantly, Hart finds that there are certain sounds which can't be divided into smaller units, but which don't already have their own letters. Therefore, a few additional characters need to be invented for sounds like *sh* and *th* (both voiced, as in *then*, and unvoiced, as in *thin*).

To show he means business, the final third of Hart's book is written entirely in his simplified orthography. This is a nifty trick: if readers want to finish the book they will have to engage with the writing system, and thus (hopefully) discover that it is not nearly as confusing as it looks. When it comes to the index, Hart includes this note about how his new alphabet should be ordered (Figure 6). For a translation, see the footnote.*

---

* An advertisement touching the order of the following table.
Because the vowels and consonants are divided into such parts as before, this table doth keep them in the like order: to-wit first a, e, i, o, u, and then the four pairs which are made with a stopping breath: to wit b, p: d, t: g, k: and j, ch. Then the other three thoroughly breathed pairs, to wit th [voiced, as in *then*], th [unvoiced, as in *thin*]: v, f: and z, s. Then the 5 semi-vocals l, m, n, r, and [syllabic] l, and the two breaths sh, and h: also, for that in the order before used, these new letters are not comprehended. Wherefore this table is placed and set in such order as followeth.

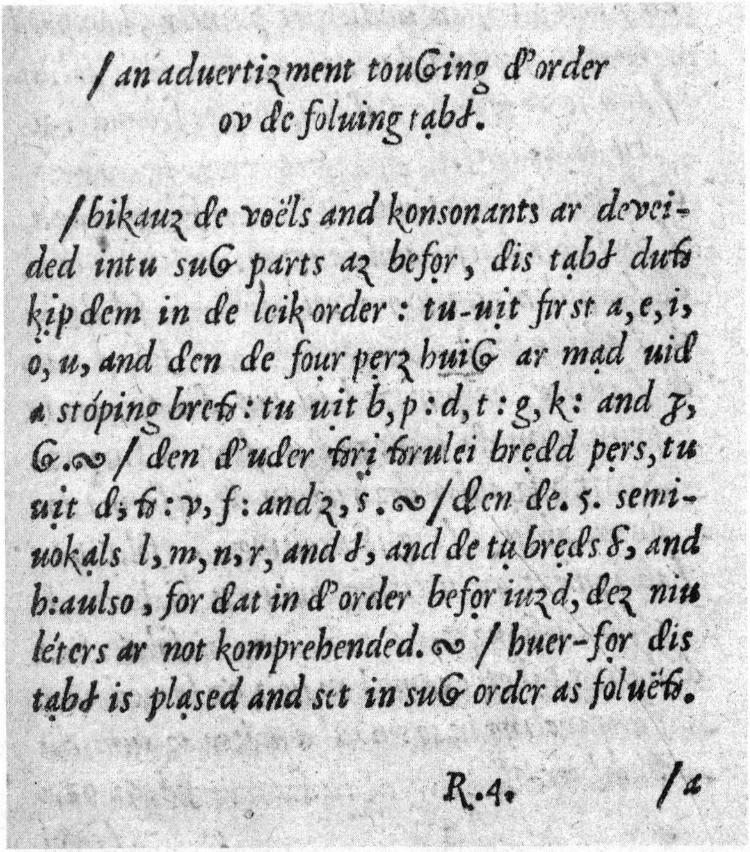

/ an aduertiȝment touƣing d'order
ov de foluing tabƚ.

/ bikauȝ de voëls and konsonants ar deveided intu suƣ parts aȝ befor, dis tabƚ duƚ ƙip dem in de leik order : tu-uit first a, e, i, o, u, and den de four perȝ huiƣ ar mad uid a stóping breƚ : tu uit b, p : d, t : g, ƙ : and ƺ, Ƣ. ∾ / den d'uder tri torulei bredd pers, tu uit d, ƚ : v, f : and ȝ, s. ∾ / den de. 5. semi-uokals l, m, n, r, and ƚ, and de tu breƚs Ƨ, and h:aulso, for dat in d'order befor iuȝd, deȝ niu léters ar not komprehended. ∾ / huer-for dis tabƚ is plased and set in suƣ order as foluëƚ.

R.4. / a

Figure 6: Prefatory paragraph to the index in Hart's *Orthographie.*

The exercise ends as it begins, by reminding readers that the index that follows will be arranged according to new principles. The alphabetical order is not one which readers will have learned at school. Hart states that the table is 'placed and set' following the rules of his new orthography. It is, in other words, a new-spelling native (*niu-speling nativ*), born under the new dispensation. In this, Hart has saved himself some strenuous effort. Switching, after the fact,

43

between two orderings – two alphabets – can be a problematic process.

Vladimir Nabokov's 1962 work *Pale Fire* is a novel dressed as a poem, or rather a novel dressed as a critical edition, its central poem bookended by editorial apparatus: introduction, notes, index. The poet is JoÙ Shade, recently deceased, longstanding faculty member at Wordsmith College in the small Appalachian town of New Wye; the editor is his colleague and neighbour Charles Kinbote, a recent arrival from across the Atlantic; and the novel plays on the literary relationship between the two as Kinbote does what no editor should: overshadows his author and steals the limelight for himself. In endnotes that become increasingly wild, catty and narcissistic, Kinbote ultimately leaves Shade's poem behind to tell his own deranged backstory as an exiled monarch, Charles the Beloved, deposed and driven from his homeland of Zembla.

The index, supposedly compiled by Kinbote, maintains his waspish, complaining tone. Academic rivals are haughtily snubbed in the lengthy entry for Kinbote himself – 'his contempt for Prof. H. (not in Index), 377 . . . his final rupture with E. (not in the Index), 894 . . . shaking with mirth over tidbits in a college textbook by Prof. C. (not in the Index), 929' – while Shade's wife, Sybil, in fact a major presence in the poem, is jealously dismissed with a single blunt line: 'Shade, Sybil, S's wife, *passim*'. Hovering over all this is the presence of Nabokov himself, so that a sniping, over-detailed entry such as 'Marcel, the fussy, unpleasant, and not always plausible central character, pampered by everybody, in Proust's *À la recherche du temps perdu*, 181, 691' is at once pure Kinbote in its phrasing and a metafictional skewering of *Pale*

Fire's own fussy, unpleasant and not always plausible central character.

Pale Fire ends with a final, incomplete index entry: 'Zembla, a distant northern land'. In an interview given the year the novel was published, Nabokov expanded on the meaning of this ending: 'No one has noted that my commentator committed suicide before completing the index to the book. The last entry has no numbered reference.'[28] Zembla has no locator. It is unlocatable, both nowhere, the fantasy of a delusional mind, and also everywhere, all-pervasive, the idealized stand-in for Kinbote's – and Nabokov's – lost homeland, Russia.[29] It is a devastatingly poignant ending, one that pulls the rug from under us, a sharp change of tack from the fireworks, zaniness and comedy of cringe that have gone before. But this transition, while abrupt, is nevertheless remarkably unobtrusive. The index form allows Nabokov to hide his workings, disguising the emotional manipulation at play. Alphabetical order protests its innocence: it is only arbitrariness, the fact that the Z of Zembla comes after all the other letters, that has brought us out at this point, an entry without a closure, pondering the longing and the madness of exile.

There is, of course, nothing arbitrary about this, but rather a certain sleight of hand, the same trick as Ballard's: aligning one's narrative needs, for plot, for emotional payoff, with the stations of the alphabet. But what if, having determined that the novel should end on this particular note, Zembla *didn't* come at the end of the index? It was Nabokov's widow, Véra, who first translated *Pale Fire* into Russian.[30] It was Véra, therefore, who first encountered a sticky problem: the Cyrillic alphabet has a different ordering from the Roman. In

Russian the letter З, the equivalent of Z, is the ninth of thirty-three letters. Given Nabokov's – and Véra's – own history of forced emigration, the Russian translation of *Pale Fire*, and in particular its final moment of unbearable nostalgia, is profoundly poignant. And yet, thanks to the different orderings of the two alphabets, the conceit doesn't work at all. That distant, northern land should be filed somewhere near the front. For *Pale Fire* to finish in the same way in Russian, Véra would have to find a way to take Zembla and its connotations of loss and peg them to a word beginning with Я, the last letter of the Cyrillic alphabet.

In Canto Three of the poem at the heart of *Pale Fire*, Shade muses on the immediate afterlife, specifically 'How not to panic when you're made a ghost'. One couplet finds him wondering 'How to locate in blackness, with a gasp, / Terra the Fair, an orbicle of jasp' (ll. 557–8), in other words, how to find one's way to the fair land, or the sphere of precious stone. In Kinbote's mad footnotes this is 'the loveliest couplet in this canto' – he is thinking, we presume, not of paradise but of his lost homeland. Thus, when Véra translates 'orbicle of jasp' as ячейка яшмы (cell of jasper), she has the material she needs. Véra's translation ends with the incomplete index entry:

ЯЧЕЙКА яшмы, Зембля, далекая северная страна
[Orbicle of jasp, Zembla, a distant, northern land]

It is an elegant solution. It bends the rules, introduces an extra element, but, in doing so, it allows the translator to repeat Nabokov's original trick, rigging the ordering in a new alphabet, allowing the author once again to have the final say.

But the artistry, the deviousness, required to ensure that the novel's emotional trajectory remains the same should be a reminder that the index is not a form well suited to narrative. It is hard to break in. Its commitment is not to the author but to the reader, and to the arbitrary order of the alphabet.

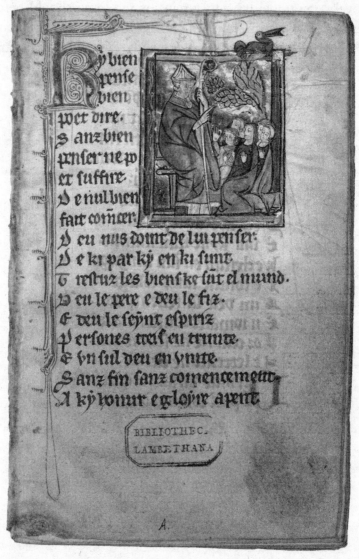

Figure 7: An image of Grosseteste preaching to a crowd, taken from a thirteenth-century manuscript of his poem *Chasteau d'amour*.

2

The Births of the Index
Preaching and Teaching

'But after you had fled from the schools to the
cloisters, you became as it were an unlearned man
and a despiser of letters, pursuing neither
reading nor teaching.'
Alexander of Ashby, *De artificioso modo predicandi*

'Ky bien pense bien poet dire.' A line that practises exactly
what it preaches: it is difficult to render it in English without
clogging up its rhythm, the succinctness and clarity of the
thought it contains. *Who thinks well speaks well*, perhaps. That
will have to do. It is the opening line of the long poem *Chasteau d'amour* (*The Castle of Love*), in which the Christian idea of
redemption is given a courtly make-over, the Crucifixion
explained in an allegory of princes and princesses and told in
elegantly rhymed couplets of Anglo-Norman. It was written
in the first half of the thirteenth century, and the poet was
Robert Grosseteste. We can see him in an illumination that
accompanies the poem in a manuscript now at Lambeth Palace. There he is, seated on the left, his long index finger
extended, the classic gesture of the storyteller. Perhaps it is
this very poem that he is declaiming to the audience at his feet.
Certainly they look rapt. The women clutch their hearts, a man
raises his hand in amazement (or maybe he has a question).

The listener on the right gazes adoringly upwards, locking eyes with Grosseteste. Only the large pelican, squatting in the trees, can break the connection, a symbol of bad audience, staring insolently, resolutely offstage. But she is being gradually struck out, her colours fading as the original red and gilt borders reassert themselves reprimandingly from beneath, the manuscript exacting a slow punishment for the sin of inattention.

Who thinks well speaks well. A tidy adage. One that might serve as a motto for anyone starting out as a lecturer, perhaps, or as a preacher. Indeed it might serve as the perfect epitaph for Grosseteste himself, one of the great polymaths of the English Middle Ages, a man who was, in his time, both lecturer and preacher, Chancellor of Oxford and Bishop of Lincoln (hence the mitre and crosier in the illumination). A poet too, of course, but also a statesman, a mathematician and a religious reformer. He translated Aristotle from the Greek, was the first to argue that rainbows are caused by light refraction, and imagined the birth of the universe as an expanding sphere of luminescence, taking science and scripture and blending them into a kind of Big Bang Theory that still leaves room for God to start it all off with 'Let there be light'. It is perhaps little wonder then that Grosseteste should devise – should *need to* devise – a method of imposing order on the vast breadth of his reading. Grosseteste's great table – or *Tabula* – brings cosmos out of chaos by categorizing the concepts he encountered, whether in patristic or pagan writings, keeping similar ideas together, and storing their locations for future reference. An encyclopedic mind needs an encyclopedic index to provide it with structure.

Necessity, then, is the mother of invention. But it would be wrong to treat Grosseteste as a man out of time, isolated from his culture. The necessity which gives rise to the *Tabula* is not uniquely felt by Grosseteste; rather, it is a version of a need that is coming into focus throughout the sphere in which he operates. By the thirteenth century, the tools for index-making – the codex and alphabetical order – have long been available. The spark that will bring them together will come from two forms of speaking well: teaching and preaching. Both take on renewed importance in the late Middle Ages thanks to the arrival of two new institutions: the universities and the mendicant orders, the friars – Dominicans and Franciscans – who lived and preached among the wider population. In these institutions there is a growing demand for new, more efficient ways of reading – of *using* books – to drive their respective vehicles for orderly speech, the lecture and the sermon. We are about to witness the birth of the index, or rather the *births* of the index, two versions of the same idea, arising simultaneously, one in Oxford, one in Paris. Taken together, both can tell us something about the index in our present, twenty-first-century moment, the Age of Search. Between them, they set up the axes by which we think about indexing: word versus concept; concordance versus subject index; specific versus universal.

Grosseteste, naturally, represents the universal. His grand *Tabula* is an attempt to boil down the whole of knowledge, of the Church Fathers – Augustine, Jerome, Isidore – but also of an older, non-Christian tradition – Aristotle, Ptolemy, Boethius – into a single resource, a place where concepts are non-sectarian and turn up as they please. It is what we now call a subject index, an index of ideas, and as such it is alive to the play of synonyms, able to identify a concept even where the text does not explicitly name it. It is also, then, a *subjective* index, the work of a particular reader, thinking and parsing their reading a certain way. Concepts are slippery things. We make a choice when we say that a text is *about* something; that, say, the story of Noah's Ark is about forgiveness, or anger, or rain. By contrast, another type of index – another way of searching – is more straightforward. Its terms are simply the words of the text under analysis: if the text uses a particular word, then that word will be in the index. Unsubjective, this type of index leaves little room for interpretation – a word is either there or it isn't. Alongside Grosseteste's *Tabula*, this type of index – the word index, or concordance – will be the second birth we witness in this chapter. Let us meet our second creator, Hugh of St Cher.

In the convent of San Nicolò at Treviso in Italy, a few miles north of Venice, a fresco running around the upper walls of the chapter house takes the form of a series of portraits. Each features a man wearing the white robe and black cappa of the Dominican Order – the Black Friars – and each man is shown seated at a desk, in the act of either reading or writing. These are the leading lights of the Dominicans. Taken as a whole, the fresco is a kind of hall of fame for the order's first century or so (the order was founded in 1216; the fresco, by Tommaso da Modena, was painted in 1352). It stresses the Dominicans' commitment to Bible study and to scholarship, and no portrait conveys this more than the image of Hugh of St Cher. Here he sits, with inkpot and quill, three heavy volumes at his feet and another open for reference at eye-level. The tassels of his galero, the red hat that indicates Hugh's status as a cardinal, dangle, twin irritants between his body and the page. His brow is furrowed, his expression severe. He is writing, but with a curious form of attention. The left hand, index finger extended, marks a place on the page, holds a thought, while the wrist rests on a second sheet of parchment with further

Figure 8: A bespectacled Hugh of St Cher at his writing desk in Tommaso da Modena's mid-fourteenth-century fresco for the Chapter House at the convent of San Nicolò.

notes on it. This is a writing act that is not fluent, abundant, the spontaneous overflow of powerful emotion; rather, it is patient, analytical, the writer synthesizing ideas from multiple sources. As if all this were not enough for us to get the message, the picture contains one more timeless symbol of intellectual endeavour. Tommaso's portrait of Hugh is the earliest known image of a man wearing spectacles.

obviously a moral

In fact, this final detail is a mistake, an anachronism. Hugh died a couple of decades too early to have benefitted from this invention: two magnifying glasses bound together by a rivet in their handles. But it tells us what Tommaso wants us to know about Hugh: that reading and writing are essential to how we should think of him. In his treatise on rainbows, who else but Robert Grosseteste – a contemporary of Hugh's, and another reader who would not quite live to put on a pair of specs – was able to glimpse blurrily the possibilities that the fledgling science of optical refraction might open up:

> This part of optics, if fully understood, shows us the way in which we can make objects at very long distance appear at very close distance, and large things, closely situated, appear very small, and small things at a certain distance we can see as large as we want, so that it is possible for us to read the smallest letters at incredible distance, or count the sand, or grain, or grass, or anything else so minute.[1]

But Hugh here is not counting sand, or grain, or grass. The rivet spectacles tell us that he is a man of letters.

As a writer, Hugh's work will trace a narrow orbit around the Bible. He will produce a monumental set of Bible commentaries which will endure well into the early modern period, along with a huge 'correctorium' – listing variants across different versions of the scriptures – which will not. Alongside the centrifugal impulse of an intellect like Grosseteste's, Hugh's writing offers something different: patience, focus. Let us consider him as a miniaturist beside Grosseteste's maximalism. Let us picture Hugh, not with a sheet of writing paper, but with a Bible before him. But let us still imagine those spectacles, spirited impossibly backwards across time and clamped to Hugh's nose to enable him to sift this Bible's words like sand, or grain, or grass. For Hugh will be the first to produce a concordance to the Bible, to break the book down and rearrange it into an alphabetical index of its words.

These, then, are our players, two midwives who will deliver the index into the world – simultaneously, independently – in or around the year 1230. But so far we have no backdrop, and no plot driving us to our denouement. Robert, Hugh: what is their motivation? The *idea* of the index must be in the aether if two people, hundreds of miles apart, are to chance upon it at the same time. What is the context, the need? What are the precedents? Let us leave our two heroes offstage, waiting in the wings for their entrances, while we pause to consider the *mise-en-page* of our books, the way they present their text.

Imagine a book. A paperback, a novel. Now imagine one of its pages, halfway through; not the start or the end of a chapter, just somewhere in the middle. In your mind's eye, what does it look like, this page? A single, wide column of text, surrounded by white space? Is it justified so that both sides have a straight edge? Perhaps the white space makes a few incursions into the text block: a bite coming in from the right where a paragraph finishes without reaching the margin; a nibble from the left where the next paragraph begins. A page number – where? Top right, or centred below the main text? And that is pretty much that: a standard page of modern prose.

Except that it is by no means the only standard. Imagine a different kind of book: a reference book this time – an encyclopedia, perhaps, or a bilingual dictionary: the kind of book you would use to look something up, but which you'd be unlikely to read from start to finish. What happens to the page layout now that the book is being used as a container for many discrete pieces of information, rather than for a single, continuous narrative? Is the text in multiple columns now? Maybe it is heavily abbreviated, words reduced to italicized morsels, *n.* for *noun, d.* for *died.* Maybe it's flecked with cross-references, **emboldened**, (parenthesized). How are the headwords marked out? A different typeface or larger lettering? Or maybe something in the margin, a bullet or a manicule, that Pythonesque pointing finger, telling us that this is the start of a new entry, a new unit of information? Probably there will be a running head above the text block, telling us what we can expect to find on this particular page, or how far through the alphabet we are.

All of these features are related to our story. The index, after all, did not arrive alone, but is rather the youngest sibling of a whole family of reading tools that arrived in a flurry in the few decades either side of the beginning of the thirteenth century. And all have one thing in common: they are all designed to streamline the reading process, to bring a new efficiency to the way we use books. To understand, then, why this family of interlopers should come crashing all at once onto the page, we will need to understand the need for speed.

'Blessed Lord, which hast caused al holy Scriptures to bee written for our learnyng; graunte us that we maye in such wise heare them, read, marke, learne, and inwardly digest them.'[2] We have jumped forward, briefly, by a few centuries, arriving just in time to hear the Archbishop of Canterbury telling us to slow down. The words form the opening to one of the short prayers known as collects, included by Thomas Cranmer in the *Book of Common Prayer* (1549) and intended to be spoken as part of the communion service. Hear, read, mark, learn and inwardly digest: this is how we should receive the Holy Scripture. For the most part, the terms in this salvo of advice can be understood literally. Readers today may not be as used to marking – to writing in – their books as a congregation in Cranmer's day, but *hear, read, learn*: these are all plain, unsurprising. How else would one expect to understand the Bible? But with *inwardly digest* comes something harder, more revealing. Surely Cranmer doesn't expect the faithful to eat their books. So what does the metaphor imply? Nourishment, certainly – the scriptures provide spiritual sustenance just as food provides us with physical sustenance. St Augustine draws this same parallel when he writes to a community of nuns, 'let it not be only your mouth that takes food, but let your ears also drink in the word of God'.[3] But Cranmer's metaphor surely implies something more, what we might call *rumination*, a word whose own meaning was originally linked to digestion but which has been extended metaphorically to signify a mental process: to mull, to consider.

Hear, read, mark, learn and inwardly digest. A detailed and specific programme. After all, how do we usually read? A few pages, snatched between bus stops on the way to work; snatched during our lunchbreak, while trying to ignore the pings and jingles of our mobile phones; snatched before sleep takes us at the end of the day. We read, for the most part, where we can. We read in the gaps, as we try to fit work, family – *life* – into the narrow tract of the day. But to hear, read, mark, learn and inwardly digest: there is an idea of patience, of slowness, implicit in these words, the sense of an abundance of time, or of reading – spiritual reading, at least – as being an activity that sits outside our usual fraught economies of the clock. It is an appeal to an ancient mode. How might we read if we took work and family out of the equation, if there was no commute and precious few other entertainments, if we pruned our library down to the essentials (the Bible; maybe a handful of theological works), if reading was our only responsibility, not just now but for life? Cranmer, ironically given the suppression of the monasteries that has just taken place, is asking us to read, or to hear the lessons, as though we were living in the regular, eternal rhythm of monastic time.

The monasteries put reading at the centre of daily life. After rising for prayer in the middle of the night, the Benedictine Rule stipulates that monks should then apply themselves to two hours of reading, after which they may either go back to bed, 'or if anyone may perhaps want to read, let him read to himself in such a way as not to disturb anyone else'.[4] At mealtimes, one monk will be appointed to read to the others, who must keep absolute silence 'so that no whispering may be heard nor any voice except the reader's'. Reading – and listening – have utter priority. The situation is the same in the nunnery, where St Caesarius prescribes two hours to be set aside for reading in the early morning and a nominated reader to be the only audible voice both at mealtimes and during the nuns' daily weaving. And woe betide the sister who finds herself drifting off: 'If anyone should become drowsy, she shall be ordered to stand while the others are seated, so that she can banish the heaviness of sleep.'[5] Attention is enforced. The scriptures are not to be a background noise, a radio left on quietly in the corner of the room. In the monastic tradition, reading *is* meditation, not a means to learning but an end in itself, endlessly repeated over a lifetime of ordered devotion, of devoted order.

And while monastic readers in the Middle Ages may have digested the scriptures inwardly, they ate, as it were, with their mouths open. Meditative reading engaged more senses than just the eye. As the historian Jean Leclercq, himself a Benedictine monk, puts it, 'in the Middle Ages, one generally read by speaking with one's lips, at least in a whisper, and consequently hearing the phrases that the eyes see'.[6] Reading involved a sensitivity to the image of the text as the finger traced the page, to the muscle memories that the words left on the lips as they were murmured, to the sound of the words as they were heard muttered aloud. Looking back on his first encounters with Ambrose, Bishop of Milan, in the late fourth century, Augustine remembers noticing the curious way Ambrose would read: 'his eyes would scan over the pages and his heart would scrutinize their meaning – yet his voice and tongue remained silent'.[7] This – reading in silence – is not normal, and Augustine wonders what could possess Ambrose to adopt such a practice. (Was it to preserve his voice? Or a way of avoiding unwanted discussions about the text he was reading?) Not so the tenth-century JoÙ of Gorze, who is said to have pored continuously over the psalms with a soft buzzing 'in morem apis': in the manner of a bee.[8] It is the immersive, sensory engagement of JoÙ the droner, not Ambrose the silent, that is the model for monastic reading in the Middle Ages.

But readers would not remain bee-like for ever. A century after JoÙ's buzzing, the centralizing reforms of Pope Gregory VII called for a more professionalized clergy. Church officials should now be trained administrators, versed not only in the scriptures but also in the principles of accounting and law. A papal decree of 1079 ordered that cathedrals should establish schools for the training of priests, and while these schools largely operated under the control of a single teacher, with students willing to travel long distances to study with a prestigious master, sometimes demand would outstrip supply. In a few centres – Bologna, Paris, Oxford, Cambridge – students and masters began to incorporate themselves into what were essentially guilds, to which they would apply the title *universitas scholarium* or *universitas magistrorum et scholarium*. The university had been born.[9]

While the focus of teaching in the monasteries was on quiet contemplation, in the schools and universities, where students were being trained for careers in religious or secular administration, new methods of teaching came to dominate. Disputation, the citing of authorities, the reading-out of commentaries (a format with a now-familiar name: the *lecture*): scholastic learning would favour external demonstration over inner revelation, intellectual agility over endless meditation. University readers would require new tools on the page, new ways of efficiently finding parcels of text – a word, a phrase – amidst the prose block.

Alongside this, during the twelfth century, an increasingly rootless, urban population, along with the threat of heretical sects had convinced the Church of the need for a new emphasis on preaching. A new model of religious order sprang up: the mendicants. Franciscans and Dominicans, living in poverty (*mendicant* has its root in *mendicans*: begging), not monks but friars – from *freres*: brothers – not isolated in remote monasteries but working among the wider population, evangelizing, preaching, not in Latin but in the everyday languages of the people. A renewed focus on communication, persuasion – on the sermon – that required a textual agility to match that being practised in the universities. The same fast, ordered way of thinking about the scriptures: who thinks well speaks well. Preachers and teachers: the book itself would have to shape up if it was to meet the needs of these new readers. Its pages would need to be remodelled, colour-coded, peppered with marks and dividers, designed to offer up information – morselized, tagged – efficiently. New tools, first the *distinctio* then the index, would be devised to offer these agile, demanding readers not paths, but something instantaneous, non-linear – *wormholes* – through the scriptures.

First of all, however, the text needs to be parcelled up. Pliny's table of contents works because the *Natural History* is divided into thirty-seven books. Conveniently, the Bible, of course, is similarly constituted. It is made up of the books of the Old and New Testaments, and some medieval cross-references use these alone. A margin note beside a quotation, 'Ezekiel saith', informs readers that passage is from the book of Ezekiel. But what if one actually wanted to look this up? Ezekiel is by no means a short book. Remember our fantasy of the Emperor Titus retiring in exasperation at the inefficacy of his searching. If the preachers and teachers of the thirteenth century are not to experience a similar frustration, they will need a way of arriving closer to their desired destination than simply 'Ezekiel saith'. Something more granular than the book, a system that can be shared among the entire scholarly community.

Figure 9 shows a manuscript page, taken from a commentary on Mark's gospel, produced in the last quarter of the twelfth century and now in the British Library. The image shows the first page, before the commentary itself begins. Just by looking at it – the roman numerals running down the left margin, the short(ish) passages beside each, the fact that it occurs at the front of the book – it should be possible to guess what this is. The top line, in red, introduces this page as the *capitula* – the chapters – to Mark's Gospel. Nowadays one might call it a table of contents.

Like a modern table, it is broken down into sections which are laid out so that each begins on a new line, and the large initials, in alternating red and blue ink, aid the eye by drawing it to the start of each new section. There is also a pilcrow – ¶, the paragraph mark still used in modern word-processing software – drawn in red to indicate a break that occurs within a single entry. The table breaks down Mark's Gospel into its chapters, summarizing their events and numbering them with a red numeral in the left-hand margin.

And yet anyone trying to map these chapters onto a twenty-first-century Bible would soon find that they don't quite match up. For a start, there are only fourteen of them rather than the sixteen we find in Mark today. And the episodes contained in each don't quite tally with the modern divisions. For example, the entry for Chapter 3 reads:

> iii. The disciples pluck ears of corn; he heals the man with the withered hand; the election of the twelve apostles; on Beelzebub, prince of devils.

In a modern Bible Mark 3 does indeed contain the stories of the man with the withered hand, the commissioning of the apostles and Jesus speaking about Beelzebub. What it does not contain, however, is the scene of the disciples picking grain. That happens at the end of Chapter 2. The twelfth-century commentary was produced before the chaptering of the Bible, its division into short textual units, had settled into a widely shared convention. In the new context of university teaching, of training in canon law, of citation and disputation, it is easy

Incipiunt capitula siue distinctiones super matheum euangelistam

i. De iohanne baptista. et uictu z habitu eiusdem. baptizatus ibe
Per temptatus. uicit. petrum z ceteros sequi iubet. hominem a
spiritu immundo expr̄t;

ii. Socrum petri a febribz libat. z alios multos curat. iacobum alphi
sequi iubet. et uidet dici non ē opus sanis medicum.

iii. Discipuli uellunt spicas. manum aridam b̄ntem sanat. duodecim
apostolorum electio. De beelzebub principe demoniorum;

iiii. Matrem z fratres spirt. parabolam seminantis dicit. nauigans tē
pestatem sedat. et demonium legione. m ab homine expellit.

v. Archisynagogi filiam mortuam suscitat. Nesciam in patria sua sine
honore dicit. Duodecim discipulos pmittit cum pceptis. De capite

vi. Regressi ad ihm apli. De quinqz panibz z duobus pisc. iohannis;
cibo. quinqz milia hominum saturat. ihe supra mare ambu
lat. Ca magis coinquinare hominem: que exeunt de ore.

vii. Filiam syrophenisse a demonio libat. surdum z mutum curat. dices
et effeta. De septem panibz in quatuor milia uirorum. monet ca
ueri a fermento phariseorum. De sputo ceco oculos apit. petrum
post confessionem suam dure increpat. in monte transfiguratur. si
posset ihm immundum eici: nisi p ieiunium z orationem dicit.

viii. Humilitatem docet. z non esse phibendum qui in nomine eius uir
tutem facit. et de calice aque frigide. uxorem non dimittendam.
Infantes a benedictione non ē arcendos. uendens omnibus he
lemosinam dandam. et quia diues difficile in regnum celorum
sit ingressurus.

ix. Cruentam sibi predicit. petitionem filiorum zebedei. de ceco in
dicante. De pullo asine;

x. Interrogatus in qua potestate hec faceret: parabolam de uinea
et colonis. et de denario cesaris. De muliere que septem fr̄s

to see how a standard system, something universal, was badly needed.

The task fell to an English cleric, Stephen Langton. Langton would go on to become Archbishop of Canterbury, instrumental in the wrangles with the king that would lead to Magna Carta; at the start of the century, however, he was a teacher in Paris. His chaptering, completed no later than 1204, was undertaken there, perhaps at the behest of the university.[10] As students completed their studies and returned to their home countries, Langton's system spread across the continent.[11] Its ubiquity was further ensured a couple of decades later when the Parisian *scriptoria*, the copyshops – the publishing houses of their day – began to incorporate it into the bibles which they produced in huge numbers.[12]

Division into verses would have to wait another few centuries, until Robert Estienne's printed editions of the early 1550s, but Langton's chapters – the chapters we still use today – provided a swift, accurate referencing system. They save time in the schoolroom, and they give us our first glimpse of the locators that Hugh will use as placeholders when he disassembles the Bible into its individual words. Langton's chapters will form the basis of the mapping between two ordering systems, between Bible and alphabetical concordance. We will have more to say about this soon. Now, however, it is time to consider another page, and to introduce the genre of *distinctiones*, older brother to the index.

At a meeting of the Church council during the latter half of the twelfth century, the assembled delegates are treated to a sermon preached by the Bishop of London, Gilbert Foliot. Foliot begins with an analogy: Christ is like a stone. To

illustrate the point, Foliot proceeds to run through a list of
biblical stones, from Psalm 118 ('The stone which the build-
ers refused is become the head stone of the corner') and the
stone that Jacob uses as a pillow (Genesis 28:10–22) to the
stone that smashes the false gods in Nebuchadnezzar's dream
(Daniel 2:34–35). At each stage, Foliot pauses, drawing out
the metaphorical implications of these different instances,
using each to shine new light on his opening analogy, enrich-
ing it by viewing it from a variety of angles. Seated in the
congregation, a scholar, Peter of Cornwall, watches with
rapt attention, awestruck at the dazzling flow of Foliot's
rhetoric, so nimble as it leaps smoothly, effortlessly, around
the scriptures. Years later, Peter will recollect the experience,
setting down his memories of how the sermon 'ran backwards and forwards on its path from its starting point back
to the same starting point'. Foliot's oration was sparkling and
learned, 'adorned with flowers of words and sentences and
supported by a copious array of authorities'.[13] But the key to
its elegance, Peter will realize, is in its organization: 'The
whole sermon was varied by certain *distinctiones.*'

Foliot's sermon was based on the principle of the *distinctio,*
of taking a topic – here *stone* – and anatomizing it, exploding
it into a variety of distinct senses, much like a dictionary
entry will list the multiple meanings attached to a single word.
Like dictionary definitions, too, these *distinctiones* could be
gathered together, compiled into one large volume. The *distinctio* collection could store up a trove of these individual
scriptural analyses, often in the hundreds, as a sourcebook
for preaching or a storehouse of ideas. Unlike a dictionary
entry, however, an individual *distinctio* is not intended to be
exhaustive. Its job is not to define a word; rather, in its
arrangement of manifold senses, it provides a memorable

format, a series of staging posts, for what is essentially a sermon in miniature.[14] As Mary Carruthers puts it:

> to divide matter into *distinctiones* in order to preach is not so much a device for objective classification as a means for easily mixing and mingling a variety of matters, and to be able to know where you are in your composition. A simple, rigorous ordering scheme is critical to the practice of oratory, for it cues the 'way' . . . It enables a speaker to enlarge a point, to digress, and to make spur-of-the-moment rhetorical side trips of all sorts.[15]

Each *distinctio* is an *aide-mémoire*, a well-ordered, bite-sized cribsheet on a given theme.

Different collections adopted different ways of setting out their analyses on the page. The diagrammatic presentation used in the *Distinctiones* of Peter the Chanter – one of the earliest examples of the genre – offers perhaps the most lucid illustration of how an individual *distinctio* actually works. Amounting to roughly 600 entries and running in alphabetical order from *Abel* to *Zelus*, Peter's collection explodes each of its topics into a sort of primitive tree diagram. Take, for example, the topic *Abyssus*, meaning *depth* (Figure 10). Here the rubricated headword gives onto five wavy lines, each one leading to a distinct sense in which the term might be understood – the depth of God's justice, or the depth of men's hearts – followed by the gobbet of scripture from which this particular sense is drawn: 'He layeth up the depth [*abyssos*] in storehouses' (Psalm 33:7), 'Deep [*abyssus*] calleth unto deep [*abyssum*]' (Psalm 42:7), and so on. It is not hard to imagine this as a preaching aid for a sermon like Foliot's: a visual aid, more memorable than a paragraph of text. It offers

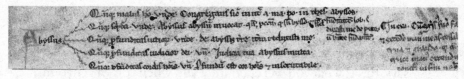

Figure 10: The distinction for *Abyssus* (or *Abyss*) from Peter the Chanter's *Distinctiones Abel*.

the security of the basics, the scaffolding – order, erudition – but leaves room for extemporization, for the preacher to take or leave particular elements, to spin from it their own elegant verbal performance.

When Peter of Cornwall heard Foliot speak, he was so inspired that he began to compile his own immense collection of *distinctiones* as an aid for preachers. At around a million words in length, Peter's *Pantheologus* may look a daunting read today, but it would be wrong to imagine that this would have been the case for its earliest users. Joseph Goering points out that, while modern scholars, looking historically at medieval manuscripts, might read them from start to finish, 'most *distinctio*-collections seem not to have been intended for consecutive reading'.[16] This is assuredly true, but *distinctiones* implicitly say something further about reading: they expect us to read *other* books in extract form as well. Far from the deliberate monotony of the monastic reading drill, of a lifetime spent patiently working and reworking one's way through the Bible, each *distinctio* sends its user on a series of targeted sorties into the source material – a phrase from the Psalms; maybe an image from one of the Gospels; a moment in Genesis. Every *distinctio* projects a different shape – a distinct snowflake – onto the scriptures, its own unique pattern of reading.

The *distinctio*-collection, then, is evidence of a type of

reading that might be thought of as indexical. A table of contents, as we saw in the Introduction, respects and reflects the order of the book to come. If you read from start to finish, it says, this is what you will encounter and when you will encounter it. The index, on the other hand, has nothing to say about orderly reading. In fact, if we wanted to reconstruct a book's sequencing from its index, we would need a spreadsheet and an awful lot of patience, and the whole exercise would probably take longer than it would just to read the book in the first place. The *distinctio* too offers, not so much a map of the book, as the mindmap of a moment of creative reading. It is neither methodical nor chronological, but *associative*, sparked by a single word or concept, firing unpredictably in multiple directions. We are inching towards a modern notion of the book index. What would happen if we took Peter the Chanter's *distinctio* for *Abyssus* and stripped out the quotations, replacing them with locators telling us where to look them up? The *distinctio* still serves a different purpose to the index headword. Focused on the senses of a term rather than the instances of it, it elucidates rather than enumerates. In the hands of an experimentalist like Grosseteste, however, the *distinctio*-collection offers a format that might be repurposed, upcycled, into something new.

And so we come, at last, to the entrance of our main players, Robert and Hugh. Grosseteste's origins are both humble and obscure. He was born in Suffolk, some time around 1175, probably into a family of tenant farmers. It was a lowly start that would be held against him even after a lifetime of service and achievement – as Bishop of Lincoln, his underlings would openly grumble that someone of such mean beginnings had been appointed above them. But the details of Grosseteste's background – so consequential to his peers – have been lost to us now. It is not even clear whether Grosseteste was the family name or an epithet applied once Robert's abilities had become manifest. *Grosse tête*: big head. In the seventeenth century, the Church historian Thomas Fuller would claim that Grosseteste 'got his surname from the greatness of his head, having large stowage to receive, and store of brains to fill it'.[17] Whatever, Robert's capacious intellect was recognized early on. Having acquired some schooling, perhaps supported by a local nobleman, the young Robert would find himself in the service of the Bishop of Hereford, arriving with a letter of recommendation from the historian Gerald of Wales:

> I know he will be a great support to you in various kinds of business and legal decisions, and in providing cures to restore and preserve your health, for he has reliable skill in both these branches of learning, which in these days are most highly rewarded. Besides, he has a solid foundation of the liberal arts and wide reading, which he adorns with the highest standards of conduct.[18]

Even here, our earliest real glimpse of the young Grosseteste, his 'wide reading', the encyclopedic nature of his learning – business, law, medicine, the liberal arts – is already the trait that captures the attention of his sponsors.

Grosseteste will serve two bishops: Hereford and Lincoln. Perhaps he will also study at Oxford; perhaps he will teach in Paris. As with his youth, his middle years must be viewed through a glass darkly, the evidence sketchy, unreliable. One thing we know for certain is that he begins to write. Scientific works: *On the Calendar*, *On the Movements of the Planets*, a commentary on Aristotle's *Posterior Analytics*. When we finally pin him down it is the late 1220s, and Robert, now in his fifties, is in Oxford, preaching to both gown and town, and lecturing at the newly established Franciscan convent. It is here too that Grosseteste is compiling his *Tabula distinctionum*, his Table of Distinctiones, the detailed, even picturesque, subject index to a lifetime of unbounded reading.

Grosseteste's index survives now in a single, incomplete copy, a manuscript kept in the municipal library at Lyon in south-eastern France. A title in red ink announces, 'Here begins the table of Master Robert, Bishop of Lincoln, with the help of Brother Adam Marsh.' Beneath it, a column of glyphs – dots, squiggles, geometric shapes, tiny illustrations, a sun, a flower – snakes downwards and then onwards, in three columns, for another four pages. Each sign is accompanied by a concept: eternity, imagination, truth . . . These are the topics, or subjects, of Grosseteste's index. Unlike the alphabetically arranged *distinctiones* of Peter the Chanter, Grosseteste's *Tabula* is ordered conceptually. The topics, all 440 of them, are grouped into nine top-level categories, broader themes like *the mind, created things, the holy scriptures*. So, taking Grosseteste's first category, *God*, as an example, it is broken down into thirty-six topics: that God exists, what God is, the unity of God, the trinity of God, and so on.

The first part of the *Tabula* then is simply a list of topics and their designated symbols. Essentially, this is a key, a way of remembering what each tiny glyph stands for. The signs are designed to be simple but distinct, a kind of shorthand that Grosseteste can jot in the margins of his books as he reads. Whenever a particular topic crops up, he can scratch the relevant glyph alongside it for later reference. Sometimes they have a clear relation to the topic – the holy trinity is a triangle; the imagination a flower – but given that the system runs to hundreds of topics, it is inevitable that some will seem arbitrary. S. Harrison Thomson, the first modern scholar to pay

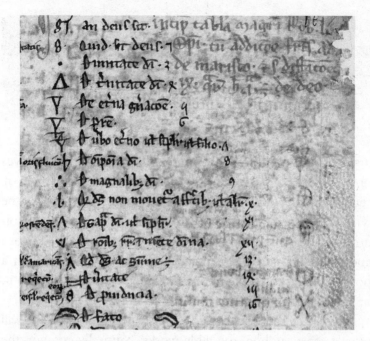

Figure 11: The opening of Robert Grosseteste's *Tabula distinctionum* showing topics on the theme of *God*, along with their symbols. The writing at the top right identifies this as 'the table of Master Robert, Bishop of Lincoln, with the help of Brother Adam Marsh'.

real attention to Grosseteste's index, neatly sums up their variety: 'All the letters of the Greek and Roman alphabets are used, plus mathematical signs, conjoined conventional signs, modifications of the zodiacal signs, and additional dots, strokes and curves.'[19] In Grosseteste's library every book would have been decorated with this pictorial annotation, thousands of glyphs running down the margins like streams of emoticons.

But this is not the index, merely its preamble. After the five-page list of symbols and their meanings, the *Tabula* returns to where it started, ready to begin in earnest. Now each topic will appear again, in order. This time, however,

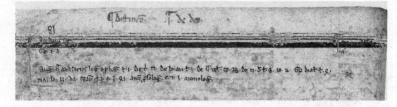

Figure 12: Grosseteste's list of references for the topic 'that God exists'.

instead of being merely an item in a list, each topic gives onto a dataset of its own. Beneath each topic is a series of references, of locators, first to Bible passages, then to the writings of the Church Fathers, and finally, in a separate column to the right, to pagan or Arabic writers. A headword and a list of locators. Grosseteste's *Tabula* is more than a book index; it is a *books* index, a subject index that aspires to be as encyclopedic as the mind of its creator.

Examining the first entry – *an deus sit* (that God exists) – will offer a sense of how the table works. Naturally enough, the entry begins with the topic and Grosseteste's symbol for it, before moving on to the list of locators. Expanding the abbreviations gives the following (where *l* indicates *liber*, i.e. book):

an deus sit

ge· 1· a·

augustinus contra aduersarios legis et prophetarum· l·1·
De trinitate ·12· De libero· arbitrio· l'·1· De uera religione·
epistola· 38· De ciuitate· dei l·8· 10· 11· gregorius dialogi l·4
·27· Ieronimus· 13· damascenus· sentenciarum ·l·1· c· 3· 41·
anselmus prosologion· c· 2· 3· monologion·

[and in the right margin] aritstoteles methaphisice l·1·[20]

What this all means is that, should a reader wish to know more about the proposition *that God exists*, they might begin by looking at the start of the first chapter of Genesis (i.e., 'ge. 1. a'). Here, of course, they would find 'In the beginning God created the heaven and the earth', reminding them that for anything to be created, a creator has to exist beforehand. The *Tabula* then directs readers to various works by Augustine – Books 8, 10 and 11 of *City of God* (*De Civitate Dei*), for example – or to Gregory's *Dialogues*, or Jerome, or JoÙ of Damascus, or Anselm. And for readers prepared to go off-piste into non-Christian thought, the *Tabula* suggests the first book of Aristotle's *Metaphysics*, where they would find the philosopher discussing the idea of primary causes.

We can test-drive the index today, using it as Grosseteste might have, thanks to the fact that some of the books he owned still survive. Thus, following up one of these references in Grosseteste's own copy of *De Civitate Dei*, now in the Bodleian Library in Oxford, I can turn to Book 8 and run my finger down the margin until I come across the topic's symbol (something like a snake holding a machine gun, or, at a squint, the letters ST). Augustine, at this point in the text, is arguing that God's existence cannot be thought of in material terms, and that the greatest philosophers have always understood this.

With Grosseteste's Augustine open in front of me and a scan of the *Tabula* on my laptop, it is easy enough to try the same exercise in reverse. Another glyph, something like a three-legged table, appears in the same section of margin, annotating the same passage. It represents the topic *de videndo deum* (*On seeing God*), and sure enough, turning to this topic in the *Tabula*, the list of references includes *De Civitate Dei*, Book 8. Having both Grosseteste's *Tabula* and some of his surviving books allows one to see both how the index worked and how he went about compiling it. Once the books had been annotated with topic symbols, filling in the index was simply a matter of skimming the margins for each sign in turn and jotting down the references.

The index as it survives is not finished. Only the first couple of hundred items from the initial topic list are treated in the index proper. Philipp Rosemann speculates that the *Tabula* was only half completed when it was copied by some of Grosseteste's students, a couple of whom were subsequently despatched to lecture at the Franciscan convent in Lyon, hence the manuscript's appearance there.[21] Perhaps Grosseteste intended the *Tabula* as a perpetual work-in-progress, something that he could carry on expanding throughout his life, and the Lyon manuscript is only a snapshot, frozen at the point it was copied, when Grosseteste still had decades of reading ahead of him. In fact, it is precisely the books which the manuscript *doesn't* include – texts that we know Grosseteste was familiar with – that allow us to put a date on the copy we have. For example, one of Grosseteste's many literary accomplishments was the translation from Greek of a work by Aristotle known as the *Nicomachean Ethics*. If he was still compiling the index by the time he translated this, we would expect to see some reference to it among the citations in the *Tabula*. It is by working backwards like this from what we know about Grosseteste's life as a reader that we are able to date the Lyon *Tabula* to around 1230.

It is not clear whether Grosseteste intended his index to be used by anyone other than himself and his immediate circle. What is certain is that the *Tabula* in its final form offered far more than simply a set of crib notes for time-pressed preachers. It was, rather, an instrument for serious scholarship. Users would need to have the primary texts to hand; they would need time to follow the references up; they would need to decide for themselves how to interpret the various senses in

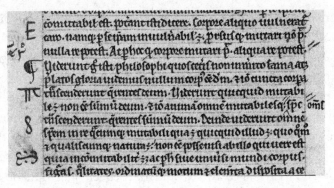

Figure 13: Grosseteste's copy of St Augustine's *De Civitate Dei* (*City of God*) with his topic symbols in the margin. The flower denotes *ymaginacion*.

which a topic has been used. Moreover, Grosseteste's index is simply *too* comprehensive to function as a convenient preaching aid. Each topic has dozens of instances, and Grosseteste's compass is far more ambitious than the *distinctiones* we have seen before. Ranging through scripture, patristic writings and classical philosophy, not to mention Islamic thinkers such as Avicenna and al-Ghazali, the all-encompassing *Tabula* is the search engine of the thirteenth century, a Google on parchment, or a divergent lens that takes its subjects and explodes them across the whole of known literature. But while Grosseteste was in Oxford, filling his margins among the Franciscans, across the Channel the index was about to be born again. A different model, as exhaustive – more – than Grosseteste's *Tabula*, but one which trains its attention with unprecedented focus on a single text. In 1230, a new prior will take over at the Dominican convent in Paris. Enter Hugh, the kind of man who would have worn glasses. ༄

If you've ever been to Paris and visited the Panthéon, the vast domed mausoleum on the Left Bank where the heroes of the

French republic are laid to rest, the chances are that you've stood at the foot of its steps and admired the view west up the Rue Soufflot to the Eiffel Tower. The area is heavily built up now, noisy with traffic, shaded by tall Haussmann blocks on either side of the road, their ground floors given over to commercial outlets: an optician, an estate agent, a couple of cafés whose crowded tables spill out onto the pavement. It is hard to imagine, then, that, had you been standing in the same spot 800 years ago, you would have been just outside the south wall of the Dominican friary of St Jacques. The Rue Saint-Jacques, which these days juts north towards the Sorbonne, cues us in, with its name, to the past, but there is little else to remind us of the calm – the cloisters, the chapel, the garden – that once characterized this busy, urban spot. In the thirteenth century, however, with painstaking care in the convent library, the friars of St Jacques were at work on an extraordinary project.

The year is 1230, and the friary, like the Dominican Order itself, is barely a decade old. The new prior, Hugo – Hugh to us now, his name Anglicized by history – is a man of thirty, and an intellectual. He was raised in what is now southeastern France, the town of Saint-Cher, just a few miles south, ironically, from Lyon, where Grosseteste's *Tabula* will come to rest. By 1230, however, Hugh has already been in Paris for more than half his life, having arrived at fourteen to study, then teach, at the university. He will spend only five years at the friary. His talents have already caught the eye of the pope; a life of diplomacy lies ahead. But, while he is at St Jacques, Hugh will oversee a grand project, one whose lasting and far-reaching impact will ultimately leave his later, more prestigious work in the shade. For it will be at St Jacques and under Hugh's leadership that the first verbal concordance to the Bible will be undertaken.[22]

The friars divide up the work. They take a letter, or part of a letter each, writing out all the words that begin with it, and all the instances of that word. They write in rough, draft versions, in multiple hands, with gaps and insertions. These will be grouped together later, put in order, copied out in neat. A task like this needs many hands; it needs oversight, a plan. When it is finished, the St Jacques Concordance – the word-by-word index to the Latin Bible – will identify over 10,000 terms and list them in alphabetical order. It will begin with the exclamation *A, a, a* (usually translated as *ah!* or *alas*) and end with *Zorobabel* (or Zerubbabel, a sixth-century governor of Judea). As well as names and exclamations, the concordance will also include the ordinary language of the Bible – common nouns, verbs, adjectives – and for each term it will list every instance of its occurrence, giving the book, chapter and chapter section in which it appears. The friars of St Jacques adopt Langton's chaptering but supplement it with another innovation, designed to add a further level of granularity. Each chapter is divided into equal sevenths, labelled *a* to *g*. A word near the start of a chapter can be given the sublocator *a*; a word in the middle, *d*; at the end, *g*. 'In the beginning': Genesis 1a. 'Jesus wept': JoÙ 11d.

Taking the first entry, then, the concordance gives us the following line of data:

A, a, a. Je.i.c. xiiii.d. eze.iiii.f Joel.i.f.

Expanding the abbreviations, this is telling readers that the search term, *A, a, a*, appears in Jeremiah 1 at position *c* (i.e. just before the middle of the chapter), as well as Jeremiah

14*d*, Ezekiel 4*f* and Joel 1*f*. Following these up, sure enough, will lead to:

> Jer. 1:6 Et dixi: **A, a, a**, Domine Deus, ecce nescio loqui, quia puer ego sum.
> [Then said I, **Ah**, Lord God! behold, I cannot speak: for I am a child.]

> Jer. 14:13 Et dixi: **A, a, a**, Domine Deus: prophetæ dicunt eis: Non videbitis gladium, et fames non erit in vobis: sed pacem veram dabit vobis in loco isto. ~ *gladiator*—!
> [Then said I, **Ah**, Lord God! behold, the prophets say unto them, Ye shall not see the sword, neither shall ye have famine; but I will give you assured peace in this place.]

> Ez. 4:14 **A, a, a**, Domine Deus, ecce anima mea non est polluta: et morticinum, et laceratum a bestiis non comedi ab infantia mea usque nunc, et non est ingressa in os meum omnis caro immunda.
> [Then said I, **Ah** Lord God! behold, my soul hath not been polluted: for from my youth up even till now have I not eaten of that which dieth of itself, or is torn in pieces; neither came there abominable flesh into my mouth.]

> Joel 1:15 **A, a, a**, diei! quia prope est dies Domini, et quasi vastitas a potente veniet.
> [**Alas** for the day! for the day of the Lord is at hand, and as a destruction from the Almighty shall it come.]

Thus, that one tight half-line of text contains everything needed to lead readers to the passages they want, while the alphabetical arrangement means that any search term can be located within seconds. Another extraordinary feature of the St Jacques Concordance is its size. Despite the vast amount of referencing information it contains, thanks to its heavy abbreviation and a five-column format on the page, it could be produced as a single small volume. One copy, in the Bodleian Library in Oxford, is about the size (fractionally shorter, slightly wider) of an index card, or a smartphone at the bulkier end of the market. It is an astonishing thought that this small, handwritten book contains location information for every word in the Bible.[23]

Nevertheless, if portability was an advantage, it brought with it a significant drawback. If we take another term from the first page, we can get a sense of the problem. Here are the first few entries for the term *abire*, to depart:

Abire, Gen. xiiii.d. xviii.e.g. xxi.c. xxii.b. xxiii.a. xxv.b.g xxvii.a. xxx.c. xxxi.b.c xxxv.f. xxxvi.a. xliiii.c.d

That's twelve separate references in the book of Genesis alone. The full list runs to hundreds of entries across several columns. In cases like these – and they are not uncommon – the concordance is in fact little use in locating the passage a reader might be looking for since the amount of work still left to do – all that page-turning and locating the term within those broad chapter divisions – is still impracticable.

The promise of the index – as a device which can bring about a new type of reading – relies on its allowing a reader to locate a passage within a timeframe that is reasonable. Where the reader is presented with an undifferentiated list running to dozens of entries, the index fails in its basic function as a finding aid. To be fair to the friars of St Jacques, if they had committed one of the cardinal sins of indexing, it was because they had literally just invented the form. Other indexers do not have this excuse. The long spool of unstructured locators is still all-too-commonly found, as in this egregious entry from the index to Ian Ker's biography of Cardinal Newman:

> Wiseman, Nicholas 69, 118–19, 129, 133–4, 135, 158, 182–3, 187, 192, 198, 213, 225, 232, 234, 317–18, 321, 325, 328, 330, 331–2, 339, 341, 342, 345, 352, 360, 372–4, 382, 400, 405, 418, 419, 420, 424–7, 435–6, 437, 446–7, 463, 464, 466–8, 469, 470, 471, 472, 474–5, 476–7, 486–9, 499, 506, 507, 512, 515–17, 521, 526, 535, 540, 565, 567, 568, 569–72, 574, 597, 598, 608, 662, 694, 709.[24]

Bemoaning this particular index in *The Times*, Bernard Levin thundered, 'What is the point of wasting space on idiocy of that order? What conceivable purpose could it serve? How *dare* the publishers print it under the noble and meaningful heading "Index"?'[25] To be fair to Jonathan Cape, who published the Newman biography, the next edition featured a vastly improved index; to be fair to the Dominicans, a second version of the concordance was soon in production.

The new concordance would become known as the *Concordantiae Anglicanae* or English Concordance since it was compiled – once again at St Jacques – by the English friars, Richard of Stavensby, JoÙ of Darlington and the wonderfully named Hugh of Croydon.[26] The innovation of the English Concordance was to add a passage of contextual quotation for each reference – what we would now call a keyword-in-context or KWIC index of the type seen in, for instance, the 'snippet view' of Google Books. Here's how the first few entries for *regnum* (kingdom) appear in one of the English Concordance fragments held in the Bodleian Library:

Regnum

Gen. x.c. fuit autem principium .R. eius Babilon et arach

[Gen. 10:10: And the beginning of his **kingdom** was Babylon, and Arach];

xx.e. quid peccavimus in te quia induxisti super me et super .R. meum peccatum grande

[Gen. 20:9: what have we offended thee in, that thou hast brought upon me and upon my **kingdom** a great sin?];

xxxvi.g. cumque et hic obiisset successit in .R. balaam filius achobor

[Gen. 36:38: And when he also was dead, Balanan the son of Achobor succeeded to the **kingdom**];

xli.e. uno tantum .R. solio te precedam

[Gen. 41:40: only in the **kingly throne** will I be above thee].[27]

With the new concordance, as well as being told the book, chapter and chapter section, users could see at a glance the sentence in which it appears.

The English Concordance, however, was not without its drawbacks, chief of which was that with so much contextual quotation, the book had now swelled to a vast, multi-volume size. An entry that might have taken half a column in the first concordance now runs over four or five lines. Scale that up for some of the commonest words – *God*, say, or *sin* – which were already running to several pages even without adding a sentence for every locator, and the sheer size of the book becomes cumbersome enough to compromise its usefulness. Before the end of the century, therefore, a third version had been compiled at St Jacques, keeping the snippet view, but shrinking it to three or four words, and it is this format which would become the standard for centuries to come. The story of the concordance, then, is a Goldilocks tale: a book that is too small, another too large, and a third format which, at last, is just right.

With the success of the concordance, the index had entered the mainstream, and in a monumental form. For a sense of its scale, of the paradigm shift it presented, we might think back to Peter the Chanter's *distinctio* for *Abyssus* which presented five different biblical instances of the term. The concordance gives us more than fifty. And where a *distinctio*-collection might run to several hundred entries, the concordance includes many thousand. We might wonder whether this capaciousness is, in fact, an advantage, at least for preachers who might previously have used *distinctiones*. Nevertheless, by the early fourteenth century, the *distinctio*-collection had passed out of fashion, while Thomas Waleys, a theology master at Oxford, could write in praise of the alphabetical concordance:

> this mode of preaching, that is, by bundles of the authorities, is very easy, because it is easy to have the authorities, since Concordances of the Bible have been made ... in alphabetical order, so that the authorities can be easily found.[28]

Moreover, within a few years of the first St Jacques concordance, people were beginning to experiment with the index form. Two florilegia – books of extracts from patristic or ancient authors – now held in the Bibliothèque municipale in Troyes in northern France both feature alphabetical indexes that are extensive, clear and easy to use.[29] They were compiled by William Montague, who died in 1246, making them near contemporaries of the St Jacques concordance.

Montague's indexes are essentially concordances, albeit ones that apply to far shorter works than the Bible. They are highly detailed usage maps of individual words. Other scribes, however, were trying out different variations on the index form, mixing the partial approach of the *distinctio*-collection – that doesn't aim for comprehensiveness, but rather picks out a number of key themes – with the bare locators of the concordance. The manuscript known as Oxford, Lincoln College MS 79 is one of four surviving copies of a work known as the *Moralia super Evangelia* or *Moralities on the Gospels*, thought to have been the work of our old friend Robert Grosseteste. The Lincoln College manuscript – dating probably from the second quarter of the thirteenth century – is distinguished by having not one, but two indexes.[30] (In fact, somewhat bizarrely, it has four: two at the front, and the same two, copied out in a different hand, at the back.) The first is non-alphabetical, though its keywords are loosely grouped together with thematically similar entries appearing close to one another. The ordering principle seems to be that of an invisible *distinctio*-list, a collection with its headwords, wavy lines, and separation between entries removed, so that a run of sins – wrath, discord, hatred, slander, speaking ill, murder, lying – now flows seamlessly into a cluster of virtues – clemency, patience, serenity. This is followed – immediately in the same hand on the same page – by a much more granular alphabetical index, where the emphasis is less on the abstract and more on the material world.

By the middle of the century then, the alphabetical subject index has arrived. And if, as E. J. Dobson speculates, Grosseteste's *Moralia* was written with its index already in mind, it wasn't long before readers were adding their own indexes to books that had not been planned that way. Here, perhaps, we recognize something we have in common with these medieval readers. I know I do: of the books I use in class, almost all of them have a list of page numbers – important scenes, useful quotations, passages for close reading – scribbled in pencil on the inside cover when I've been preparing my lessons. Extracting, navigating, using the index to find the words we need: it is a way of reading that is as old as the university itself.

3

Where Would We Be Without It?
The Miracle of the Page Number

'So much for my chapter upon chapters, which I hold
to be the best chapter in my whole work.'

Laurence Sterne, *Tristram Shandy*

I am in the Bodleian Library in Oxford with a small printed
book open on the desk in front of me. This is the text of a
sermon, and it was printed in 1470 in Cologne at the printshop
of a man named Arnold Therhoernen. The book is no larger
than a paperback, and the text itself is short, just twelve
leaves – twenty-four pages – long. But sitting here in the library
with the book before me and opened on its first page is, I
think, the most intense experience that I have had of the arch-
ival sublime, that sense of disbelief that something so
significant, something of such conceptual magnitude, should
be here on my desk among my own workaday effects – laptop,
notebook, pencil. It feels astonishing that I should be allowed
to pick it up, hold it, turn its pages as though it were a novel I
purchased at the train station. Why is it not under glass, sealed
off, labelled and exhibited where crowds of schoolchildren
might look but not touch? There's a name for this feeling:
Stendhal Syndrome, after the French novelist who, on a visit
to Florence, described the palpitations he experienced at being

so close to the tombs of the Renaissance masters. I feel like I am on the verge of tears.

The sermon was written by Werner Rolevinck, a monk from the Cologne Charterhouse. Rolevinck would become famous for writing the *Fasciculus temporum* or *Little Bundle of Dates*, a history of the world from the first day of the Creation to the bleeding edge of the present, in this case, 3 May 1481, the date on which, Rolevinck informs us, the Ottoman Emperor Mehmet II went to hell for his wickedness against Christianity.[1] But the lengthy and complex *Fasciculus* was still a work in progress when Rolevinck penned this short sermon to be preached on the feast of the Presentation of the Blessed Virgin Mary, 21 November. If the truth be told, however, it is neither Rolevinck nor his preaching that make this book special for me. It is something else, something about the book itself, there in the right-hand margin, halfway down: a single, large capital J. The ink has bled slightly, the impression slightly too strong so that the letter is a little smudgy, without the detail and clarity of the gothic lettering in the main text block. Nevertheless, I love this J all the more for its blurriness. I would rather it were this way – characterful, let's call it – than that other J (crystalline, a perfect impression) just to the left of it in the main text, beginning the name *Joachim*. Our marginal J has nothing to do with Joachim; it is pure coincidence that they should appear side by side like this. In fact, our J is not really a J at all. It is there as a numeral – 1 – announcing that this is the first leaf of the book. Our J is the first printed page number. It will revolutionize the way that we use books. And in doing so it will become such a commonplace that it will almost disappear from view, hiding in plain sight at the edge of every page.[2]

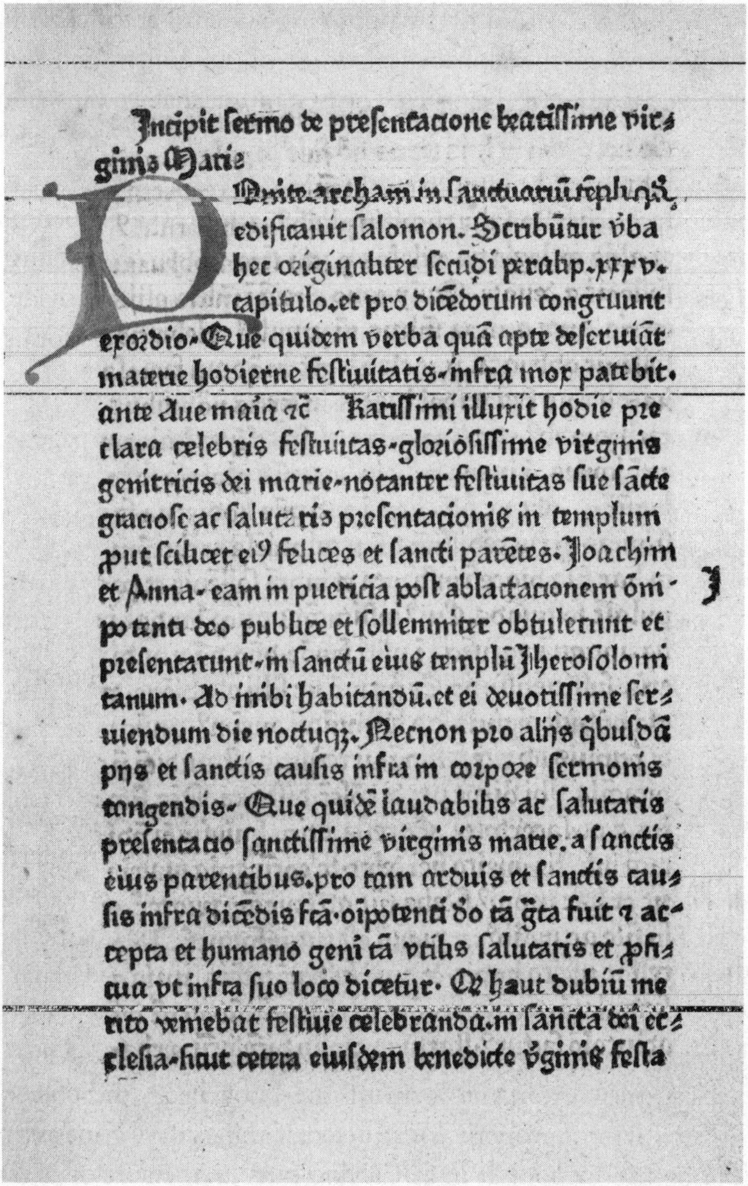

Incipit sermo de presentacione beatissime virginis Marie

Porite archam in sanctuariu seph. qd
edificauit salomon. Scribuntur vba
hec originaliter scripi pralip. xxv.
capitulo. et pro dicedorum congruunt
exordio. Que quidem verba qua apte deseruiat
materie hodierne festiuitatis. infra mox patebit.
ante Aue maia zc.   Karissimi illuxit hodie pre
clara celebris festiuitas. gloriosissime virginis
genitricis dei marie. notanter festiuitas sue sacte
graciose ac salutaris presentacionis in templum
qput scilicet ei9 felices et sancti parentes. Joachim
et Anna. eam in puericia post ablactacionem omi-
potenti deo publice et sollemniter obtulerunt et
presentarunt. in sanctu eius templu Jherosolomi
tanum. Ad inibi habitandu. et ei deuotissime ser-
uiendum die noctuqz. Necnon pro alijs qbusda
pijs et sanctis causis infra in corpore sermonis
tangendis. Que quide laudabilis ac salutaris
presentacio sanctissime virginis marie. a sanctis
eius parentibus. pro tam arduis et sanctis causis infra dicedis fca. oipotenti do ta gta fuit q ac-
cepta et humano geni ta vtilis salutaris et pficua vt infra suo loco dicetur. Ex haut dubiu me
rito veniebat festiue celebranda. in sancta dei ec-
clesia. sicut cetera eiusdem benedicte virginis festa

3

Figure 14: The first printed page number in Werner Rolevinck's *Sermo de presentacione beatissime virginis Marie* (1470).

An index is a tool of two ordering systems, a conversion table between the alphabetical order of its entries and the sequential order of the pages. The first means that we can skim quickly to the headword we require; the second means that, armed with our locator, we can move easily to the passage it indicates. Where Chapter 1 traced the story of alphabetical order, in this chapter we will look at the locators – page numbers, digital locations, even chapters themselves – that provide, with greater or lesser precision, the landing co-ordinates for us to enter a work via the index.

> Wait a minute! Look at the page number. Damn! From page 32 you've gone back to page 17! What you thought was a stylistic subtlety on the author's part is simply a printer's mistake: they have inserted the same pages twice. The mistake occurred as they were binding the volume: a book is made up of sixteen-page signatures . . . when all the signatures are bound together, it can happen that two identical signatures end up in the same copy.

An accident at the binders, the same gathering of leaves inserted twice. This is the glitch that begins the dizzying pile-up of narratives that make up Italo Calvino's postmodern novel *If on a Winter's Night a Traveller*. From here, things quickly spin out of control. Pages appear from other books, fragments from a gumshoe thriller, a spaghetti western, Chekhovian naturalism, Borgesian fantasy . . . This is a novel of compounded interruptions, a novel against order. But the chaos, in Calvino's set-up, arises from the form of the book itself, the codex. What if it's not properly constructed, if things have gone awry during production? It is, as Calvino puts it, 'the sort of accident that happens every now and then'. We have all come across misprints. Maybe we have come across other errors, pages that have been too heavily or too faintly inked, or where the type is misaligned, wonky. A book is, after all, just another piece of mass-produced tecŪology.

Most of the time, when we talk about books, about literature, we have no particular form in mind. It is not the actual book, the material object, but rather the text-in-the-abstract — words, plots, characters — that concerns us. Your copy or mine, first edition or cheap reprint, hardback, paperback or digital download, it doesn't matter: Jane still marries Mr Rochester in the end. But, reader, there is no such thing as an immaterial text. And however it is instantiated — whatever physical form it takes — we need to know that it works, that the words it delivers up to us are the right ones in the right order. What Calvino's novel does is remind us of the book itself, foregrounding its physical sequencing — something we take for granted — by removing it.

The page number, of course, is not the only sequence running through a written work. Earlier on in our history we saw how the literary critics at the Library of Alexandria divvied up Homer's *Iliad* and *Odyssey* into twenty-four books — the number of letters in the Greek alphabet — and how the friars of St Jacques used the chapters of the Bible for their concordance. These are meaningful divisions, sensitive to their texts. They try to break up the action when the viewpoint shifts, when the subject changes or the scenery needs shuffling around. As readers we still use divisions like these — sections, chapters — every day to orient ourselves in a work or to measure out our reading. And yet a modern index will seldom follow suit. A brief look at the chapter should illustrate why.

When we come to modern works — works, that is, of a slightly more recent vintage than the *Odyssey* or the Bible — we will usually assume that the author has applied their own divisions, that the chaptering was something planned at the time of writing, a unit of intention. This may not always be the case: Mrs Gaskell would submit her novels in flurries of continuous manuscript, leaving it to her editor – probably Dickens – to break them up for serialization.[3] But most writers, it is fair to say, do give some thought to the matter. Take, for example, Henry Fielding, whose 1742 novel *Joseph Andrews* is divided into four books, the second of which opens with a chapter-length disquisition on why authors divide up their works into books and chapters. Fielding describes this breaking up of narrative as something like a trade secret, a mysterious art of the novelists' guild which he will unveil to the uninitiated reader. Chapter breaks, states Fielding, provide staging posts on a long journey: 'those little spaces between our chapters may be looked upon as an inn or resting place where [the reader] may stop and take a glass.' Many readers, he goes on, read at a pace of no more than a single chapter each day. Length, then, should be set as the smallest unit a reader can read in a single sitting. By thus persuading readers to pause at regulated moments, rather than willy-nilly within the text, chaptering 'prevents spoiling the beauty of a book by turning down its leaves'.

Fielding's tongue might be firmly in his cheek here, but the point feels right: a chapter, on the whole, is a unit based on our availability as readers. Different books, different genres, calibrate this differently: the punctual half-hour instalments of the bedtime story; the short, moreish hits of the thriller or the beach read. But what should be clear is that chapters are geared primarily to be readable, not searchable. As index locators, they lack granularity. The amount of text we read in a sitting is still a rather large haystack in which to be looking for the needle of a single phrase or detail. 'It becomes an author generally to divide a book, as it does a butcher to joint his meat,' waxes Fielding, 'for such assistance is of great help to both the reader and the carver.' The indexer, however, can go whistle.

Before the thirteenth century was out, then, medieval indexers had begun to turn to another type of locator, one with a high degree of granularity, and available in any work regardless of whether an author or an editor had previously divvied it into sections. The new locator, however, would have a new relationship to the text. No respecter of the passage of thought, it would instead be ruthlessly disinterested, apt to splice a sentence – even a word – in midflow. Its allegiance would be not to the story or to the argument but to the physical book. In the chapter that follows, or perhaps we should say the pages that follow, we will have cause to think about the way our books are made, their materiality. What is a page, a leaf, a signature, a loc? And how can their numbering go awry, becoming unreliable either in the fourteenth century or the twenty-first?

Another library, another old book. It is mid-December, late afternoon. Outside it is cold, dark, a winter rain lashing the window. But I am cosy, nestled, satisfied, hunting words. It is the library of St JoÙ's College, Cambridge. The students have gone home for the holiday season, and no one is here but myself and the librarian, who has brought me a lamp, a reading stand, and a manuscript: St JoÙ's MS A.12. It contains a work known as the *Polychronicon*, written by a monk named Ranulf Higden from Cheshire in the north of England in the middle of the fourteenth century. Higden's *Polychronicon* is a history book, and, like Rolevinck's *Fasciculus*, its scope is ambitious to say the least. Its span, as its first English translator puts it, is 'from the begynnyng of the world unto our tyme'. To this end, Higden weaves together classical, biblical and medieval histories, blending them all into a narrative that starts with the division of the earth into three continents (Asia, Europe and Africa) and ends with the coronation of Edward III. It was an immediate popular success, a medieval bestseller. Over a hundred manuscripts containing the work still survive today, and there is no way of knowing how many more have been lost or destroyed in the intervening centuries.

So much for the text, but what about the book itself? The copy in front of me was made in 1386, a few decades after Higden's original. Its 200-odd leaves, wheaty yellow, darkening to a greasy black around the edges, are mottled with the blemishes of the animals whose skins they are made from. They have the musty-sweet leather smell that medieval manuscripts do. Like incense, slightly acrid. A scent that sticks on your fingers and gets into your clothes. The parchment is thick, slightly curling, and the leaves crinkle loudly when I turn them. The bottom corners, however, have been worn thin, sometimes almost to translucence, from handling. This is a well-thumbed manuscript, one that had seen several owners before coming into the College's possession. JoÙ Dee – advisor to Queen Elizabeth, mathematician, astrologer and magician – has signed his name on the first page. But the manuscript was nearly 200 years old by the time Dee got his hands on it. The oldest autograph appears not on the first page but the last. Beneath the final paragraph, in larger letters, is a colophon, a brief note by the scribe: 'And this is the end. He who wrote this book, JoÙ Lutton is his name, may he be forever blessed.' Lutton had just finished writing out the history of the world by hand, transcribing it patiently, word by word, from another copy. No wonder he felt like blessing himself. But, in fact, Lutton's work was not quite over. The colophon is not the final word in this manuscript. Like any good history book, the *Polychronicon* comes with a comprehensive index, probably compiled originally by Higden himself. Sure enough, then, right after signing his name, Lutton began a new column and started to copy again.

Like many early indexes, this one is prefaced by a paragraph of explanation, a how-to guide for the medieval reader. With the book in front of me, I try it out. 'First of all, note the leaf numbers in the top right corners; these represent the number of each written leaf.' A bit of tautology perhaps, but I get the point. What next? 'Then consult the table wherever you please.' In other words, find the entry for whatever it is you're looking for. Next:

> For example, '*Alexander destroyed the city of Tyre except for the family of Strato 72.2.3*'. This number, 72, indicates that the heading from the table can be found on the leaf where 72 is written in the top corner. And directly after this number 72 are also the numbers 2 and 3 which indicate that the matter of Alexander and Strato is discussed in the second and third columns.[4]

Hmm . . . A bit wordy, but I think I've got it. Let's give it a go. I turn to the leaf marked 72 . . . That's funny. Alexander is nowhere to be found here, either in the second column or anywhere else on this leaf, front or back. Instead there is the story of Seleucus, one of Alexander's successors. Alexander seems to be dead by this point in the narrative. Clearly, the story has moved on. Flicking backwards, I skim in reverse replay through Alexander's demise and his late campaigns, turning the pages until, finally, sure enough, I come to the story of how he laid waste the city of Tyre. It is on the reverse side of leaf number 66.[5] What is happening? Why doesn't the how-to guide work? How did this book end up with a broken index?

The answer is that the index almost certainly does work – or rather it *did* – just not for this particular book. Six hundred years ago, when Lutton wrote out the *Polychronicon* by hand, he would have had another copy of the same work in front of him to use as his exemplar. But scribes did not, as a rule, pay attention to the pagination of their writing – after all, they might be copying from a large format book into a small one, or vice versa. The copy in St JoÙ's College is about the size of my laptop – a medium-sized book. If the book that Lutton was copying from was slightly smaller, it is entirely possible that the words on page 72 of the exemplar might end up on page 66 of the copy. For index locators, of course, this is of fundamental importance. But poor old John Lutton, it seems, was unfamiliar with the tecÙology of the book index. He just transcribed the numbers as they were. A perfect copy. Just not a perfect index.

A quick look at the index itself confirms that this was the case. The introductory paragraph has escaped unscathed, but in the main table every single locator has been erased: literally scraped off the parchment with a sharp knife by a later reader frustrated at all the broken links. One can see where it has happened because the skin of the page is fractionally lighter where its top layer has been scratched away. On top, or sometimes beside, in red ink and a late medieval hand (though one markedly different from Lutton's) are a series of new locators – ones that *do* work. Evidently, the index was recognized as a dud early on. This simply wouldn't do. Readers, even medieval readers, want to be able to *look things up* in their history books. The page number – or, strictly speaking, the leaf number: only one side of the page is marked up – has brought granularity at the expense of portability: the index has to be redrafted every time it is recopied. But the problem of the broken index is a specifically medieval one, a problem from the manuscript age. In the middle of the fifteenth century – though just too late for Lutton – it would disappear at a stroke.

The life of Enea Silvio Piccolomini was nothing if not eventful. By the end of it, he would no longer be Enea but Pope Pius II; along the way he would be an envoy to the pope's ambassador in England, poet laureate to the Holy Roman Emperor in Vienna and father to two children – one in Strasbourg, one in Scotland – though neither would survive into adulthood. Later, as pope, he would persuade the prince of Wallachia, a certain Vlad Dracula – otherwise known as Vlad the Impaler – to go to war with the Ottoman Sultan, something which Vlad initiated with characteristic brutality: by nailing the Sultan's emissaries' turbans to their heads. If all

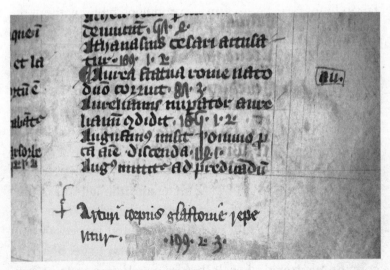

Figure 15: A medieval broken link. The darker patch of parchment beneath the numerals shows how the original incorrect locator was scraped off and overwritten with a new – correct – folio number.

this were not enough, in his writing, Piccolomini also serves – at nearly 600 years' distance – as our earliest surviving witness to something of more world-shattering importance even than the wars and crusades in which he had a starring role.

It is the spring of 1455, and Piccolomini, a few months shy of fifty, is still in the foothills of his steep, late ecclesiastical career. He has been made bishop of his native Siena, but he resides in Vienna, at the court of Frederick III. On 12 March, he sits down to write a letter to his mentor, Cardinal Juan Carvajal. After a few preliminaries, he picks up a thread from his previous letter, a rumour that he has passed on to his old friend, and which has clearly aroused the Cardinal's attention. Piccolomini jokes, 'I can imagine your grace's great desire to know how matters stand from the fact that the messenger you sent was quicker than Pegasus!'[6] The news is that a 'marvellous man' has been trumpeting a new invention at the trade fair in Frankfurt: a way of mass-producing bibles without the need to copy them out by hand. The man, of course, is Johannes Gutenberg. And where previously Piccolomini had been able only to pass on gossip, today he tells the Cardinal that he has seen with his own eyes the output from Gutenberg's printing press: 'What was written to me about that marvellous man seen at Frankfurt is entirely true. I have not seen complete Bibles but only a number of quires of various books [of the Bible]. The script is extremely neat and legible, not at all difficult to follow.' With an afterthought that might remind us of another bookish cardinal, he adds, 'Your grace would be able to read it without effort, and indeed without glasses.' Piccolomini promises that he will try to get hold of a copy on his friend's behalf, before sounding a note of caution: 'But I fear that won't be possible ... because buyers were said to be lined up even before the books were finished.'

Gutenberg's Bible – the first major production of the print-ing press – had sold out on pre-orders alone.

Although Gutenberg's invention (or rather series of inven-tions: the metal letter sorts – tiny, individual, reusable – and the method of casting them; the oily ink that could be slopped across a page of type without running off as pen ink would; the press that would distribute pressure evenly across the page) was initially a trade secret in his home city of Mainz, soon, inevitably, it would spread across Europe. In 1462, Mainz was sacked as part of a bitter conflict that saw many of its citizens flee the region. The refugees included trained printers, and before long printshops sprang up in Ulm, Basel, Venice, Rome. Around 1473, an English merchant named William Caxton was on a visit to Cologne when he saw a press there. This invention, he reasoned, might be just the thing for a problem he had been having with some extracurricular activity. For some years, Caxton had been living in Bruges, where he had become close to the circle of Margaret of York, wife of the Duke of Burgundy. Lately he had translated a popular poem on the legends of Troy into English, and his version had proved popular with the English speakers of Margaret's court. But the poem was long, and copying it out for everyone who wanted it was a daunting task. 'My penne is worn,' wrote Caxton, 'my hand wery & not stedfast myn eyen dimed with ouermoche lokyng on the whit paper and my cor-age not so prone and redy to laboure as hit hath ben.'[7] In setting up a printworks, Caxton would be able to rattle off enough copies to satisfy demand without straining his eyes or spraining his wrist. (Rather, he would employ trained com-positors to work all day setting the tiny letters of type and pressmen to tirelessly operate the heavy machine.)

Caxton's *Recuyell of the Historyes of Troye* would be the first printed book in English. In a note at the end of the text, Caxton states that the printing was 'begonne in oon day and also fynyshed in oon day'. This is certainly an exaggeration, a moment of entrepreneurial overclaiming, but the point nevertheless is a crucial one: the time it takes to produce a book in bulk has been radically cut. Gutenberg's invention has ushered in the age of the print run, of the mass production of literature. Caxton trumpets the speed of the press, but there is an undocumented feature too – a side-effect, perhaps, whose lasting importance had not yet come fully into focus at the time Caxton was writing. Mass production brings uniformity. Across a print run, every copy of a work will have not just the same text, but the same layout, the same pagination. Readers would no longer need chaptering to be able to share accurate references with each other. As long as they were looking at the same edition, they could use the physical book instead. 'Last leaf, recto side, half way down: claims he printed the whole thing in one day.' And there it is. Now we're on the same page.

This is all well and good in this instance, when the quotation in question is on the final leaf, a location that is easy to describe. But what if the desired passage was buried deep in the middle of a text running to hundreds of pages? Alexander at Tyre, say, about a third of the way into the history of the world? Gutenberg's invention might have brought stability to the page; but it was those smudged, marginal numerals in an obscure sermon from Cologne, a decade and a half later, that pointed the way to how this uniformity might be exploited, a shared locator for disparate readers. The page number has become the universal referencing unit, the second basic ingredient – along with alphabetical order – of pretty much any book index in the last 500 years. Glance at any of the endnote citations in the book you are holding – in *any* book, for that matter – and invariably it will direct readers to a particular numbered page, some descendant of that first marginal J.

Except . . . what if you are reading this on an eReader, with its percentage bar and its 'Time left in chapter' message (a metric that might have been dreamed up by Fielding)? Because screen text is 'reflowable' – because readers can expand or contract their margins, shrink or enlarge their font, swap it to a generous Palatino, a parsimonious Times – the page, so reliable for so long, has gone off the rails again. Or, to put it another way, a screen is not a page. For our convenience, for continuity between formats, ebooks *may* come with page numbers coded into them so that readers – no matter what their screen settings are – can still navigate to a point of reference from the print edition. But this is by no means a given. Ebooks are just as likely to pitch us back into the world of JoÙ Lutton, where Alexander reaches Tyre six screens earlier on your device than on mine.

And yet, behind their search bars, eReaders still keep an index (a concordance, really) of every book stored on them. Type in a search term, and the device will bring up a list of every time it appears; click on one of these instances, and the device will take you through to the passage in which the word appears. How are these locations marked, if not by page numbers? On the eReader, location stability comes not from the physical device, but from the file one downloads whenever one purchases an eBook. Like the printed book, the file offers portability across an edition: your device or mine, large font or small, if we download the same file, we can divide it up the same way to share locations. On the Kindle, the locator of choice is the loc#, a division based on numbered units of 150 bytes. Like the page number, this is a blind splicing, one that pays no attention to what is being said, to the passage of thought, the appropriate pause. The loc# doesn't care what any of its 150 bytes represent, whether they are letters of the authorial text or mark-up instructions telling the eReader that a passage should be displayed in italics or indented or as a hyperlink. It is a crude algorithm, but it makes for a highly granular system of locators, one which can pinpoint a search term to an area shorter than a tweet.

For all their accuracy, however, file locations are still a long way from being socially acceptable. The *Chicago Manual of Style*, for example, is cool on them, suggesting that *textual* divisions – chapters or numbered paragraphs: non-arbitrary, format-neutral – are preferable when citing an eBook. Portability trumps granularity. If one absolutely must cite an eBook locator, the manual suggests including both the specific location and the total number of locations – 'loc 444 of 3023' – so that readers of other formats can work out, at least roughly, how far through the work the reference occurs.

Five and a half centuries ago, the situation was not so very different. Numbered leaves, in fact, did not catch on as quickly as we might have expected. For several decades after that primal J, the printed page number remained a rarity. By the end of the fifteenth century, it was still only found in about ten per cent of printed books.[8] To understand why this might be, let us look at a pair of documents, inspecting them carefully, thinking about how they were produced, and how they were used. They are from the same year, both printed in 1470. The second, naturally, is the Rolevinck *Sermo* printed by Arnold Therhoernen. For the first, we must return to Mainz, to the cradle of the printing press, and to a man who was there from the beginning.[9]

*

We are in the printshop of Peter Schöffer, Gutenberg's first foreman before the relationship turned sour. Schöffer is now a successful printer in his own right, and on the press today is a sales list, a single sheet, printed on one side, advertising his wares. This will be used by the travelling salesmen who cart Schöffer's books around the country, selling to students, clergy and other educated readers. Arriving in a new town, the salesman will leave copies of the handbill wherever interested buyers might find it, adding details of how to contact him. We do not know how many copies of the list were printed; only one survives today, discovered in the late nineteenth century having spent four centuries as padding inside the covers of another book. Now it is in the Bayerische Staatsbibliothek, the library of the Bavarian state, in Munich. It is the earliest known printed book list.

Actually, though this is how it is usually described, to call this sheet a printed book list is to simplify how it really worked. This book list, in fact, is a little more complex, more hybrid than that. At the top of the sheet, a printed paragraph in lustrous gothic type instructs anyone wishing to acquire one of the listed books to 'come to the place of habitation written below'; at the bottom, scratched in fading brown ink is a handwritten address. *Venditor librorum reperibilis est in hospicio dicto zum willden mann*: 'The bookseller can be found at the hostel known as the Wild Man.' This is a document in which print and handwriting interact. It has the mechanics of a form, of 'insert address here'. It draws at once on print's reproducibility and the flexibility of script. Today the Wild Man Inn at Nuremberg, tomorrow monastic lodgings in Munich: the same sheet, the same advertising flyer, will do the job, just so long as the salesman has packed multiple copies plus ink and quills. The book list serves as a reminder that when we speak of the 'print era' we are making a convenient generalization; that, even now, manuscript has never really gone away; and that, in decades immediately after the Gutenberg revolution, the relationship between script and print was a complicated one. There will be more to say about this soon, but first let us inspect the items on Schöffer's list.

The twenty named books begin, naturally enough, with 'a beautiful Bible printed on parchment' before rattling through a medley of religious, legal and humanist classics: psalms and scriptures, Cicero and Boccaccio. Most items take up no more than a single line, just the name of the work and its author. But the fifth title, St Augustine's *On Christian Doctrine*, comes with a little extra sales patter: 'with a noteworthy table of great use for preachers'. For Schöffer and his salesman, in other words, the book's index was considered a major selling point, a detail not to be overlooked. It was, after all, the first of its kind in a printed book.[10]

But Schöffer is not, in fact, pitching his index as a novelty. The flyer makes no mention that it is a first. It is, after all, a very good index in its own right, both comprehensive – a seven-page index to a work that is only twenty-nine pages long – and sophisticated, with subheadings, cross-references and multiple points of entry for the same complex phrase.[11] The book's preface, something potential buyers might inspect before committing to purchase, again trumpets the 'extensive alphabetical index which has been compiled with great care' and adds that this alone would be worth the asking price since it makes the rest of the book so much easier to use.[12]

Both in his sales flyer and in the work itself, then, Schöffer wants to draw attention to the index because of its quality and its usefulness and not because of its originality. Manuscript indexes, sometimes comprehensive and sophisticated ones, had been around for centuries, and, like much else in the early

Volētes sibi oparare infrascriptos libros mag
cū diligētia corrrectos· ac in hūōi lra mogunūe
impssos· bn ōnuatos· vemāt ad locū habitatio=
nis infrascriptū·

Primo pulcram bibliam in pergameno.
Item secdam secde beati thome de aquino.
Item quartū scriptū eiusdē.
Itē tractatū eiusdē de eccie sacris a articlis fidei.
Itē Augustinū de doctrina xpiana·cum tabula
notabili pdicantib9 multū pficua.
Itē tractatū de rōne et osciētia.
Itē mgrm iohāne gerson de custodia lingue.
Itē osolatoriū timorate osciē wnerabilis fratris
iohānis in der sacre theologie pfessoris eximij.
Itē tractatū eiusdē de otractib9 mercatoz.
Itē bullā pij ipc sedi contra thurcos.
Itē historiā de psentacōe beate marie vginis.
Itē canōe misse cū pfacōibs a paratoriis suis.

annplionis in magna ac grossa littera.
Itē iohānne ianuensem in catholicon·
Itē sextumdecretaliū·Et clemētinā cum apparatu
iohannis andree.
Itē in iure ciuili· Institicōnes.
Itē arbores de osanguinitate a affinitate.
Itē libros tullij de officijs·Cū eiusdē paradoxis.
Itē historiā griseldis·de maxia ostantia msierū·
Item historiam Leonardi aretini ex bocatio de a=
more Tancredi filie sigismūde in Guiscardum.

het est littera psalterij

Venditor librozx reynbilus est in hospicio dato zwi wilsin man

Figure 16: The book list for Peter Schöffer's press (Mainz, *c.* 1470). At the
bottom, the bookseller has written where he can be found: 'at the Wild Man Inn'.

days of print, Schöffer's intention was not to make an obvious break with the past, but rather the opposite: to make books that had been produced on the press look as much like manuscripts as possible so that readers would hardly notice the difference. *Cheaper, but just as good* might be the cautious motto of the print trade in its first decades. Typefaces were designed to resemble written letterforms, while fancy initials and flashes of red ink were added after printing to make the page look as though it had been produced in the painstaking scribal tradition. Schöffer's Bible, the marquee item on his sales list, was even printed on parchment. For its locators, Schöffer's Augustine index uses numbered paragraphs – divisions of the text, not of the book. There is nothing radical about this table, nothing that could not have been produced a century earlier. When the printed index makes its first appearance, it is as a direct import from the manuscript tradition, elegant and fully formed, trying not to look like print, with a studied obliviousness to the new possibilities of the printed page.

While Schöffer is busy with his booklist, using his press like a photocopier to run off flyers for his salesmen, a hundred miles to the north, Arnold Therhoernen is in his printshop in Cologne. Rolevinck's *Sermo* is on the press, and the first page of proofs, ink still wet, has just been pegged to a line that hangs across the room. An aproned Therhoernen is standing before it, inspecting the sheet, skimming the glistening letters with a magnifying glass. His hand pauses. He is leaning in, squinting. He looks down, then turns to his foreman, shaking his head. The J is splodgy.

Why should this be? If we look closely at the first page of the *Sermo* – ignoring the swirling red initial which was added by hand – we will notice that nearly all the text on the page fits into a single rectangular text block. Only the J sits outside. When it comes to locking the type so that it doesn't spill out onto the floor during printing, the fewer page elements there are the better. A single rectangle is perfect. Anything else, any outliers or appendages, brings an extra layer of work and multiplies the chances of error or inconsistency. This one little J is troublesome, fiddly. It needs to be locked in separately, it might be squeezed up off its feet, a fraction of an inch higher than the other letters, or catch an extra nick of ink.

Let us imagine Therhoernen, then, looking at his page and thinking fast. A little over-inked, he reasons, but nothing a small adjustment shouldn't fix. Loosen the type, give it a tap, then lock it all in again and try another pull. (The Bodleian's J may be blurry, but the Berlin Staatsbibliothek have a copy of the *Sermo* whose J is neat, well-defined, a perfect impression.) The process may be slightly hit-and-miss, he tells his workmen, but at least the number is legible. It's not the end of the world. Turning away, however, he performs a silent calculation. Has the extra effort been worthwhile? Who will use these numbers? Will they help to sell this slim sermon for a minor feast day?

An index represents value added, something for booksellers to work into their patter, 'worth the asking price alone'; the poor old page number, by contrast, has yet to demonstrate that it is worth the printer's trouble. In fact, a number of early printers were alert to the possibilities for indexing that the printed page opened up. They just didn't see page numbers as the way forward, since there was already another marker that could potentially do the job. Take, for example, the *Chronicles of England*, yet another immense history book, printed in St Albans in around 1486. As with the St JoÙ's *Polychronicon*, its index comes with a brief paragraph of instructions:

Her begynnys a schort & breue tabull on thes Cronicles. And ye must vnderstond yt eueri leef is markid vnder with A. on. ij. iiij. & iiij, & so forth to viij, all the letters. And what sum er ye fynd shor[t]li writin in this table ye shall find openli in the same letter.

If you are reading this and thinking that these don't sound like ordinary numbers – what's the capital A for? What does it mean, 'all the letters'? – you are quite right. These are not page numbers; they are signature marks – the codes used by bookbinders to head off exactly the type of sequencing disaster that triggers the action in Calvino's *If on a Winter's Night*.

This is how they work. Imagine a newspaper. A short one, sixteen pages long. Now imagine opening it up at the middle, the centrefold. These pages – 8 and 9 – are, of course, two halves of the same sheet, folded down the centre. And if we took the sheet out and turned it over, we would find pages 7 and 10 on the reverse.

In fact, our whole newspaper is made up of just four sheets stacked on top of each other, each with that fold down in the

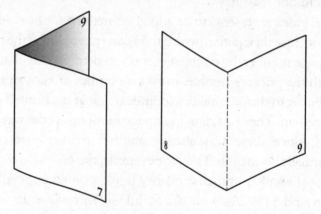

Figure 17a: 2 sheets, 8 pages.

middle. As readers, we want our pages numbered sequentially from 1 to 16. But the person who puts the newspaper together only needs to make sure that these four sheets – let's call them i to iv – are stacked in the right order. The relationship between sheet numbers and page numbers, however, is not a simple one:

Sheet	Pages
i	1, 2, 15, 16
ii	3, 4, 13, 14
iii	5, 6, 11, 12
iv	7, 8, 9, 10

To stop our newspaper coming apart, we might staple the sheets together down the central fold like a magazine or a comic, or stitch them, again along the fold, like a chapbook or poetry pamphlet. A book – a hardback book, at least – is made up of series of these stitched gatherings, also known as signatures. The longer the book, the more signatures are

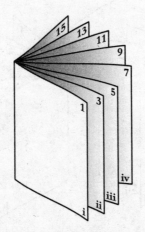

Figure 17b: 4 sheets, 16 pages.

needed. And if we call our first signature A, then B, then C, and so on, we can label each sheet with a mark indicating its signature and its position within it:

Signature	Pages
Ai	1, 2, 15, 16
Aii	3, 4, 13, 14
Aiii	5, 6, 11, 12
Aiv	7, 8, 9, 10
Bi	17, 18, 31, 32
Bii	19, 20, 29, 30
Biii	21, 22, 27, 28
Biv	23, 24, 25, 26
Ci	33, 34, 47, 48
Cii	35, 36, 45, 46
Ciii	37, 38, 43, 44
Civ	39, 40, 41, 42
...	

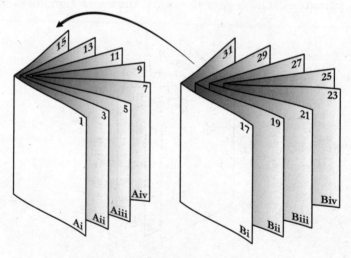

Figure 17c: 2 signatures, 32 pages.

In Calvino's novel, instead of the B signature being followed by C, the binder has inserted another gathering of B leaves. 'Look at the page number. Damn! From page 32 you've gone back to page 17!'

Returning to the *Chronicles of England*, then, what the St Albans printer has done is rather clever. Keyed neither to chapters nor to numbered paragraphs, his table makes use of the book itself, piggybacking off the marks he would have needed to supply anyway to prevent the signatures from being bound willy-nilly. A nifty idea, but there is a snag. Thinking back to our sixteen-page newspaper, since the sheets are folded in the middle, we only really need signature marks on *half* the leaves. Get these in the right order and the other half will be in the right order too since they're made up of the same sheets of paper. Commonly, then, when books are bound in gatherings of eight leaves at a time, the printer only includes signatures on the first four. As one turns the pages, in the bottom corner one sees *a1, a2, a3, a4, blank, blank, blank, blank, b1, b2, b3, b4, blank, blank, blank, blank, c1,* etc. Which means that the St Albans printer hasn't quite found an effortless solution for his table; he has actually gone out of his way – if only a little – to provide the hooks on which to hang the locators for his table of contents.

Other printers were not so conscientious. A legal textbook known as the *New Tenures*, produced in London in 1482, also includes a table of contents keyed to signature marks. Here, however, the printer has followed the normal practice of only marking leaves on the first half of each gathering. This means that half the entries in the table point to places in the book that aren't actually marked. Want to know about the law on *Collusion*? It's on page *b viii*. Just find *b iv* and then count four along from there . . . This might look like laziness to the point of uselessness, a half-hearted shrug towards a device that *might* have been useful if only it had been done properly. But it is a further reminder that the printed book, at this stage, still has one foot in the world of manuscript. Readers, it seems, were willing to pick up the slack and complete the foliation themselves. The British Library holds a copy of the *New Tenures* in which signature marks have been written in by hand, but only on leaves referenced by the table. Even Aldus Manutius, the greatest printer of the age, was not above making this type of demand of his readers. His *Dictionarium graecum* of 1497 includes a copious index but not the foliation necessary to use it. Instead a note merely instructs readers to 'Mark the book with a number in the corner of each leaf.'[13] In other words: do it yourself. The index at the beginning of the sixteenth century is still in a hybrid zone, halfway between manuscript and print. But between the *New Tenures* and the Aldine dictionary there has been a shift from semi-present signature marks to non-existent page numbers.

Though indexes had been around for centuries, the printed page number would turbocharge their pervasiveness. In the century after Gutenberg, they will appear in works of every kind: religious and historical and legal works, as we have seen, but also medical books and maths books, storybooks and songbooks. In Ludovico Ariosto's great epic *Orlando Furioso* (1516) there is a lovely detail when the English knight Astolpho – who, many chapters earlier, has been gifted a spell book by a generous fairy – finds himself in an enchanted castle. Unfazed, Astolpho knows just what to do:

> He tooke his booke and searcheth in the table,
> How to dissolue the place he might be able.

And straight in th'index for it he doth looke,
Of pallaces fram'd by such strange illusion. (22.14–15)*

By Ariosto's time, even fairy books come with a thorough
index (one which, though this late Elizabethan translation
leaves out the detail, is keyed to pages).

As the use of indexes spread, so too did their sophistic-
ation, such that, by the mid sixteenth century, high-end
indexes by the likes of Theodor Zwinger in Basel and Conrad
Gessner in Zurich would attain a level of detail that remains
unsurpassed.[14] Extolling the importance of the index to
scholarship, Gessner links it to the printing press, ranking it
as second only to Gutenberg's wondrous invention:

> It is now generally accepted that copious and strictly alpha-
> betically arranged indexes must be compiled, especially for
> large, complex volumes, and that they are the greatest con-
> venience to scholars, second only to the truly divine invention
> of printing books by movable type . . . Truly it seems to me
> that, life being so short, indexes to books should be consid-
> ered as absolutely necessary by those who are engaged in a
> variety of studies.[15]

Yet Gessner will also sound a note of caution about how
these tools are to be used. In a curious passage, he implies
that there is a right and a wrong way to use an index:

---

* The translation is that of JoÙ Harington, godson to Queen Elizabeth and
inventor of the flushing toilet. Harington was banished from court and told
not to return until he had finished his *Orlando* translation, a task he completed –
to both surprise and acclaim – in 1591. The detail of the index to Logistilla's
spell book is present in Ariosto's original: 'all'indice ricorse, e vide tosto /
a quante carte era il rimedio posto', which might be rendered literally as 'to the
index he turned, and soon saw / in which pages the remedy was situated'.

Because of the carelessness of some who rely only on the indexes . . . and who do not read the complete text of their authors in their proper order and methodically, the quality of those books is in no way being impaired, because the excellence and practicality of things will by no means be diminished or blamed because they have been misused by ignorant or dishonest men.

The reputation of the book index has been tarnished by 'ignorant or dishonest men' who use it *in place of* the main text. Gessner is quick to deflect blame away from the index itself; others, as we shall see in the next chapter – in the pages or the locs that follow – will not be so generous.

4

The Map or the Territory
The Index on Trial

'I cannot promise such exactness in our Index, that
no one Name hath escaped our inquiry.'
Thomas Fuller, *A Pisgah-sight of Palestine*

On 2 November 1965, New Yorkers went to the polls to vote
for a new mayor. The race was a close one, with the Republican candidate JoÙ Lindsay coming out ahead of his
Democratic rival Abraham Beame by 45 per cent to 41 per
cent. Way off in a distant third was another candidate, William F. Buckley, Jr, a conservative intellectual and editor of
the *National Review*. Buckley had always been a longshot for
mayor. Back in June, when he announced his decision to run,
the *New York Times* had poked ironic fun at the gulf between
Buckley's opinion of himself and that of the general public:

> He regards New York as a city to be saved from crisis and,
> with his usual diffidence, himself as the man to do it.
> Whether New York is also ready for Mr. Buckley is another
> matter. Popular demand that he become a candidate has
> been thunderously absent.

Buckley's hardline conservatism, however, began to exert an
influence on the election, drawing the vote rightwards, something which ultimately worked in Lindsay's favour. Meanwhile,

Buckley's oratory – lofty but witty, a blend that before long, and for the rest of the century, would see him installed as host of the *Firing Line* current affairs show – caught the popular imagination. Though polling only 14 per cent of the vote, he had played a galvanizing role in the election, and delivered some of its best lines, including his famous, off-the-cuff answer to the question of what he would do if he won: 'Demand a recount.' In the wake of this public attention, then, it was little surprise that Buckley should spend the next winter following the tried-and-tested path for politicians with time on their hands after an election defeat: he wrote a book about it.

Buckley's *The Unmaking of a Mayor* arrived the following October. One of its minor spats – among many major ones – is played out in a footnote and concerns Buckley's friend and rival as a public intellectual Norman Mailer. (It was, in Mailer's words, 'a difficult friendship'.) Buckley accuses Mailer of refusing to allow him to quote from their correspondence in his book, 'perhaps because he regrets a pleasantry directed towards myself', a jibe that speaks as much about their friendship as their enmity. Given that the pair had disagreed about whether their private communications should be made public in Buckley's book, it was only appropriate that Mailer should be the recipient of a complimentary copy when it came out. At the back, on page 339, beside the index entry – 'Mailer, Norman, 259, 320' – Buckley had scribbled a personal message in red ballpoint: 'Hi!'.

It's a good joke: Buckley knows that the very first thing Mailer will do on receiving the book will be to turn to the back, to the index, and look up all the references to himself. It's a wink at his friend's narcissism, another dig in the two men's scrappy, irascible friendship. It's something we can smile at – at Mailer's weakness for himself – and if the guilty thought crosses our mind that we may, once or twice, in the past, have Googled ourselves – and isn't that really the same thing? – we can surely swiftly suppress the notion, convincing ourselves that, no, it's a different thing completely. Maybe you've come across the story before. It is the anecdote I've heard most often when I tell people that I'm writing this book. And it happens to be true. The book and its handwritten annotation are shelved with the rest of Mailer's library at the Harry Ransom Center in Austin, Texas.

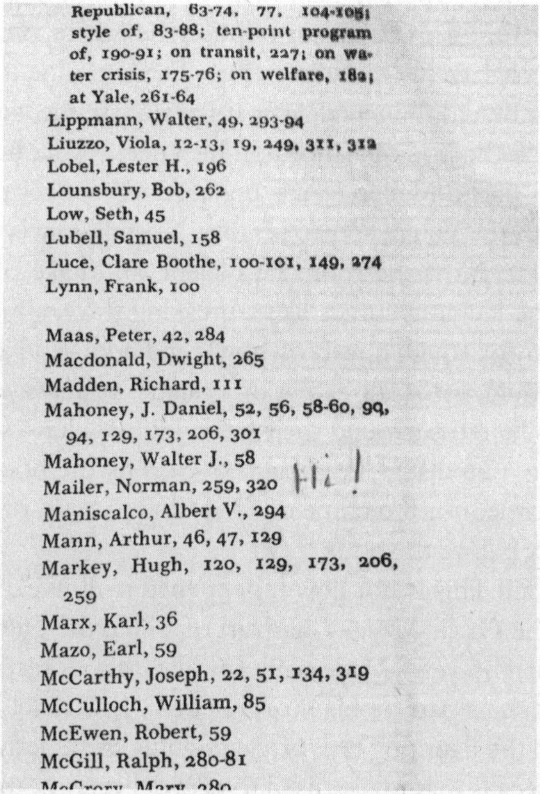

Republican, 63-74, 77, 104-105;
style of, 83-88; ten-point program
of, 190-91; on transit, 227; on wa-
ter crisis, 175-76; on welfare, 182;
at Yale, 261-64
Lippmann, Walter, 49, 293-94
Liuzzo, Viola, 12-13, 19, 249, 311, 312
Lobel, Lester H., 196
Lounsbury, Bob, 262
Low, Seth, 45
Lubell, Samuel, 158
Luce, Clare Boothe, 100-101, 149, 274
Lynn, Frank, 100

Maas, Peter, 42, 284
Macdonald, Dwight, 265
Madden, Richard, 111
Mahoney, J. Daniel, 52, 56, 58-60, 90,
94, 129, 173, 206, 301
Mahoney, Walter J., 58
Mailer, Norman, 259, 320 *Hi!*
Maniscalco, Albert V., 294
Mann, Arthur, 46, 47, 129
Markey, Hugh, 120, 129, 173, 206,
259
Marx, Karl, 36
Mazo, Earl, 59
McCarthy, Joseph, 22, 51, 134, 319
McCulloch, William, 85
McEwen, Robert, 59
McGill, Ralph, 280-81
McCrory, Mary, 280

Figure 18: 'Hi!' Norman Mailer's copy of Buckley's *The Unmaking of a Mayor*.

But whenever I hear the tale, I can't help thinking there's more to it than meets the eye. How did the prank pan out? It's fun to imagine how it *might* have happened. At a cocktail party, perhaps, Uptown Manhattan, an opulent apartment packed tight with the leading lights of Buckley's and Mailer's varied *milieux*: TV, politics, literature. Neither is surprised to see the other. Buckley hands the book over to Mailer, earnest, stoical – 'Thank you, friend, for your support this difficult last year' – and Mailer, grubbily, gracelessly receives it, turning it over, not even looking up, thumbing greedily, breathlessly to the index, to the punchline. Buckley points, smirking, a bony finger hovering over the inscription he wrote only hours before. No, let's say minutes before. Let's imagine it was the last thing he did, hunched against the doorframe, snickering to himself, the book balanced on his knee, before he walked into the party. Mailer looks up, puzzled, open-mouthed: 'What's this?' 'You're so predictable, Norm!' drawls Buckley. Checkmate. Now the room falls silent, an intake of breath before the laughter surges like a breaking wave, a modernist symphony of rough music, of howls and hoots and jeers, fingers pointed, a roaring circle of ecstatic *schadenfreude* as the delirious literati surround their fallen idol. Mailer – sweating, shrinking, humiliated, emasculated – drops the book to the floor, shamed for the crime of Googling himself, of reading the index before the book . . .

But wait! This is not how it happened it all. We'd know if it was: the Great Mailer Charivari of 1966, the literary sensation of the year. More likely by far, Mailer received the book alone as part of his morning post. J. Michael Lennon, who had the daunting task of cataloguing the elderly writer's library, recalls that Mailer used to take delivery of about half a dozen books every day.[1] Maybe he flicked to the index there

and then, standing by the mailbox in dressing gown and slip-
pered feet; or maybe the book, unexamined, sat on his desk
for days, weeks, for ever. In truth, it doesn't matter. The
beauty of Buckley's trick is that we *can't* ever know if Mailer
looked himself up; we just feel that he might have. Nobody
actually gets to see Mailer opening the book, but as soon as
the inscription is written the anecdote has the *potential* to be
true. It's a joke that succeeds from the second Buckley makes
the inscription, a trap that is sprung at the moment it is set.
But even if Mailer *did* check the index first, why not? The
pair had quarrelled over the contents of this very book, with
Mailer saying, 'You can't print my letter.' Is it not a reasonable thing to do, first of all, to see whether your express
instructions have been followed or defied? After all, reading
a book from cover to cover is an investment of hours, something we have to make time for; with the aid of a good index,
checking a reference is the work of seconds.

And this, for me, is the crux of the tale. It is an awful
thing, of course, to take a perfectly good joke and ruin it by
overthinking it. It is, after all, just a story about two dislike-
able men trying to get one over each other. But to me it is also
a story about a curious kind of doublethink – a cognitive
dissonance about the way we read, the relative amounts of
time it takes to read a book right through and to look something up in it and the hierarchy that obtains between those
two acts. Is it that we're not *supposed* to turn to the index
before we read a book? Is that not OK? In 1532, the greatest
scholar of the age, Erasmus of Rotterdam – a public intellectual on a scale that Buckley and Mailer could only dream
of – wrote a whole book in the form of an index, quipping
in the preface that he had to write it this way because these
days 'many people read only them'.[2] It's a lovely piece of

snark, an arch version of Conrad Gessner's more plaintive worry, a decade later, that indexes were being 'misused by ignorant or dishonest men'. The printed index was only just coming into its own, and already alarums were being sounded that indexes were *taking the place of* books, that people didn't read *properly* any more, that there was something seedy, shameful – something Mailerish – about starting at the back. It is an anxiety that will rise to a fever pitch around the start of the eighteenth century – that will be the subject of the next chapter – and perhaps we are feeling its digital avatar today: is Google making us stupid? But was anybody *really* reading only the index, or were Erasmus and Gessner exaggerating things, a canny piece of doomsaying that implicitly brags, by contrast, of their own scholarly rigour?

Step forward, the first witness for the prosecution: an edition of the Roman historian Lucius Florus, published in Venice in 1511. At the back of the work is a lengthy alphabetical index, laid out two columns to a page in the exquisite wide type of the period. And at the top of the index is a short verse:

> Read, dear reader, the following table,
> And soon under its guidance you will hold the entire work in
>   your mind.
> The first number written is the chapter, then the book,
> The third number gives the paragraph.[3]

It is far more elegantly expressed in the original than in my translation, a distinctly stylish take on the how-to paragraphs we've seen before. The last couple of lines explain what locators are in use, since, as we have seen, the page number has yet to dominate, and folio, signature, chapter, paragraph are all still common options. But what interests us most here, of course, are not the locators, but the instructions in the first two lines. Read the index – or rather, read *the whole of* the index: read it thoroughly (the Latin is *perlege* – *read through* – rather than merely *lege*). It's a striking suggestion: we are not used to really *reading* indexes. We *use* them, *refer* to them, *dip into* them, plunder them for our immediate needs – that's why they are in alphabetical order, after all. But that is not what is being proposed here. Read through the index and soon you will hold the *entire work* in your mind. I don't think the verse is really encouraging people to read the index *instead of* the book – to read it first then not bother with the rest – but its claim about the fullness on offer is a revealing one. If this is the way that the index is conceived of – as containing the entire work – then it is surely easy for us to imagine the type of time-poor scholar denounced by Gessner and Erasmus, the kind who reads indexes only. Life is short. 'Time wastes too fast' as Tristram Shandy puts it. What is to be gained by reading a book if everything in it is more succinctly expressed in the index?

Another prosecution witness: in the winter of 1565, Peter Frarin, a distinguished lawyer from Antwerp, was invited to deliver a lecture at the University of Leuven. On 14 December, Frarin stood for two hours in the cold, excoriating Protestantism as a heresy of 'boutchers, traitors, madmen, [and] wicked Church robbers'.[4] The lecture was a roaring success and was hurried into print. Within five months it was available both in its original Latin and in an English translation, *An Oration Against the Unlawfull Insurrections of the Protestantes of our Time*, printed in Antwerp and ready to be shipped across the Channel. The printer of the latter was clearly hoping for as wide an audience as possible, since the book came supplied with a curious index under the following heading: 'The Table of this Booke set out not by order of Alphabete or number,

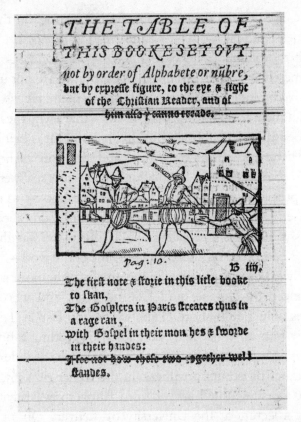

Figure 19: The first page of the multimedia table to Frarin's *Oration*. The printed locators are signature marks rather than page numbers. This would have been unusual even to the book's original audience, and in this copy an early reader has added in a more straightforward locator by hand: 'Pag[e]: 10'.

but by express figure, to the eye and sight of the Christian Reader, and of him also that cannot Read'. There's a lot to unpack here, but surely the detail that jumps out is the idea of a table that could possibly be any use to 'him that cannot reade'. What follows is a series of woodcuts illustrating key sections of the main text: a church being set on fire; a man having his guts drawn out at a public execution; a pyre of books in a university quad. These illustrations are effectively the table's headwords. Beneath each is a locator directing readers to the passage in which Frarin considers the particular atrocity depicted. A visual index, then, and hence one that could not possibly have been arranged 'by order of alphabet'.

Each entry, however, has a further element in addition to the images and locators. Each is accompanied by a short verse, summarizing the scene, boiling it down into a rough quatrain. The first entry, for example, consists of a woodcut in which a band of doubleted men run riot, swords drawn, through the streets. From the lips of one emerges a single word, 'EVANGELIE', i.e. 'the Gospel'. A locator beneath the image directs the reader to a passage in which Frarin denounces the hypocrisy of Protestants who preach peace while practising violence. In particular, he describes a 'Companie of desperat & wicked personnes that ran lyke men up and down the streates of Paris with glistering naked swordes in theyr handes, and cried out, "The Gospel, the Gospell".' Frarin's text – an oration, after all – is an unambiguous piece of tub-thumping. But when, in the index, this scene is forced into a rhymed vignette, it becomes stranger:

> The first note & storie in this litle boke to skan,
> The Gospelers in Paris streates thus in a rage ran,
> With Gospel in their mouthes and sworde in their handes:
> I see not how these two together well standes.

Verses like this come down to us with a tone that is difficult to get to grips with now. That last line – 'I see not' – is it scornful or outraged, arch or appalled? In the doggerel of the index, sneering and horror seem to take on the same voice, becoming indistinguishable. Another early entry treats

Frarin's allegation that the theologian JoÙ Calvin fathered a child with his landlady, a former nun:

> Calvin in his chamber five yeres taught a Nonne
> Tyll she was great with Gospell and swolne with a Sonne.

Here the verse is playful, the slander delivered with a rhetorical relish, pitching the sacred and profane together as parallels: 'great with Gospel and swollen with a son'. This is nudge nudge wink wink stuff: Calvin has been teaching her more than just the scriptures. But when the table moves on to a lengthy series of examples of Protestant brutality, the rhymes remain stuck in the same mode. Here, for example, is the extraordinary tale of a priest forced to eat his own genitals before having his belly cut open:

> Yet another olde Prieste they tooke most cruelly,
> And cut his membres most villainously,
> And broyled them on the coles, and made him thereof eate,
> And ript his belie to see, how he could digest such meate.

Eat, meat. We must resist seeing the same arcÙess, the same irony here as before. That would certainly not be true to Frarin's intention. But it is hard – the index is already so bizarre, so singular, it does not handle changes in tone well. Having it both ways, being satirical on one page and pitiful the next, requires a flexibility, a change of gear that the compressed form of the table can hardly offer.

In fact, the *Oration*'s multimedia table is all about having it both ways. On the one hand, for one set of readers, it really is a functioning index, a way of navigating the book: you can identify a scene from its illustration then follow up the locator in the main text. At the same time, however, the table also offers up a compressed, self-contained adaptation of Frarin's

The Bookseller to the Reader.

T He Reason why ther is no Table or Index added herunto, is, That evry Page in this Work is so full of signal Remarks, that were they couchd in an Index, it wold make a Volume as big as the Book, and so make the Postern Gate to bear no proportion with the Building.

CHR. ECCLESTON.

Figure 20: The publisher's non-apology for the lack of an index in James Howell's *Proedria Basilike*.

work, albeit one that is transposed into a different key, a tabloid voice, wryer, harder. Finally, on a third level, it even works, as promised, for people who do not read at all, serving up the *Oration* in graphic novel form, one long parade of hangings and burnings and dismemberments. For these readers – or rather, viewers – the table is a work unto itself, operating wordlessly without the support of the original Leuven lecture.

Our third witness for the prosecution, James Howell's *Proedria Basilikē* (1664), has no index at all. Instead, placed on its own in the middle of the last page, there is a note, signed by the publisher, Christopher Eccleston:

The Bookseller to the Reader

The Reason why ther is no Table or Index added herunto, is, That evry Page in this Work is so full of signal Remarks, that were they couched in an Index, it wold make a Volume as big as the Book, and so make the Postern Gate to bear no proportion with the Building.

Chr. Eccleston.[5]

This is a pretty bold excuse. There is a distinct *hauteur* here, a contemptuousness of tone that is certainly intentional.[6] This is part of Eccleston's gambit: if you're not going to apologize then don't bother sounding apologetic. But Eccleston is not just unapologetic; more than that, he turns the lack of an index into a selling point for the book. It would have been easy to say nothing, to end the book on the last page of Howell's text and hope that readers wouldn't mind too much: a full stop and a guilty silence. Instead, Eccleston draws attention to the omission, arguing that it had to be this way, that the work is uniquely abundant in 'signal remarks' so that the task of selection and compression would have been an impossible one. No handy crib, then, for Howell's readers; they will just have to start at the beginning and read to the end.

This is, of course, pure brass neck. There really is nothing remarkable about this book's contents, nothing about the density of Howell's observations that would cause it to stand alone, a category of one, set apart from all those lesser history books whose inferiority is signalled by that dead giveaway, an index. Nevertheless, there is something rather appealing – and rather telling – about the terms in which this excuse is couched, the architectural metaphor and the way it makes explicit something that we take for granted: that there is an implicit relation of scale between an index and the work it serves. Of course there is! One must, by definition, be smaller than the other. We might think of the fantastic mapmakers imagined by the Argentinian writer Jorge Luis Borges:

> In that Empire, the Art of Cartography attained such Perfection that the map of a single Province occupied the entirety of a City, and the map of the Empire, the entirety of a Province. In time, those Unconscionable Maps no longer satisfied, and the Cartographers Guilds struck a Map of the Empire whose size was that of the Empire, and which coincided point for point with it.[7]

The joke is in the oxymoron: unconscionably perfect. The map should not match the territory; the index should not be as big as the book. To produce an exact reflection would be to fundamentally misconstrue their function.

For Shakespeare this difference in scale is precisely the point. In his *Troilus and Cressida*, a play set in the Trojan War, a duel is proposed between Achilles and Hector, champions of the Greeks and the Trojans respectively. Although it is framed merely as sport, the elderly prince Nestor reasons that such a contest would serve as a weather vane for the course of the wider war:

> . . . for the success,
> Although particular, shall give a scantling
> Of good or bad unto the general;
> And in such indexes, although small pricks
> To their subsequent volumes, there is seen
> The baby figure of the giant mass
> Of things to come at large. (Act 1, Scene 3)

The 'baby figure of the giant mass' – the scaled-down version of the whole – how *could* an index be anything other? But the problem that Borges and Eccleston hit on so wittily is that if the only perfect map is on a 1:1 scale, then perhaps we should be concerned about the imperfections of our 'baby figures'. Something inevitably will be lost in the shrinking process. Does it matter? It is not a problem, perhaps, when we're talking about the Bible in a medieval clerical setting. An index can certainly help to speed things up here, but it's not as if those particular readers aren't already deeply familiar with that particular text. Things are not going to slip through the cracks, as it were. But as the index becomes more prevalent, so too does the chance that readers will use it *first*. Rather than an *aide-mémoire*, a reminder of material we know already, the index might be used as the way into a book. In the same way that much of our reading nowadays begins on the results page of a Google search, the index has always contained within itself the possibility of being our primary port of entry to a book, and our first sense of its contents.

This is the other sense implied by Shakespeare's image above: the index as precursor. Just as the volumes of the main text are 'subsequent' to the index – they are 'things to come' – so the duel between Achilles and Hector will serve as a premonition of how the Trojan War will end. Similarly in *Hamlet*, when the prince confronts his mother in her closet and rages at her, she demands to know, 'What have I done, that thou darest wag thy tongue / In noise so rude against me?' (Act 3, Scene 4). Twelve lines later, when Hamlet's hotheaded, long-winded reply still hasn't got to the point, the Queen sighs witheringly, 'Ah me, what act, / That roars so loud and thunders in the index?' Indexes come first, and they should neither outweigh nor outroar the work that follows.

In these lines, Gertrude may be thinking not just of how readers use indexes, but also how books were physically arranged. In many, though by no means all, fifteenth- and sixteenth-century printed books, the index was bound at the front of the work (as is still the case with tables of contents). It will, in time, undertake a slow migration to the position it occupies today at the back of the book, a move that is accomplished by the early eighteenth century, so that the *Grub Street Journal*, in 1735, can muse that 'an *Index* . . . in most of the books I ever saw printed before 1600, stood in the same place where our *Preface* does now'.[8] But this anonymous reflection overstates the case. Indeed, binders or their customers could decide for themselves at which end of a book their indexes should go, since they were generally printed on separate gatherings from the rest of the work, often with signatures that stand outside the usual alphabetical order, using other signs from the printer's case such as asterisks (*1, *2, *3, etc.).[9] The fact remains, however, that in the days of the early printed book, the back-of-book index was often the front-of-book index. But the idea of the index coming first is more important as a figurative statement than a bibliographical fact, and this is what comes across loud and clear in the Shakespeare examples: the index is the baby figure of things *to come*.[10]

Not that this is *necessarily* a bad thing. In the last chapter we saw Gessner praise the book index as the greatest gift to scholarship bar only the printing press, only to then concede that it can be misused by people who no longer read the whole book. But let us have a closer look at how Gessner makes that pivot:

> Truly, it seems to me that, life being so short, indexes to books should be considered as absolutely necessary by those who

are engaged in a variety of studies . . . *whether one will be reminded of something one has read before, or so that one might find something new for the first time.* Because of the carelessness of some who rely only on the indexes . . .

The switch comes when Gessner considers the two ways you might use an index: *after* reading the main text, and *before*. In other words, as a *reminder* and as a *foretaste*. Both are valid, of course. Using an index as a way back into a book we have already read is one particular mode of reading, one particular way of using an index; but, of course, it is not the only way. When we are writing an essay, or a lecture, or standing in a bookshop wondering whether this book *that we have never read before* will have something useful or interesting on a particular topic we flick to the index and use it predictively. And Gessner is not saying that one way is good and the other bad. Not exactly. It is just that this distinction seems to track the drift of his thought from 'absolutely necessary' to 'the carelessness of some'. And it is not only Gessner who seems anxious about this. We can find something similar in the index prefaces – those how-to paragraphs – of William Caxton, in books that are among the very earliest to be printed in England.

Take, for example, the *Legenda aurea sanctorum*, otherwise known as the *Golden Legend*, a hugely popular book of saints' lives written in the mid thirteenth century, which Caxton first printed in English in 1483. Caxton's presentation of the work is rather innovative in that he gives it not one but two tables. Firstly, a list, with folio numbers, of the 200 or so saints in the order in which they appear in the book. This is immediately followed by another table which uses exactly the same headings – the same group of saints – but rearranges them, listing them in alphabetical order. In other words, Caxton has included both a table of contents and an index. And here is what he has to say about them:

> And to thende eche hystoryy lyf & passyon may be shortely founden I have ordeyned this table folowyng / where & in what leef he shal fynde suche as shal be desyred / and have sette the nombre of every leef in the margyne.
>
> [And so that each history, life and passion might be found quickly, I have had this table compiled showing where and on what page you can find what you're looking for, and I have had each leaf numbered in the margins.]

So the book is helpfully provided with tables and folio numbers so that readers can *shortely* find whichever saint's history, life or passion they're looking for. And that phrase 'suche as shal be desyred' is a reassuring one. It seems to cover all eventualities: *whatever you're looking for, look it up in the index and follow the reference.* Caxton is not about to admit publicly that there might be things in the book that you would want to look up but which are not included in the index, that the index might be an inadequate representation of the main text. Why would he? 'He shal fynde suche as shal be desyred': it seems a perfectly reasonable thing to say, as long as one doesn't wilfully read too much into it.

Here is another perfectly reasonable thing to say, this time introducing the index to Caxton's edition of Cicero (1481): 'Here foloweth a remembraunce of thistoryes comprysed and touchyd in this present book entitled *Tullius de Senectute*, Tully of old age, as in the redyng shal more playnly be sayd al a longe.' The passage states that the main text of a book will describe things 'more playnly' and at more length than the entries in the index. Of course it will: the map is not the territory. If we expected anything else, we would be fundamentally misunderstanding what an index is. Moreover, there's something very telling about that word *remembraunce*. Something we might have spotted over the past chapter or so is that the term *index* does not quite come into focus until relatively late. In English, we hear of *tables* or *registers* or *rubrics*, but the terms are used vaguely, interchangeably. Sometimes they refer to alphabetical indexes, other times they are nothing more than chapter lists that follow the order of the text.[11] To these terms we could add many others, all used during the late Middle Ages to refer to what we now know as an index: *repertorium, breviatura, directorium*. In sixteenth-century English it was sometimes a *pye*; in the Latin of Martin of Opava it was a *margarita*. They are all, however, frustratingly imprecise – they might refer to an alphabetical index, or to a table of contents – but even among such motley company, *remembraunce* stands out as a magnificent oddity. Semantically quite separate from *tabula* or *register*, it doesn't describe the form itself, but rather its proper usage: a memento, something conspicuously backwards-facing. It implies that you should have read the book already, that a table is not a shortcut to an initial reading.

Caxton's printed version of the *Polychronicon* (1482) contains another caution about how the table should be used: 'And folowynge this my prohemye [i.e. Prologue] I shal set a table shortly towchyd of the moost parte of this book.' That phrase 'the moost parte' doesn't exactly inspire confidence, does it? It sounds a very different note from the idea that 'he shal fynde such as shal be desired'. An admission, or perhaps a warning: it's not just that the entries in the table are, of necessity, briefer – less plain – than the main text; there seems to be an implication here that parts of the book are uncharted territory as far as the table is concerned. Perhaps this seems like overreading, a paranoid type of literary criticism that sees doubt or admonishment creeping in where really there is none. But a couple of years later, in Caxton's edition of the Latin proverbialist Cato (1484) the point is made explicitly. The table concludes with the following note:

> And over and above these that be conteyned in this sayd table is many a notable commaundement / lernynge and counceylle moche prouffitable whiche is not sette in the sayd regystre or rubrysshe.
>
> [And over and above those contained in this table are many notable commandments, learnings and profitable pieces of advice that are not in this register or rubrics]

A table that immediately professes its insufficiency? It's rather wonderful – it sounds so contemporary, the kind of thing that professors teach their students in introductory Research Skills training: an index can be a wonderful labour-saver, but never mistake the map for the territory. There is a prudence here, a diligence in these instructions for use that argues eloquently for the defence in the face of the index's accusers. Caxton's tables come with a pre-emptive warning, an advisory sticker outlining when and how they should properly be used: retrospectively and with caution. If delinquent readers abuse them nonetheless, let the blame lie with those readers. The index pleads not guilty.

We have found ourselves right back with the very earliest books to be printed in English, and already anxieties about the index – its use and abuse; the dangers of overdependence – are apparent. We have looked forwards to our own time, touching on a parallel with twenty-first-century fears about

Google's effect on our capacity for deep reading. Now, let us round off an anxious chapter by looking backwards to the earliest iteration of the same worry. Plato's *Phaedrus* is a dialogue between Socrates and his young friend Phaedrus as they stroll outside the city walls of Athens before resting under a plane tree. (The pair, it seems, are more than just friends – the opening exchanges are brim-full of flirting and what's-that-under-your-cloak innuendo.) Like much of Plato's writing, the *Phaedrus* contains a number of satirical attacks on the literary world of fourth-century Athens. When Socrates first bumps into Phaedrus, the latter is on his way from spending the morning with the great orator Lysias, listening to him give a speech on the subject of love. Socrates asks his friend to repeat the speech to him as they walk along, to which Phaedrus replies in shock: 'What are you saying, my dear Socrates? Do you suppose that I, who am a mere ordinary man, can tell from memory, in a way that is worthy of Lysias, what he, the cleverest writer of our day, composed at his leisure and took a long time for?'[12] Socrates teases Phaedrus – *I bet you asked to hear it twice, then borrowed the script so you could memorize it* – and this, it turns out is precisely what happened. Phaedrus produces Lysias' written speech from under his cloak, and the pair settle themselves down in the shade so that Phaedrus can read it out. At the end of the reading, Socrates is deeply moved. He declares the reading 'miraculous' and himself 'quite overcome'. But it was not Lysias' words that produced such an emotional response; rather it was Phaedrus' performance of them: 'This is due to you, Phaedrus, because as I looked at you, I saw that you were delighted by the speech as you read. So, thinking that you know more than I about such matters, I followed in your train and joined you in the divine frenzy.'

The scene so far has, of course, been about love – Lysias' high-toned oratory on the nature of love, and the teasing, playful love between Socrates and Phaedrus. But it has also, subtly, been about speaking and writing: the disappointment that Phaedrus can't remember Lysias' speech by heart; the distinction between enjoying a performance and enjoying the script that underlies it. Through these almost incidental narrative details, we are gently being introduced to the idea that speech has something about it – a presence, let's say – that writing lacks. It is a theme that bubbles away quietly for much of the dialogue, but, near to its close, Socrates addresses it head on in one of the *Phaedrus*' most famous passages. Here, Socrates recounts an Egyptian myth about the inventor god Theuth. It is Theuth, says Socrates, whom we have to thank for arithmetic, geometry, astronomy, draughts and dice. The greatest of all his creations, however, is writing. One day, Theuth takes his inventions to show Thamus, the king of the gods, hoping to be allowed to share them with the people of Egypt. Thamus goes through them in turn, praising some, throwing others out. When he comes to writing, Theuth chips in to explain: 'This invention ... will make the Egyptians wiser and will improve their memories; for it is an elixir of memory and wisdom that I have discovered.' But Thamus is unimpressed, and his response is a withering one:

Most ingenious Theuth, one man has the ability to beget arts, but the ability to judge of their usefulness or harmfulness to their users belongs to another; and now you, who are the father of letters, have been led by your affection to ascribe to them a power the opposite of that which they really possess. For this invention will produce forgetfulness in the minds of those who learn to use it, because they will not practise their memory. Their trust in writing, produced by external characters which are no part of themselves, will discourage the use of their own memory within them. You have invented an elixir not of memory, but of reminding; and you offer your pupils the appearance of wisdom, not true wisdom, for they will read many things without instruction and will therefore seem to know many things, when they are for the most part ignorant and hard to get along with, since they are not wise, but only appear wise.

For Socrates, the myth illustrates how writing is the poor relation of speech. Even finely crafted speeches, like that of Lysias, become dead language when they are written down: 'every word, when once it is written, is bandied about, alike among those who understand and those who have no interest in it, and it knows not to whom to speak or not to speak; when ill-treated or unjustly reviled it always needs its father to help it; for it has no power to protect or help itself'. In the Theuth myth, moreover, writing stands accused of leading us into bad habits, of making us forgetful as we cease to exercise our powers of attention. People hear without learning, lulled by the convenience that writing offers, the possibility of another opportunity, the chance to read it later. (Remember how this criticism echoes the narrative detail of Phaedrus' inability to memorise Lysias's speech, and his borrowing of the manuscript instead.) The show of wisdom without the reality: any of us who have books on our shelves that we haven't got round to reading yet might concede that Socrates has a point here. But hard to get along with? That's a low blow.

I wheel out the example of the *Phaedrus* not to poke fun at it, but simply because it is the ur-text in terms of our suspicions and anxieties about information tecÙology. These fears are as old as writing itself, and they are clearly not naive – one could hardly hope for more illustrious company than Socrates. And yet, though we can perhaps appreciate the logic of the argument, who among us feels today that, as far as learning and wisdom are concerned, things went downhill after the invention of writing? Reading the Theuth story, we find, surely, a resistance in ourselves, an inability to buy into its scepticism about the value of writing. Perhaps we sense that the *concept* of learning itself is an adaptable one, evolving in response to the tecÙology of its time; that what might once seem a diminution, the betrayal of an ideal, can come to be seen as essential, an ideal itself; that scholarship, rather than being timeless and immutable, is shifting and contingent, and that the questions that we ask as scholars have a lot to do with the tools at our disposal.

For the book index in the first two centuries of print, the jury remains split between those who, like Socrates, view the rapidly expanding tecÙology with wistful exasperation, and those like Phaedrus, who are only too happy to avail themselves of it. We are not yet done with the naysayers. In the next chapter we will see matters come to a head, and the idea of 'index scholarship' pilloried in the coffee-houses of the late seventeenth century. But beyond that we will also see the wits lose out as their jibes about the book index only serve to cement its place as an indispensable part of the new scholarship of the Enlightenment.

5

'Let No Damned Tory Index My *History*!' *Sparring in the Back Pages*

'I have added a ludicrous index purely to show (fools)
that I am in jest.'
William Shenstone, *'The School-Mistress'*

It is a curious thing, the way our skill for effective internet searching has developed over the last couple of decades. In the early days of the search engine, we were not so adept at finding what we were looking for. One late-1990s site introduced natural language processing into its coding, the idea being that users would struggle to leave behind the syntax of everyday life. One could simply type as one spoke: 'Please could you tell what the capital of Mongolia is?' The site was called AskJeeves, so that we might think of it as the all-knowing gentleman's gentleman to our hapless online Woostering. Twenty years on, however, we *have* left everyday syntax behind. When it comes to searching, we have learned to dress ourselves (metaphorically speaking). We have come to express ourselves in terms less like the way we talk to each other and closer to the synthetic languages of the databases that drive the engines themselves. These days even my mother just types, 'Mongolia capital'. 'Brevity is the soul of wit,' opines *Hamlet*'s Polonius – himself, ironically, an incorrigible windbag. It is also, we have all learned, the essence of good searching. For the compilers of indexes, this discovery was nothing to write home about. They have known it for centuries.

Given this formal similarity between the economical index entry and the perfectly honed *bon mot*, it was only a matter of time before literary wags discovered the index as a convenient vehicle for their wit. Whether it's the mock-serious paraphrase of bad poetry ('Jewsbury, Miss, cheats time with stuffed owl, 151'), the razor-sharp skewering of a disgraced politician ('Aitken, Jonathan: admires risk-takers, 59; goes to jail, 60'), or the caustic take-down of one's colleagues ('Peterhouse [College]: high-table conversation not very agreeable, 46; main source of perverts, 113'), the index presents a perfectly sized nook for the deployment of discreet snark.[1]

Paradoxically for something that seems to celebrate the possibilities of the index form, index wit has its origins in precisely the kinds of anxiety we saw in the previous chapter about the index's potential for abuse, about whether it is really a useful invention at all, or merely something – as in the case of writing according to Plato's *Phaedrus* – that, through its very convenience, silently deskills its users. We will pick up this anxiety, then, as it intensifies at the start of the eighteenth century, at a time when wits like Jonathan Swift (of *Gulliver's Travels* fame), had this to say about the difference between reading habits in ancient and modern times:

> The whole Course of Things being thus entirely changed between Us and the Antients; and the Moderns wisely sensible of it, we of this Age have discovered a shorter, and more prudent Method, to become Scholars and Wits, without the Fatigue of Reading or of Thinking. The most accomplisht Way of using Books at present, is twofold: Either first, to

serve them as some Men do Lords, learn their Titles exactly, and then brag of their Acquaintance. Or Secondly, which is indeed the choicer, the profounder, and politer Method, to get a thorough Insight into the Index, by which the whole Book is governed and turned, like Fishes by the Tail.[2]

People don't read books any more, he gripes. The worst offenders reel off the titles of books they have never touched; the best read nothing but the index, which gives them a flavour of the argument. It is a theme that Swift relishes, and he returns to it in another work of the same year in which he decries lazy readers pretending to a scholarship that they have not justly acquired: 'These are the Men who pretend to understand a Book, by scouting thro' the Index, as if a Traveller should go about to describe a Palace, when he had seen nothing but the Privy.'[3] The palace and the privy: if we admired Christopher Eccleston's architectural metaphor in the last chapter – the building and its postern gate – Swift's has even more bite. Meanwhile, Alexander Pope, the most acid wit of the age, joins the fight with a well-turned couplet: 'Index-learning turns no student pale / Yet holds the eel of science by the tail'.[4] For Pope and others, students are *supposed* to be pale. Knowledge is supposed to be hard-won. The effort of reading, the time invested – burning the candle down late into the night – is an indispensable part of becoming learned.

How did we end up here? Who do these wits, these great literary figures, have in their sights with these attacks? And what does it have to do with funny indexes? In this chapter we will look at three controversies – or literary arguments – that were waged in the two decades between 1698 and 1718, each one taking place in an index. And because the chapter, organized around these three bouts, is shaping up a little like

the fight card at a boxing club, we'll pause between each contest and take some time out for an intermission.

Before we move back to the late seventeenth century, however,
let's start with something closer to our own time. These days,
when we read a mainstream non-fiction book – a history or a
biography, say – it will almost certainly come provided with an
index. And if the publisher is worth their salt, there is a very
good chance that the index was compiled by a professional,
most likely a member of a trade organization such as the American Society for Indexing, the Nederlands Indexers Netwerk,
the Australia and New Zealand Society of Indexers, the Indexing Society of Canada, and so on. Of these, the oldest is the
Society of Indexers, founded in Britain in 1957. Shortly after its
formation, the Society received a letter from the Prime Minister, Harold Macmillan, wishing them success and sharing a few
of his favourite anecdotes about indexes. This might seem an
extraordinary thing – that a head of state should find time to
honour this new and, let's be honest, rather niche organization;
that he should be able to reel off a list of his favourite indexes;
that he even sounds plausible when he says 'But I must resist
the temptation to go on quoting . . .' We should bear in mind,
however, that Macmillan had publishing in his blood. His
grandfather Daniel founded the publishing house – still going
strong – that bears the family name, and where Harold worked
for many years both before and after his parliamentary career.

   Of Macmillan's index stories, the one which catches my eye
is the last one, the only one, in fact, that is about politics. Here
Macmillan – a Tory – recalls ('with all proper regret') hearing
of 'the reported instructions given by Macaulay: "Let no
damned Tory index my *History*!"' Macaulay here is Thomas
Babington Macaulay, the nineteenth-century Whig politician

and historian, who began his most famous work, *The History of England*, in the 1840s and was still working on the fifth volume at the time of his death in 1859. Perhaps this was a deathbed scene – his last, whispered instructions to his publisher: 'Let no damned Tory index my *History*'. What Macaulay is getting at, of course, is the idea that an unscrupulous indexer can radically change the emphasis of a text. And what is implicit in this is a real understanding about the way that people read history books – especially a five-volume magnum opus like Macaulay's: that for the most part they read them from the back, jumping in via the index, consulting the work for the sections they need. If this is the case, then the actions of a rogue or partisan indexer *matter*. What Macaulay was all too aware of was a particular moment, about a century and a half before he wrote his *History of England*, when the rogue index – the index weaponized against its primary text – had become a fashion.

At the beginning of the eighteenth century British politics was arranged broadly into two factions, the Tories and the Whigs. At the heart of their contentions was a bitter disagreement over the role of the monarchy, and over the status of the Stuart royal line, a Catholic dynasty, deposed in the Glorious Revolution of 1688. Much of the public skirmishing between the two factions was conducted through the medium of the political pamphlet, a rough-and-tumble warfare in which pamphleteers were always acidic, regularly anonymous and sometimes ventriloquized their enemies to make them seem rabid, obtuse or both. Into this febrile publishing environment came the mock index. Here a book by a figure of one persuasion would be treated to an index compiled by someone of the other, with entries designed to ridicule the main text, to draw attention to its moments of banality or pompousness, its sympathy for foreigners or Catholics, or sometimes even just

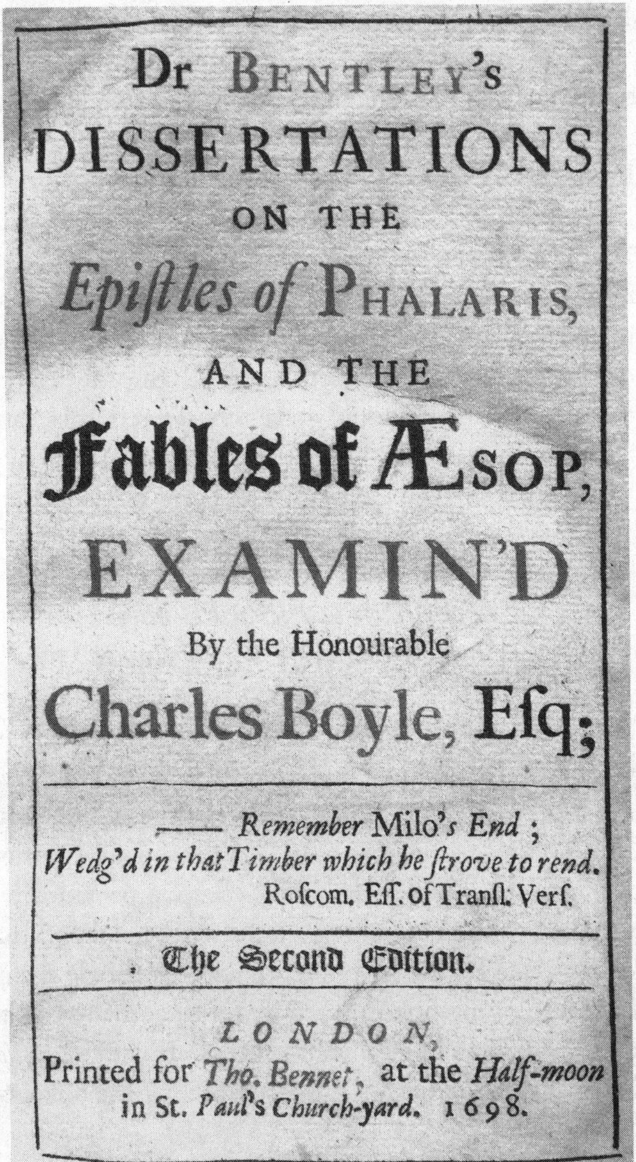

Dr Bentley's

DISSERTATIONS

ON THE

Epistles of PHALARIS,

AND THE

𝕱𝕒𝕓𝕝𝕖𝕤 𝕠𝕗 ÆSOP,

EXAMIN'D

By the Honourable

Charles Boyle, Esq;

—— *Remember Milo's End* ;
Wedg'd in that Timber which he strove to rend.
Roscom. Ess. of Transl. Vers.

𝕿𝕙𝖊 𝕾𝖊𝖈𝖔𝖓𝖉 𝕰𝖉𝖎𝖙𝖎𝖔𝖓.

LONDON,
Printed for *Tho. Bennet,* at the *Half-moon*
in St. *Paul's Church-yard.* 1698.

Figure 21: Contrary to its title page, *Boyle against Bentley* was written largely by Boyle's tutor and a few of his university friends.

its sloppy grammar. Macaulay may have thundered at such indexes, fearing that – even in the mid nineteenth century – he might fall victim to one himself, but he was also able to concede their genius. In his own library – and now preserved at the Bodleian in Oxford – he possessed a satirical work from 1698 which featured as its climax a spectacularly derisive index. The work, attributed to Charles Boyle, was entitled *Dr Bentley's Dissertations on the Epistles of Phalaris, Examin'd,* and on its rear flyleaf, in a page of scrawling, pencilled annotation, Macaulay has declared it 'a masterpiece in its way'.[5] In order to understand why Macaulay should have considered this satire a masterpiece – and why he would qualify that appraisal by adding 'in its way' – let us turn to our first bout: Boyle vs Bentley.

Charles Boyle vs Richard Bentley: A Short Account, By Way of Index

In 1695, a young nobleman named Charles Boyle published a new edition of an ancient Greek text. Boyle had been a student at Christ Church, Oxford, a college with staunchly Royalist political affiliations. It had served as Charles I's court during the Civil War half a century previously, and while many young noblemen attended the college during the second half of the seventeenth century, Boyle is said to have been the only one in thirty years to actually complete his degree. Encouraged by his tutors, Boyle's *Epistles of Phalaris* was intended as a showcase both for the college and for its star pupil.

The *Epistles* were reputed to be a collection of letters written by Phalaris, the tyrant ruler of Agrigento in Sicily during

Figure 22: (a) Charles Boyle (1674–1731); (b) Richard Bentley (1662–1742).

the fifth century BCE. However, some uncertainty existed about their authenticity, and Boyle's edition prompted Richard Bentley, the King's Librarian, to publish his *Dissertations on the Epistles of Phalaris* in which he asserted that the letters could only have been written several centuries after Phalaris' death. Bentley's entire career, while eminent and distinguished, was also marked by an inordinate number of blistering spats. He emerges as one of those figures who might not exactly relish combat but is constitutionally incapable of moderating his tone to avoid it, his brilliance unmingled with any soothing affability, putting backs up and noses out of joint on every side.

And so it was with his response to Boyle's *Epistles*. Since the *Epistles* had not been entirely Boyle's own work – it was widely, and justly, rumoured that he had had considerable help from his tutors at Christ Church – it was no surprise that the college should respond *en masse* to Bentley's criticisms. First to publish was Anthony Alsop, then a student at the college, who took aim at Bentley in the preface to his edition of Aesop's Fables, in which he describes 'a certain Richard Bentley, a diligent enough man when it comes to turning the pages of dictionaries'.[6] This is an odd, cryptic insult, but from the preceding chapters we can probably get a whiff of what is afoot. This is about *proper* reading versus *extract* reading, being familiar with literary texts versus being familiar only with reference works. It is an attack on Bentley's working methods, portraying him as a drudge or an automaton, competent only at looking things up.[7] It will set the tone for the Christ Church pile-on against Bentley that will follow.

We will need to understand *why* Alsop uses this barb about dictionaries as a way of punishing Bentley for calling the epistles into doubt. First, however, let us look, for comparison, at the case that was made by William Temple for their authenticity, since it illustrates some of the battle lines that are being drawn:

> I know several Learned Men (or that usually pass for such, under the Name of Criticks) have not esteemed them Genuine . . . But I think, he must have little skill in Painting, that cannot find out this to be an Original; such diversity of Passions, upon such variety of Actions, and Passages of Life and Government, such Freedom of Thought, such Boldness of Expression, such Bounty to his Friends, such Scorn of his Enemies, such Honor of Learned Men, such Esteem of Good, such Knowledge of Life, such Contempt of Death, with such Fierceness of Nature and Cruelty of Revenge could never be represented, but by him that possessed them.[8]

*

Logically speaking, it is an easier task to demonstrate the falsity than the truth of something. One only has to find one flaw in a document to demonstrate that it is a fake, whereas proving that it *isn't* will always be based on assumptions, the balance of probabilities and the absence – so far – of evidence to the contrary. Nevertheless, in modern terms, Temple's argument, such as it is, seems extraordinary in its high-toned vagueness. Essentially, Temple's case is that the quality of majesty is inimitable; therefore, since the Phalaris epistles possess it in spades, they can only be the work of the majestic tyrant himself.

The way that Bentley constructs the case for the opposition could not be more different. Firstly, triangulating from the accounts of various classical historians, he establishes the dates when Phalaris must have reigned. This allows him to identify anachronisms in the letters, such as a loan of money from the citizens of Phintia. Since we know from the ancient Greek historian Diodorus that Phintia was founded around 280 BCE, this means Phalaris would be 'borrowing Money of a City, almost CCC [300] Years before it was named or built'.[9] Elsewhere, Bentley seizes on a reference to ten pairs of 'Thericlean cups' given by Phalaris to his physician. Again he deduces that this must be a slip by the forger since Thericles, the Corinthian potter who first designed this particular type of cup, lived over a century after Phalaris. In the course of demonstrating this point, Bentley draws on multiple etymological works from the classical and medieval periods to corroborate that the cups were named after their inventor, and cites the second-century grammarian Athenæus for the dates of when Thericles lived.

All of which, not to mention Bentley's habit of casually switching between English, Latin and Greek, makes for an exhausting read: compressed, highly tecÙical and hinging on minute details. It is no surprise that Bentley's enemies derided him as a pedant. In contrast to Temple's bufferish defence of the epistles, there is nothing lofty about Bentleian rhetoric, no fine phrases or thundering oratory; rather, Bentley's style is painfully tecÙical, still dripping in classical quotation, but every reference forensically serving a purpose in the larger argument. It is easy to see why Alsop portrays Bentley with his dictionaries – single words and their histories are key elements of his evidential method. Where Temple is a windbag, Bentley is a nitpicker.

While Alsop's dig at Bentley was nothing more than a jibe, written in Latin and buried in a preface, the next of the Christ Church faction's attacks came on an entirely different scale. *Dr Bentley's Dissertations on the Epistles of Phalaris, and the Fables of Æsop, Examin'd* – better known as *Boyle against Bentley* – is a book-length character assassination of the King's Librarian. Credited to Boyle on the title page, its composition was really a joint effort by a confederacy of Christ Church men: Boyle himself, his tutor Francis Atterbury and recent students William Freind and William King.[10]

Boyle against Bentley opens with some familiar hell-in-a-handcart rhetoric about the imminent demise of 'Learning' at the hands of modern editors and annotators. The preface also rehearses Alsop's line that Bentley's criticism is drawn from dictionaries, but takes this observation radically further by stating plainly that this is a wholly invalid mode of scholarship: 'I am not therefore engag'd to defend [the Phalaris epistles'] Reputation against the Attacks of Dr. *Bentley*, or any other person, who, by the help of Leisure and Lexicons, shall set up for a Critic in this point'. In other words, anyone with a dictionary and enough time on their hands can find arguments to make about great literature, but these will be contemptible – inherently worthless – so there is no need to address them. It is an extraordinarily bold statement, but in case we were in any doubt whether Boyle and his cronies mean it, the claim is repeated liberally throughout the work. For example, 'Dr. *Bentley*'s Appendix [i.e. the *Dissertation*] has all the Pomp and Show of Learning, without the Reality'. Bentley is accused of having *only* used indexes and dictionaries: 'Dr. *Bentley* methinks should have dug deeper for his materials, and consulted Original Authors'. Finally, a pair of rather wonderful coinings sum the situation up: Bentley, accused of a purely mediated form of scholarship, is a '*Second-hand Critic*', while his working method, reliant on reference works, is dismissed as '*Alphabetical* Learning'. But dictionaries are not, of course, the only sites of alphabetical learning, and the index comes under fire too, with Boyle (or whichever of his friends is ventriloquizing him at this point) stating, 'I take *Index-hunting* after Words and Phrases, to be, next *Anagrams* and *Acrosticks*, the lowest Diversion a Man can betake himself to'.

For all its wounded acerbity, however, by far the most notable feature of *Boyle against Bentley* is its wit. One section, by William King, mimics Bentley's original critique of the Phalaris epistles, suggesting that, should critics in the far-off future ever chance to read Bentley's *Dissertation* ('which I am far from thinking they will'), they will look at its tedious and tecÙical writing style and conclude that it cannot have been composed by an Englishman, but must be the work of a later impostor. It is King too who provides the book's most ingenious piece of comedy: an index.

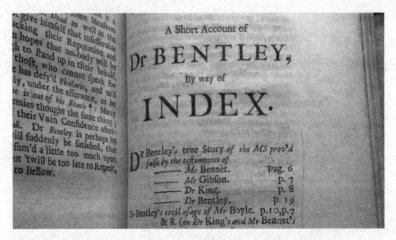

Figure 23: William King's 'Short Account of Dr Bentley, By Way of Index', included in the final leaves of *Boyle against Bentley*.

This four-page table, inserted at the back of the book, is entitled 'A Short Account of Dr Bentley, By Way of Index', and sure enough, each of its headwords relates to some aspect of Bentley's low character. Users will find where to turn if they need to know about such important matters as:

His egregious dulness, p. 74, 106, 119, 135, 136, 137, 241

His Pedantry, from p. 93 to 99, 144, 216

His Appeal to Foreigners, p. 13, 14, 15

His familiar acquaintance with Books that he never saw, p. 76, 98, 115, 232

It is a glorious twofold attack. Part of the great fun of King's index is that the locations are real ones. If we follow the reference to 'His Collection of *Asinine* Proverbs, p. 220', we do indeed find ourselves at a page where Bentley is accused of citing the same proverb – about an ass – at two different points in his *Dissertation*. The surface-level joke of 'A Short Account of Dr Bentley', then, is that a time-poor reader really might need to check the details of some particular facet of Bentley's awfulness and be delighted at the provision of a functioning index. At the same time there is a covert attack, a sneer at the 'second-hand critic', dependent on indexes and always at one remove from literature itself.

Boyle against Bentley was a considerable success. By taking shots, not at the detail of Bentley's arguments – which were both watertight and obscure – but at Bentley himself, the Christ Church faction had produced a witty and accessible piece of invective that made Bentley an object of ridicule in the taverns and coffee-houses. There was even rumoured to be more of the same should Bentley dare to respond, with one coffee-house wag offering this memorable piece of fighting talk: 'Let the Dr. come out with his Answer as soon as he will, they are in readiness for him; to my certain knowledge . . . they have *Rods in Piss* against him'. The metaphor comes from horse riding, and the practice of soaking riding whips in urine to preserve their suppleness.[11] For all its obnoxiousness, *Boyle against Bentley* is an extremely entertaining read, something which could never be said for Bentley's *Dissertation* itself. Macaulay thought it was a masterpiece, though only in its own way: the limited field of tag-team attacks on worthier opponents. He later expands on this view, dubbing it 'the best book ever written by any man on the wrong side of a question of which he was profoundly ignorant', a neatly double-edged evaluation of the Boyle group's wit and their ability as classicists.[12]

But *Boyle against Bentley* had a curious side effect. King's masterstroke, devising a mock index as a sneer at index-scholarship, had only whetted his appetite. The mock index was a form with all sorts of potential. It could be mobilized again, against different targets. There is, however, a catch. If the mock index ceases to be a reflexive joke, a joke *about* indexes – *against* them – then it starts to work in the opposite direction, promoting the index, making it innocuous, showing off its strengths. Time for our first interlude before the next bout.

Intermission: William King's New Toy

With *Boyle against Bentley*, the notion of the satirical index had been set loose in the world.[13] In the two years after its appearance, King would produce three more satirical works, two of which come with spoof indexes, while the other, *Dialogues of the Dead*, still harps on the Phalaris controversy with a character called Bentivoglio who reads dictionaries as if they were literary works. Even when King leaves Phalaris behind, he takes the comic index with him. In *A Journey to London*, the object of satire is Martin Lister's *A Journey to Paris* (1699), a travelogue which King judged to be too sympathetic to the French.[14] While Lister's book had no index, King's parody includes one. Here, rather than a personal attack on the author, the humour of the index is based on whimsy. Entries in the alphabetical list include 'Mushrooms', 'Naked Statues Commended' and 'Kitling in an air Pump', an indication of the silliness of the text being indexed, and by extension the ludicrousness of the text it parodies.[15]

The following year, King would refine this method to a format in which the satirized material is presented almost verbatim. The target this time is the *Philosophical Transactions*, the journal of the Royal Society. The Society had been founded in 1660, and its journal came into being five years later. Rather than simply writing up the papers and experiments that were given by the Society's more eminent members at its London headquarters, the *Transactions* would publish correspondence from amateur scientists the length and breadth of the country.[16] In 1700, the editor was Hans Sloane, and King was infuriated by both Sloane's style and the material he included, seemingly unquestioningly, as editor. In the preface to *The Transactioneer*, published anonymously, King complains that

> All who read his *Transactions* either in *England*, or beyond the Seas, cry out that the Subjects which he writes on are generally so ridiculous and mean: and he treats of them so emptily; and in a Style so confused and unintelligible, that it is plain he's so far from any usefull Knowledge that he wants even common Grammar.[17]

King decides that the best way to satirize the journal is simply to quote from it: the inherent ridiculousness will be evident. He claims that Sloane's shortcomings are 'so Notorious from every line he has published, that his own Words will be the best Proof of what I say, and I have been so carefull in producing them, that I defie him to shew he is once Misrepresented'. But in the index these selective quotations are summed up in a phrase, a mocking synopsis that pricks the pomposity of the original by puckishly shining a light on its latent preposterousness. It is a method which King has developed from *A Journey to London*, and the index to *The Transactioneer* is a wonder of intentional silliness. Here, for example, is a passage on the effects of the opium poppy, quoted verbatim from an article published in the *Philosophical Transactions* a couple of years before.[18] The author reports on a Cornish apothecary, Charles Worth, who has 'caus[ed] a Pye to be made of the said Poppy':

> eating of the said Poppy Pye, whilst hot, [he] was presently taken with such a kind of a Dilirium, as made him fancy that most that he saw was Gold, and calling for a Chamber-pot, being a White Earthen one, after having purged by stool into it; he broke it into pieces, and bid the by-standers to save them, for they were all Gold . . . *But these were not all the Effects of* Papaver Corniculatum [yellow horned poppy]. *For,* The Man and Maid Servants, having also eat of the same Pye, strip'd themselves quite naked, so danced one against another a long time . . . The Mistriss, who was gone to Market, coming home, and saying how now? What is here to do? The Maid turned her brich against her, and purging stoutly, said there Mistriss, is Gold for you.[19]

Too Much Information? King certainly thinks so. *The Transactioneer*'s index sums up all we need to know, in glorious fashion: '*Charles Worth* his man and Maid, all merrily besh-t. p. 39.' Further entries include:

Mr. *Ray*'s Definition of a Dil-oe. p. 11.
A China Ear-Picker. p. 15
Picking the Ears too much, Dangerous. *ibid*
That Men can't swallow when they're dead. p. 28
That a Shell is not a Crust, p. 31
Dr Lister bit by a Porposs, and how his Finger fell sick thereupon, p. 48
The Head that was a Bag, p. 56
Hoggs that sh-te Soap. p. 66
Cows that sh-te Fire. p. 67

King's index invites us to read the *Philosophical Transactions* as he does, with a dogged focus on the material and a wilful blindness towards any scientific value that might be implicit in its observations.

Across three separate works, then, King has been honing a method of satire where the index is used to turn an author's own words against them – where a witty indexer can draw attention to the ludicrousness or inconsistencies in an otherwise innocuous-looking text. It is a device which others will soon begin to imitate. Time for our second bout.

William Bromley vs Joseph Addison: Tories, Whigs and Travelogues

The initial trigger for the next spate of mock indexes was the election, in October 1705, for Speaker of the House of Commons. The incumbent was Robert Harley, and among the challengers was William Bromley, a Tory, and another former Christ Church man.

In 1691, while in his late twenties, Bromley had done what many young noblemen of the time did and taken the Grand Tour, visiting France and Italy. On his return, again like many noblemen before him, he had written up and published an account of his travels. In a slightly defensive preface, the young Bromley acknowledges that it has already become a cliché to publish a report of one's trip. Of course, Bromley goes ahead and publishes anyway, though he takes the precaution of bringing the book out anonymously, so that he cannot be accused of seeking to make a name for himself by

Figure 24: (a) William Bromley (1663–1732); (b) Joseph Addison (1672–1719).

such an unoriginal act. The title page modestly informs us only that the author is 'A Person of Quality'.

Nevertheless, some thirteen years later this anonymity would not be enough to conceal Bromley's *Remarks* from the attentions of his political rivals. On 22 October, three days before the election – the precision-timing is remarkable: just long enough for gossip to spread, but not long enough for it to go stale – a second edition of Bromley's travels appeared. More than a decade after its first publication, Bromley's *Remarks* was in print again, though Bromley had not authorized the reprint. The title page innocuously announces the sole change between this and the 1692 text: 'The SECOND EDITION. To Which is added A Table of the Principal Matters'.

Following King's example in *The Transactioneer*, the second edition of *Remarks in the Grand Tour* leaves Bromley's words wholly unaltered. The addition of an index, however, draws attention to any aspect of that text which might show Bromley in a bad light. For example, where Bromley sounds pedantic or confused, the index picks this up: '*Chatham*, where and how situated, *viz.*, on the other Side *Rochester* Bridge, though commonly reported to be on this Side, p. 1.' When he states the obvious, the index is there to point this out for the reader: '*Naples* the Capital City of the Kingdom of *Naples*, p. 195.' Moments of popisÙess are hardly likely to escape the indexer's censure: 'The Author kiss'd the Pope's Slipper, *and had his Blessing*, though known to be a Protestant . . . p. 149.' But it is when Bromley is simply banal or idiotic that the table is most fun, as when he is caught pondering about the fish in Lake Garda, and the index gives us a po-faced recap of his musings: '*Carpioni* a Fish in the Lake *di Guarda*, by the Similitude of the Fish and of the Name, the Author much questions if they are not the same with our Carps, p. 50.'

When Bromley lost the election, he was furious, seeing his humiliation by the satirical indexer as having been instrumental in his failure. In a handwritten note on the flyleaf of his own copy, he rants sarcastically against his political opponents:

This edition of these Travels is a specimen of the good-nature, and good manners of the Whigs, and I have reason to believe of one in the Ministry (very conversant in this sort of calumny,) for the sake of publishing '*the Table of principal Matters, &c.*' to expose me, whom the Gentlemen of the Church of England designed to be Speaker of the House of Commons . . . This was a very malicious proceeding; my words and meaning being plainly perverted in several places; which, if they had been improper, and any observations trifling or impertinent, an allowance was due for my being very young, when they were made.[20]

Bromley's suspicion that the plot came from within the Ministry was correct. The reprint and its index had been arranged by none other than Robert Harley, the outgoing Speaker, who kept a personal stash of the offending volume at his home, and handed them out delightedly to anyone who came to visit.[21]

As Bromley's marginalia shows, the attack on his *Remarks* had left Tories smarting, as well as presenting a new model for satirically attacking the publications of one's political enemies. For Joseph Addison, then, a notable Whig, it was diabolical timing that his own travelogue should be slated to appear only weeks after the vote for Speaker. Addison was emerging both as a writer and as a politician, and in 1705 he was an Under-Secretary of State. So when in November that year his *Remarks on Several Parts of Italy* appeared, it presented an unignorable opportunity for Tory satirists to subject it to the same index of its flaws as had been dished out to Bromley. Thus, in addition to the perfectly sensible alphabetical index published as part of Addison's book, not one, but two satirical tables with almost identical titles were rushed out as standalone pamphlets, along with a deluxe edition – combining the two – the following year.

The first, rather than simply leaving Addison's words to implicate themselves, adds sarcastic comments in italics after each entry, hauling Addison over the coals for tautology ('Uncultivated Plants rise naturally about Cassis. (*Where do they not?*). 1'), for poor grammar ('*Same* us'd as an Adjective Relative without any Antecedent. *Send him to School again.* 20, 21'), Catholic sympathy ('The Popes are generally Men of Learning and Virtue. *Vid. View of Popery.* 180'), or simply for banality ('The Author has not yet seen any Gardens in Italy worth taking notice of. *No matter.* 59').[22]

The second sticks to the model of King's *Transactioneer*, placing all the pithiness and irony in the index entries themselves. Sample entries include: 'Colour does not lie within the Expression of the Chissel. 330,' and 'Water is of great Use when a Fire chances to break out. 443.'[23] The indexer even manages to return fire for the attack on Bromley's interest in Carp with an entry imputing a similar banality to Addison: 'The Lake of Mount Ceunis is well stocked with Trouts, 445.' Unlike the first pamphlet, this one includes a preface, first of all noting that another satirist has beaten the author to the punch of skewering Addison, then using this fact to infer sarcastically that the work must be wonderful and wise: 'I am not surprised to find a great many Heads at Work in Common-placing and Indexing so vast and Inexhaustible a Treasure of Knowledge.' The preface goes on, however, to aim a kick at an old enemy:

> I am glad that this Table has not interfered in above one or two things with the other, and that my Labours also are like to be of advantage, and benefit to the Learned World. It is not indeed of the same bulk with some *Dutch* Lexicons and Glossaries, but I do not however despair of its finding a place, (as it is an Index) in the most Letter'd, Renowned and *Humane* Dr. *Bentley*'s Library. 'Twill be of singular use to him in his next Controversy; for tho' there is not one word in it of *Phalaris*'s Epistles, yet it will be as Applicable to that, or any other Argument, as a great many of the Books he has quoted in his Polite and refin'd *Dissertation*.

Reigniting old hostilities with Bentley, accusing him once more of being a connoisseur of indexes, implying that his *Dissertation* was larded with irrelevant quotation: this is an index with William King's fingerprints all over it.

This section is fun!

Intermission: John Gay's Poetical Indexes

William King died on Christmas Day 1712, a year short of his fiftieth birthday. His contemporaries suggested that his was a talent wasted – an ingenious man who might have been a serious poet or a successful judge if he had not been 'so addicted to ye Buffooning way, that he neglected his proper Business, grew very poor, and so dyed in a sort of contemptible manner'.[24] He was reputed to have read 22,000 books during his eight years at Christ Church (a claim which Dr Johnson would later demonstrate, with a few quick calculations, could only be a wild exaggeration).[25] His later years, however, found him drunk and broke. When Jonathan Swift managed to find him a job as a journal editor – on condition that he be 'diligent and sober' – King lasted only two months in the role.

His innovations as a rogue indexer, however, buffoonish as they might have been, outlived him. The year before King's death, the poet and dramatist John Gay had mentioned him in a work entitled 'The Present State of Wit'. Gay observes that King's career has floundered. His gift for humour, reasons Gay, was vast but one-tracked and so 'the Town soon grew weary of his Writings'.[26] Nevertheless, Gay has clearly taken some of King's methods on board. His long poem *The Shepherd's Week* (1714) comes with a whimsical index – 'An Alphabetical Catalogue of Names, Plants, Flowers, Fruits, Birds, Beasts, Insects, and other material Things mentioned by this Author' – which gets some comic mileage out of mingling people and things: 'Goldfinch, 6, 21; Ginger, 49; Goose, 6, 25, 45; Gillian of Croydon, 42'.[27] But it is Gay's second poetical index, published with the mock-heroic poem *Trivia, or the Art of Walking the Streets of London* (1716), that shows he has learned from the master. *look for This!*

Trivia itself is a glorious piece of urban comedy in rhyming couplets, in its way as much a travelogue as Bromley's or Addison's Grand Tours. The terrain it covers, however, is London in the early eighteenth century, serving as a guide to the types one might encounter on a walk through the city. Its index, meanwhile, functions much in the manner of King's *Transactioneer* table, the humour coming from the surprising spin which is put on scenes in the index entry. To take an example, here is a passage about football, giving us a picture not so much of the beautiful game as of something wild and mucky which anyone in their right mind would want to avoid (a margin note printed next to this scene says simply 'The Dangers of Foot-ball'):

Where *Covent-garden*'s famous Temple stands,
That boasts the Work of *Jones*' immortal Hands;
Columns, with plain Magnificence, appear,
And graceful Porches lead along the Square:
Here oft' my Course I bend, when lo! from far
I spy the Furies of the Foot-ball War:
The 'Prentice quits his Shop, to join the Crew,
Encreasing Crouds the flying game Pursue.
Thus, as you roll the Ball o'er snowy Ground,
The gath'ring Globe augments with ev'ry Round;
But whither shall I run? the Throng draws nigh,
The Ball now Skims the Street, now soars on high;
The dext'rous Glazier strong returns the Bound,
And gingling Sashes on the Pent-house sound.[28]

The scene, then, is of young men, apprentices, running out of their shops to kick a ball round the snowy streets of Covent Garden. It ends with one of them – a glazier – kicking the ball so high that it smashes the sash windows on an upper floor of one of the houses in the street. So how does the index represent this vignette? With an entry that is entirely deadpan, and seemingly almost irrelevant: 'Glasier, his Skill at Foot-Ball, p. 36'. A strangely specific thing to focus on: why not have the entry under *Apprentices* instead? And why say that he is *skillful* when he is the one who smashed the window? Perhaps this is another sarcastic index, like the ones written against the earlier travelogues. However, I think not. There is something altogether subtler going on. The wit here is not sarcasm, but innuendo. After all, who smashed the window? The glazier. How convenient. Could it be that he did it on purpose to get work? If so, he'd have to be a skilful footballer . . . and that is exactly what the index tells us. What seemed like a coincidence when we read the main text of the poem becomes something more calculated once the index informs us that he is *skilled* at football. Smashing the window is a method of making sure there's work for himself and his master. The index contains buried information – it holds the key to some of the poem's satire.

At the same time, there is another type of comedy at work in the *Trivia* index, not reliant on the main poem but intrinsic to the index itself, and which goes beyond King's innovations. There is a humour of juxtaposition, whereby the index creates its own miniature narratives. Like many indexes at this time, the alphabetical ordering applies only to the initial letter of the headword; after that, entries are ordered by the sequence in which they appear in the poem. This gives Gay some leeway to orchestrate what entries go next to each other in the index. Thus we have this medley from the Cs:

> Christmas, A season for General Charity, *ibid.*
> Coaches, those that keep them uncharitable, p. 42
> Charity most practiced by walkers, *ibid.*
> – Where given with Judgment, *ibid.*
> – Not to be delay'd, *ibid.*
> Chairs, the Danger of them, p. 46
> Coaches, attended with ill Accidents, *ibid.*
> – Despised by Walkers, p. 49
> – Kept by Coxcombs and Pimps, p. 50

A narrative emerges about the uncharitability of coach riders, ending with the twin punchlines of an accident befalling a coach and the type of person most likely to keep one. Similarly the list of character types that makes up almost the whole of the B section is evidence of a certain amount of design in compiling the index:

> Brokers keep Coaches, p. 8
> Bookseller, skill'd in the Weather, p. 11
> Barber, by whom to be shunn'd, p. 23
> Baker, to whom prejudicial, ibid.
> Butchers to be avoided, p. 24
> Bully, his Insolence to be corrected, p. 25
> Broker, where he usually walks, p. 31

There is a consistency in the syntax of the entries here, a sort of poetry is going on: a series of tradesmen and a humorous take on each. They belong together even though they don't appear next to each other in the work.

Gay's index also has its share of plainly amusing single entries: 'Cheese not lov'd by the Author', 'Asses, their Arrogance', or 'Nose, its Use'. Though it pokes gentle fun at various urban stereotypes – the sly glaziers, aggressive coachmen and butchers to be avoided – the whole performance seems to have shaken off the viciousness and bile that characterized the index wit that went before it. Not so in our third and final bout – the bitterest of all.

Laurence Echard vs JoÙ Oldmixon: Indexing in Bad Faith

So far, the indexes in this chapter have been, effectively, literary performances. They have been jokes that take the index as their form. As such, there has been plenty to say

Figure 25: Laurence Echard (c. 1670–1730).

about the creators of the indexes as well as the people they were satirizing. These were notable figures – celebrities, if you like – from the world of literature or politics, or from the nobility. We have even been able to look at portraits of them because these were the types of people who had their portraits done. The index in our final bout is rather different. It is still very much a part of the cut-and-thrust of early eighteenth-century politics, of Tories versus Whigs, but this time it is a *real* index, one compiled by a professional indexer – a hard-up, hardworking member of the literary industry, someone who was neither a nobleman nor a celebrated writer.

His name was JoÙ Oldmixon, and while we have no image of what he looked like, we do have an acidic pen portrait from Alexander Pope who pictures Oldmixon flinging himself 'in naked majesty' into the open sewer of Fleet Ditch.[29] A devoted propagandist for the Whig cause, he is described by Pope as 'a virulent Party-writer for hire', a dig which makes him sound both mercenary and extremist, if such a thing is possible. Nevertheless, Oldmixon's publishers imagined him less rabid as a compiler of indexes than as an author in his own right. And so it happened that towards the end of 1717 the publisher Jacob Tonson the Younger hired Oldmixon to index a work with strong Tory sympathies: the three-volume *History of England* by Laurence Echard.

Unlike Oldmixon, hard-up and languishing in obscurity in Devon, Echard was very much an establishment figure. He was archdeacon of Stow, and, again unlike Oldmixon, we have a portrait to show us what he looked like. Not only that, but we have surviving correspondence in which we can hear Echard rather vainly suggesting improvements to said portrait. The image was made for the frontispiece to Echard's

History when it was reissued in 1720, and here is a letter to the publisher about it:

> The Inclosed Picture answers mighty well on the Face and Wigg, only some few think that the highest and middle Part of the Forehead want a small amount of covering from the Wigg. But I cannot say I am of that Opinion. I think indeed that the Hands, and some of the lower Parts of the Cut, still want *finishing*.[30]

The request is a masterclass in genteel command, moving down the portrait from the wig to the hands, while modulating from jolly satisfaction, through the first glimmers of critique – 'some few think . . . ' – before ending up at the crux of the matter: the portrait will require alteration. Ha ha, no but *really*. This is the tone of someone used to getting their own way.

Oldmixon, on the other hand, is no such master of diplomacy. He really has only two modes – whining and snarling – and his letters are characterized by an oscillation between these. Here he is negotiating his payment for the index to Echard's *History* and comparing it with another indexing job he did for a different publisher (White Kennett's *Compleat History*, published by William Nicolson):

> Tis very Large and if I demanded 12gs for it woud be little . . . I had for the Index to Kennets 3 Voll. 35l. pd me by Nicolson this I am sure is better in proportion and I was 3 hard Weeks about it. *Under 10l. I am positive not to take* . . . Pray let me have the Books I wrote for & the Third Vollume of Eachard to do that Index also . . . You shall have ye other next Week well done. That now sent has cost me a great deal of Pains & richly deserves 12l. it being but a 3d Part of what I find for Kennets of so stingy a Creature as Nicolson.[31]

It's a wild piece of haggling. Reading it is like listening to one side of a phone conversation, possibly about selling a car. But of course this is a letter: no one is interrupting Old-mixon as he veers from demanding twelve guineas, to ten pounds, then twelve pounds, takes a swipe at the 'stingy' Nicolson and calls into question how good his own last index was. Not exactly a smooth operator, then. But Oldmixon, it turns out, has a few tricks up his sleeve.

In 1729, a good decade after Echard's *History* first went on sale, an anonymous pamphlet appeared, presenting an out-raged exposé of the index to that work. The pamphlet is called *The Index-Writer* and on its title page it rages at the 'WHIG HISTORIAN' (all angry caps) who had the 'parti-ality' and 'disingenuity' to misrepresent the great archdeacon. The second page gives us more of an idea of what Oldmixon has done, as well as a sense of how professional indexers were viewed in the publishing foodchain of the early eight-eenth century:

It may not be amiss to acquaint the Reader, that when Arch-Deacon Echard had finished his 3d vol of the History of England, the Drudgery of compiling an Index, was left to one who was thought not unfit for so low an Employment as giving an alphabetical Epitome of that Volume: it was not suspected that one thus employed should be so utterly void of all shame as to pervert the meaning of his author where the abuse must be so easily discovered and his unfair-ness laid open to public View; But it has so happened that the strong Propension this Person had to serve the Faction, and the little regard he bore the Truth, put him upon fram-ing an Index, in many places contrary to the History, which the Reader will, to his Surprise, find giving one Account, and the Index another. This unfair practice is the Subject of the following Tract.[32]

Reading this, it is difficult not to feel some sympathy with Oldmixon. 'Not unfit for so low an Employment' – a phrase that surely makes us bristle. To the modern reader, at least, this passage is self-defeating: it sets us up to feel a certain relish that the lowly indexer should have found a way to undermine his supposed superiors: a worm who has turned. Whatever he has done, we want to side with poor, awkward Oldmixon against the vain, smooth-tongued archdeacon and his supporters.

So how, in fact, has Oldmixon managed to undermine his author? In truth, Oldmixon's methods are not dissimilar to William King's *Transactioneer*. He uses the form of the index entry – its brevity, its snappiness – as a sarcastic counterpoint to the main text. Here, for example, is Echard telling the story of Richard Nelthorp, implicated in the Rye House plot to assassinate Charles II:

> [Nelthorp and his accomplice] were brought from *Newgate* to the *King's-Bench* Bar; where being ask'd, 'Why Execution should not be awarded against them, in regard they stood attainted by Outlawry of High-Treason, for conspiring the Death of King *Charles* the Second;' and having nothing to say, that cou'd avail them, the Court made a Rule, That they shou'd both be executed on the *Friday* following, and accordingly they were then hang'd.[33]

The point Echard is making is that Nelthorp was guilty of high treason and hanged accordingly. Oldmixon's index, however, gives it thus: '*Nelthorp, Richard*, a Lawyer hang'd without a Tryal in King *James*'s Time'. The shift in emphasis couldn't be starker. For Oldmixon, the outrage is that these people were denied a proper trial. They were asked if they had anything to say by way of mitigation, and didn't – but this hardly constitutes due process. This leaves the pamphlet writer furious: 'I don't here charge the *Index-writer* with saying what is in Terms false, but for suppressing the true Cause of their being hang'd without Tryal, *viz.* That they stood attainted by Outlawry, and on that Account had by Law forfeited all Right and Title to it.'[34]

Another example of Oldmixon's wiliness concerns the birth, in 1685, of a baby boy to James II and his Queen. After a series of miscarriages it seemed that James was not going to produce a male heir. For many in the country this was seen as no bad thing since James and his Queen were Catholic, whereas James's nephew – who stood to inherit the throne if there was no direct heir – was a Protestant. Among the Whig faction, then, a convenient but far-fetched conspiracy theory sprang up that the baby was not really Mary's, and therefore not a rightful heir. The baby, they said, was some other boy child smuggled into her bed in a warming pan – a kind of early modern hot-water bottle – so that the royal couple could raise him as their own to continue the Catholic dynasty.

This is how Echard reports the rumour: 'As to the Warming-Pan, it was reply'd . . . that it had been impossible to put a new-born Child, with the After-Burden, in the narrow Compass of a Warming-Pan, without stifling it.'[35] And here is how the book's index refers to this passage: 'Warming-pan, very useful to King *James*'s Queen'. Not only is Oldmixon pulling in the absolute, polar opposite direction to Echard, he is doing it with a sardonic wink. Echard's readers were apoplectic. The pamphleteer rages,

Now here the Fellow sneers at a Lady of sublime Quality, and at the same time ridicules his Author; and tho' this envenom'd Writer had no regard to Majesty, one would think, as an hireling, he might have shewn some to the Person who paid him: His Master . . . is far from being ridiculous, when 'tis considered that a Warming-pan is usually about 7 Inches or 7 and a half over, and a New-born Child in Length about 16 Inches.[36]

This is a boiling admixture of professional and personal accusation. Oldmixon has been unfaithful to the text he is indexing, he has been disrespectful to royalty, taken liberties with his status as 'an hireling'. After all this outrage, there is something unintentionally hilarious about those very precise details – the average sizes of warming pans and babies respectively – a bathos that comes from the shift in tone from fury to wounded pedantry. Where previously we saw Echard being suavely commanding about a portrait that made his forehead too big, here we see that his supporters at least can be made to lose their cool over an index.

At the end of his life, Oldmixon wrote the devastating, depressing *Memoirs of the Press*, a record of his struggles in the world of publishing and as a footsoldier in the political tussles of the time. Looking back on the Echard incident, he remains unrepentant. The history book, he reasons, was intolerably partisan, full of 'bold and false Allegations' – so much so that it 'could not but keep alive that Ardour in my Breast, which I ever felt in the Whig Cause, Liberty and the Reform'd Religion'.[37] There is here something rather satisfying about Oldmixon – the put-upon indexer, without the flair or showiness of someone like William King, but instead working deep undercover, like one of the downbeat spies in a Le Carré novel, quietly putting a radical spin on the books of his political enemies. It is surely Oldmixon that Macaulay, writing his own *History of England*, has in mind when he thunders, 'Let no damned Tory index my *History*!' It is, therefore, Oldmixon again who echoes in Macmillan's letter to the Society of Indexers. Oldmixon comes down to us via a Whig historian and a Tory prime minister, but these political affiliations have faded to insignificance. The weaponized index – an invention of the High Tory, High Church men of Christ Church – has become common property, and anyone, on any side, can use it.

We are a few years into the eighteenth century, and the index has become both an object of disdain and a tool for expressing that disdain. There is a paradox here, a tension that will break, ultimately, in the index's favour. Returning to Pope's scornful couplet – 'Index-learning turns no student pale / Yet holds the eel of science by the tail' – the meaning, surely, is unequivocal. Eels are slippery, elusive. Trying to hold one by the tail is not something to be recommended. Rather, this is a warning against superficial scholarship, a restatement of another of Pope's famous lines: 'A little learning is a dang'rous thing'. And yet by 1751 a geometry textbook can begin its preface with a rhapsody on the *usefulness* of index-learning. Shamelessly, paradoxically, it pulls in Pope's jibe, repeating it not as derision but approval:

> It is justly observed that, the present Age is remarkable for its Attachment to Essay or Index-Learning; which is a compendious and easy Way of acquiring a moderate Skill in Science, to the Content of many, without the Trouble of studying Systems, and examining their fundamental Principles. Such a Disposition the immortal Pope has beautifully

described in these Words: 'Now Index-Learning turns no Student pale, Yet holds the Eel of Science by the Tail'.[38]

In this looking-glass world, grabbing one by the tail seems a perfectly sensible way of handling eels. The battle against index-learning has been lost, to the extent that Pope's metaphor can be repurposed with a new, positive spin. For the index, the eighteenth century will be a time of experiment. As the Age of Enlightenment reaches maturity, indexes will appear not just in textbooks and histories, but in essays, poetry, drama and novels, and even figures like Pope and Dr JoÙson – who elsewhere cavil and harrumph at index-learning – will be found toying with the form, and testing its boundaries.

6

Indexing Fictions
Naming was Always a Difficult Art

'I think that indexing fiction would be a terrible idea.'
Jeanette Winterson

'Stepping the other morning into a publick coffee-room, in order to run my hand over the newest pamphlets, it happened that the first I laid my hand on was a sermon'.[1] So begins the 'Adventures of a Quire of Paper', a magnificently strange tale. No sooner has our narrator picked up the sermon than its pages start to ruffle and 'a low, yet articulate voice issue[s] from amongst them'. The pamphlet is talking, and what it has to say has nothing to do with the words printed within it. It is the paper, not the text, that wants to speak, to recount its long and woeful life story. It begins with a handful of flaxseed. The seed grows, is harvested, and then spun into linen, which in turn is woven into a handkerchief, the property of a notorious rake who uses it to wipe up unspeakable things in a brothel. The handkerchief is then discarded and recycled into paper, some low grade – used for cigarettes and wrapping in a grocer's shop – some fine. But the fine paper fares little better than the cheap stuff. It is bought by a dandy who uses it to write a love letter for his mistress and some rotten poetry for his friends. His mistress, however, uses the letter to wipe her bottom, while his foppish friends use the poetry to wrap their hair into curls at night. In both cases, the paper ends up flushed down the toilet. Other parts are used for newspaper – then reused as the shroud for a dead kitten, the tail of a kite, a rag to rub grease off a cooking pot, a makeshift coaster for a jug of ale . . . Only a small, fortunate scrap – the piece that becomes a printed sermon – survives to tell the whole sordid tale.

Funny but also fatalistic, pious but also obscene, the 'Adventures of a Quire of Paper' is a perfect example of the wild, inventive 'It Narrative' genre that flourished in the mid eighteenth century – others include 'The Adventures of a Bank-Note', 'The Adventures of a Black Coat' and 'The History and Adventures of a Lady's Slippers and Shoes'. The talking object, the object that circulates between different owners, different strata of society, offers the ideal basis from which to spin a picaresque, possibly satirical, yarn. But it can also shine a light on the minutiae of everyday life. In the case of the 'Adventures of a Quire of Paper', the tale draws our attention to the distinctions we make about how we treat our reading matter.

Do you still buy a newspaper? Every day? At weekends? Or perhaps you pick up a free advertiser on the bus or on the tube, skimming it for as long as your journey lasts then leaving it on the seat for the next reader. How do we treat these ephemera, compared to other print objects? I can easily buy a novel – second-hand or in a cheap edition – for less than my weekend newspaper, but I'll invariably treat the two very differently. I'll read my paper at the breakfast table, turn the pages with buttery fingers, use it as a coaster for my mug so that it's marked with spills and tea-rings. I may tear a page out, or keep a section to show a friend, but soon enough – a matter of days at most – the whole paper will have found its

cf.
Notting Hill

way, crumpled and stained, into the recycling bin. 'Today's news is tomorrow's fish and chip paper', as the saying goes. Not so with the novel – not even the cheap one. If it doesn't end up on my shelf in perpetuity it will go, at some point, to the charity shop. I'm a page-folder (I admit it) and I might make the odd margin note in pencil, but the book will be spared the types of abuse that the newspaper is subjected to almost ritually.

But not every periodical feels as throwaway as a news-paper. Some occupy a liminal position, not exactly precious – not like a *book* – but not quite disposable either. Glance into the office of any university lecturer you'll see that some of the shelves are given over to academic journals – yard upon yard of identical spines, collected over many years. Most of these publications will have migrated their archives online now – one can access their entire back catalogue with a few clicks *too* of the mouse. But old journals are hard to throw out. Own- *true!* ing them, and having them on display, is part of the theatre of expertise. They symbolize membership of a scholarly community, not to mention learning patiently accrued over time, and they call back to the pre-digital need to have the collected wisdom of one's peers physically present in the room in order to be able to draw on it, to take it down and look something up. Likewise, magazines such as *History Today* and the *New York Review of Books* do a brisk trade each winter selling binders and slipcases in which to store the previous year's issues. The merchandise is telling us something: that there is something about these papers that readers want to hang on to, to have around them; that just because it's periodical doesn't always mean it's ephemeral.

Many of the journals of the eighteenth century fall into this intermediary zone, and none more so than the *Spectator*.

Founded in 1711 – and no direct relation of modern magazine of the same name – the *Spectator* was a cheap, daily, single-sheet paper that featured brief essays on literature, philosophy or whatever took its writers' fancies. Its editors were Richard Steele and Joseph Addison (whom we met in the last chapter having his Italian travelogue mauled by ironic indexers), and, although it ran only for a couple of years, it was immensely popular. The *Spectator* started off in a print run of 555 copies; by its tenth issue, this had ballooned to 3,000. This, however, was only a fraction of the true readership. The editors claimed that there were twenty readers to every copy, and deemed that even this was a 'modest Computation'. The *Spectator* was a paper designed for the emerging public sphere, a conversation piece to be read at 'Clubs and Assemblies, at Tea-tables, and in Coffee-Houses'.[2] A paper to be read and passed on.

What's more, the *Spectator* was only the best known in a long list of similar sheets. The *Tatler*, the *Free-Thinker*, the *Examiner*, the *Guardian*, the *Plain Dealer*, the *Flying Post* – papers like these were able to capitalize on a perfect storm of rising literacy rates, the emergence of coffee-house culture, the relaxation of formerly strict printing laws, and a growing middle-class with enough leisure time to read. The eighteenth century was gearing up to be what scholars now call the age of print saturation.[3] That term *saturation* has some interesting suggestions. Certainly, it implies excess – too much to read – but also something else: too much to keep hold of, a new *disposability* of printed matter. Our poor, abused quire of paper was born at the wrong time. Flicking through original copies of the *Spectator* preserved in the British Library, one certainly sees the signs of coffee-house use. You won't find stains like this in a Gutenberg Bible. And yet the essays are among the finest in English: wryly elegant, impeccably learned. If you had bought the paper for self-improvement you might well want to come back to it.

And so it was that the news-sheets found themselves being republished, almost immediately, in book form. These editions, appearing within months of their broadsheet originals, anticipated how the kind of reader who would want the *full run* of the *Spectator* would want to use it: not simply as a single sheet – a single thought – for a few minutes' entertainment with one's coffee, but as an archive of ideas that one might return to. Benjamin Franklin, for example, describes coming across a collected edition of the *Spectator* as a boy and reading it 'over and over', jotting down notes from it and trying to imitate its style in his own writing.[4] The movement from coffee-table to bookshelf implies a different mode of reading, one of reference, reuse, of finding the thought, the phrase, the image, and bringing it into the light again. If the *Spectator* was to be a book it would need an index.

The indexes to the early volumes of the *Spectator*, along with those of its older sister the *Tatler*, are a joy in themselves, full of the same ranging, generous wit as the essays they serve. Rifling through them, a century later, Leigh Hunt would compare them to 'jolly fellows bringing burgundy out of a cellar', giving us 'a taste of the quintessence of [the papers'] humour'.[5] Who, indeed, would not want to sample more after reading a tantalizing entry like 'Gigglers in Church, reproved, 158' or 'Grinning: A Grinning Prize, 137' or 'Wine, not proper to be drunk by everyone that can swallow, 140'. The *Tatler*, meanwhile, offers us 'Evergreen, Anthony, his collection of fig-leaves for the ladies, 100', or 'Love of enemies, not constitutional, 20', or 'Machines, modern free thinkers are such, 130'. Elsewhere, two entries run on together, oblivious to the strictures of alphabetical order:

Dull Fellows, who, 43
Naturally turn their Heads to Politics or Poetry, *ibid.*

There is something at once both useless and compelling about these indexes. Is 'Dull Fellows', listed under the *d*s, really a helpful headword? Of course not. But it catches our attention, makes us want to find out more. This is as much about performance as about quick reference. Each entry is a little advertisement for the essay it points to, a sample of the wit we will find there. The *Tatler* and *Spectator* indexes belong to the same moment as the satirical indexes we saw in the last chapter, but unlike William King's work there is nothing cruel or pointed about them. Instead, they are zany, absurd, light. 'Let anyone read [them],' declares Leigh Hunt, 'and then call an index a dry thing if he can.' The index has made itself at home in the journals of the early eighteenth century, adapting to suit their manners, their tone. Moreover, it signals the elevation of these essays produced at a gallop for the daily coffee-house sheet to something more durable, to a format that connotes value, perhaps even status. At the midpoint of the second decade of the eighteenth century, the index is primed to offer the same sheen to other genres, to epic poetry, to drama, to the emerging form of the novel. And yet, we know how this story ends. In the twenty-first century novels do not have indexes. Nor do plays. Poetry books are indexed by first line, not by subject. Why, then, was the index to fiction a short-lived phenomenon? Why did it not take? To shed some light on this question, let us turn briefly to two literary figures from the late nineteenth century, both still indexing novels long after the embers had died down on that particular experiment. What can these latecomers tell us about the problems of indexing when it comes to works of the imagination?

'It was a glorious victory, wasn't it?' With these words, in *Through the Looking-Glass*, the White Knight introduces himself to Alice. He has just rescued her from her captor, the Red Knight, and yet it is a curious introduction, since the victory has been anything but glorious. Both knights, bashing at each other with clubs – which they hold with their arms rather than their hands, like Punch and Judy dolls – have been tumbling again and again off their horses, landing without fail on their heads, then remounting, swinging and losing their balance once more. After a final double lunge sees both knights fall off together, they shake hands, and Red retires from the field. A victory for White, to be sure, but *glorious* is not the term that springs to mind. Words, as so often in the Alice stories, are slippery, problematic things; they don't lead us where we expect.

As Alice walks on with her rescuer, he reveals himself, in his kindly, crackpot way, to be quite the renaissance man: an inventor – the portable beehive; shark-repelling anklets for horses – and with vast experience of falling off horses. He is also something of a troubadour, and before the pair part ways the White Knight insists on singing Alice a song which he introduces as follows:

'The name of the song is called "Haddocks' Eyes".'

'Oh, that's the name of the song, is it?' Alice said, trying to feel interested.

'No, you don't understand,' the Knight said, looking a little vexed. 'That's what the name is called. The name really is "The Aged Aged Man".'

'Then I ought to have said "That's what the song is called"?' Alice corrected herself.

'No, you oughtn't: that's quite another thing! The song is called "Ways and Means": but that's only what it's called, you know!'

'Well, what is the song, then?' said Alice, who was by this time completely bewildered.

'I was coming to that,' the Knight said. 'The song really is "A-sitting On A Gate": and the tune's my own invention.'

Pedantic and confusing, absurd but scrupulously logical, the Knight's discourse on the calling of names is as good a distillation of Carrollian wit as you'll find in the Alice stories. It plays on the difference between what things are and what we call them. We can do our best to make the two align, to find *le mot juste*, but naming is always a difficult art.

In a writer so keenly interested in this type of matter – the business of naming; the play between subjectivity and accuracy – it should come as little surprise that the practice of indexing should have held a particular appeal. In fact, Carroll had been indexing – and playing with indexes – since his childhood. At the family home at Croft Rectory in North Yorkshire, the teenaged Charles Dodgson – the pen name 'Lewis Carroll' (more playing with names) was still some way off – had produced for the entertainment of his siblings a handwritten journal, the *Rectory Magazine*, 'being a compendium of the best tales, poems, essays, pictures, &c. that the united talents of the Rectory inhabitants can produce'. In the archives of the Harry Ransom Centre in Texas, the magazine survives, copied out in neat into a fresh notebook when Carroll was eighteen, its title page boasting that this is the 'fifth edition, carefully revised, & improved'. And there, at

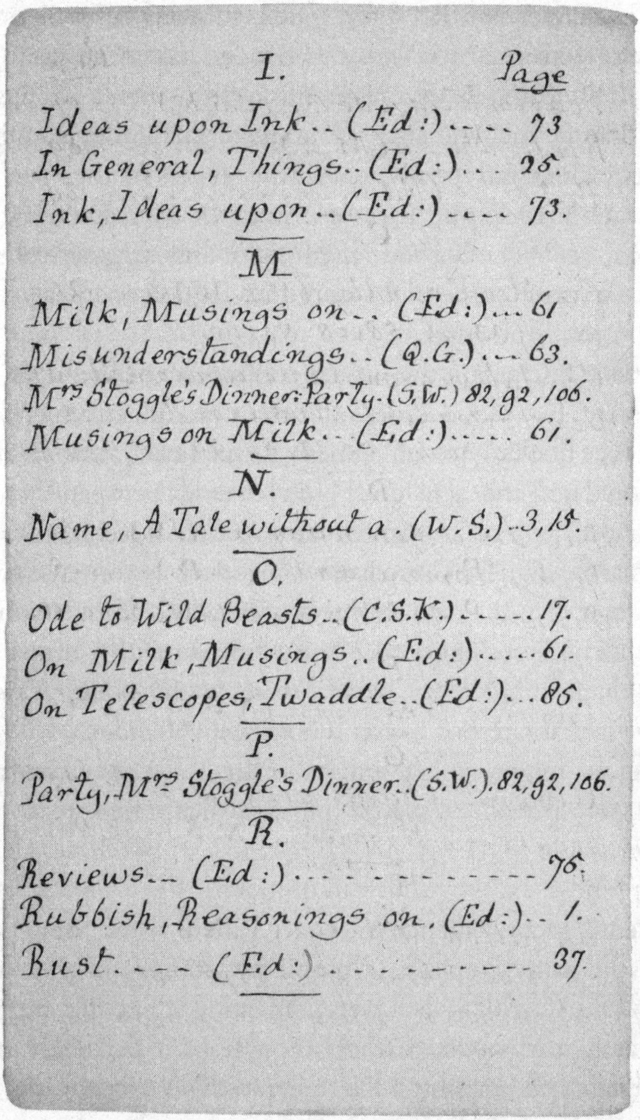

I. Page

Ideas upon Ink.. (Ed:)..... 73
In General, Things.. (Ed:)... 25.
Ink, Ideas upon.. (Ed:).... 73.

M

Milk, Musings on.. (Ed:)... 61
Misunderstandings.. (Q.G.)... 63.
Mrs Stoggle's Dinner-Party. (S.W.) 82, 92, 106.
Musings on Milk.. (Ed:)..... 61.

N.

Name, A Tale without a. (W.S.) 3, 15.

O.

Ode to Wild Beasts.. (C.S.K.)..... 17.
On Milk, Musings.. (Ed:)..... 61.
On Telescopes, Twaddle.. (Ed:)... 85.

P.

Party, Mrs Stoggle's Dinner.. (S.W.). 82, 92, 106.

R.

Reviews... (Ed:)............... 76.
Rubbish, Reasonings on. (Ed:).. 1.
Rust.... (Ed:)........... 37.

Figure 26: Index to the Dodgson family's handwritten *Rectory Magazine* showing page numbers as well as which member wrote each entry. The initials are coded but most of them refer to Carroll himself, who signed his pieces 'Ed.', VX, BB, FLW, JV, FX or QG.

the back, is a tidy, five-page index, showing off a pleasingly developed sense of whimsy. The index has entries for 'General, Things in, 25', not to mention 'In General, Things, 25' and 'Things in General, 25'. The tale of 'Mrs Stoggle's Dinner Party', which ran serially across three issues of the magazine, appears in mixed-up form as 'Stoggles, Mrs, Dinner Party, 82, 92, 106'. The baroque rhythms of indexing syntax seem to have stirred something – some fascination or amusement – in the youthful writer.

It is a fascination that would endure for the whole of Carroll's life. In 1889, decades after the extraordinary success of the Alice books, he would publish his last novel, *Sylvie and Bruno*. It would be a critical failure. Flitting uneasily between Victorian England and a realm named Fairyland, the novel mixes social drama with familiar Carrollian features such as nonsense poetry and logic play. It is also a somewhat mawkish consideration of death, childhood innocence and Christian faith – a distinctly late-nineteenth-century blend. More to the point, *Sylvie and Bruno* is that rarest of beasts: a novel with an index.

As we might expect, entries in the *Sylvia and Bruno* index lean determinedly towards the whimsical. 'Bed, reason for never going to, II.141' and 'Eggs, how to purchase, II.196'; 'Happiness, excessive, how to moderate, I.159' and 'Sobriety, extreme, inconvenience of, I.140'. There is the same pleasure, the same comedy of garbled syntax, as in the *Rectory Magazine*. Carroll is, as it were, repeating a joke that he made privately forty years earlier, though in a decidedly more sophisticated retelling. Like much of his logician's wit, Carroll's index parodies the loose, woolly rules of everyday life – in this case, indexing syntax – by pushing them to absurdity, as in the redundant, ludicrously pedantic second comma in 'Scenery, enjoyment of, by little men'.

At the same time, the *Sylvie and Bruno* index includes numerous examples of another type of redundancy whereby the same entry appears several times in slightly different formulations and under different headings: 'Falling house, life in a', 'House falling through Space, life in a', 'Life in a falling house'. Again, it is a joke he has been making his whole life – remember 'General, Things in', 'In General, Things', 'Things in General' – but again it feels as though Carroll is working intuitively, through the medium of silliness, towards something profoundly humane. These verbal round robins recall Alice's exchange with the White Knight, reminding us that settling on the best keyword is rather like finding a title for the Knight's song, that there is a whole world of possibilities. Indexing – indexing a novel, moreover – is an act of interpretation, a job of trying to second guess what future readers might want to look up, and in what terms. How does one choose? Why is one term – *life, house, falling* – better than another? Carroll's contemporary, the great Victorian indexer Henry Wheatley, would argue that 'it is in the point of selecting the best catchword that the good Indexer will show his superiority over the commonplace worker.'[6] But in leaving the choice unresolved, Carroll lifts the lid on the process, showing us his workings. Indexes are the work of individuals, they are linguistic and therefore human exercises, steeped in the same paradox, redundancy and subjectivity as all language use. Here *Sylvie and Bruno* is perfectly of a part with discussions such as Alice's with Humpty Dumpty:

> 'The question is,' said Alice, 'whether you can make words mean so many different things.'
> 'The question is,' said Humpty Dumpty, 'which is to be master – that's all.'

The *Sylvie and Bruno* index is pure Carroll – a recollection, at the end of his writing life, of an idea formed at its outset – and while later editions of the novel have tended to omit it, this feels like editorial slackness. The index is not a supplement to the novel but a coda, a final dose of wit, playfulness and even satire, beyond the story's end but still very much part of the same work.

One can see how editors might be confused, though. Part of the joke, of course, is that an index should be there at all. For the most part, we know the rule: non-fiction has an index (should have, anyway); fiction doesn't. Hence the quip, usually attributed to JoÙ Updike, that 'most biographies are just novels with indexes'. We don't expect to find an index in a novel unless the novel is playing at being another type of work – Virginia Woolf's mock-biography *Orlando*, for example, or Nabokov's mock-poetry book *Pale Fire* – and this was already as true in the nineteenth century as it is now. The *Sylvie and Bruno* index is a rule-breaker, winking at the reader as it smudges the line separating fiction from non-fiction.

What's more, while it is a good joke, it is also a bad index. *Scenery*, *Eggs*, *Bed*: these heads are not, in fact, much use for any reader earnestly trying to locate a particular moment. If anything, they serve as a decent illustration of just how hard it is to predict the features of the terrain, the narrative staging posts that will have been memorable to readers returning to something as textured as a well-crafted piece of fiction. How should a story be indexed? By names and places, certainly. What about things, the material world of the tale: the handkerchief in *Othello*, the 'sweet lemony wax' of the bar of Sweny's soap in *Ulysses*? Or ideas, since literature is no doubt where much of a culture's thinking happens? What about emotions?

A couple of years before *Sylvie and Bruno*, an index appeared in another novel, this time at the front of the book, not the back, and this time compiled not by the novel's author but by its editor. The novel was Henry Mackenzie's *The Man of Feeling*, originally published over a century earlier in 1775, and the editor was Henry Morley, Professor of English Literature at University College London. Morley had been commissioned to write the introductions for a series called Cassell's National Library which reprinted classic works for a wide audience. Priced at threepence in paperback or sixpence in hardback, the Cassell's series were pocket-sized and printed on the flimsiest paper, with their back cover and flyleaves crammed with advertisements: baby food, custard powder, Wright's Coal Tar Soap. They look, and feel, quite unlike any novel we might purchase nowadays, and this unusual appearance tells us something important about their intended market. The Cassell's Library was aimed at a readership eager for culture but for whom fine editions were out of reach: children, autodidacts, the new generation of readers that had emerged after the Education Acts of the decade before. Morley's introductions are brief – they would need to be since Cassell's brought out a new book in the series every week for four years – but they are instructive and lively, often wry, quickly situating each work within its historical context.

In the case of *The Man of Feeling*, Morley cannot resist some high Victorian disdain for the emotional incontinence of the late eighteenth-century novel. To show just how sentimental Mackenzie's tale is, Morley draws up an 'Index to Tears': a list, with locators, recording every time a character weeps. Each entry includes a brief label indicating how the crying is described, from the commonplace ('Not an unmoistened eye, p. 53') to the classical ('Tears, like Cestus of

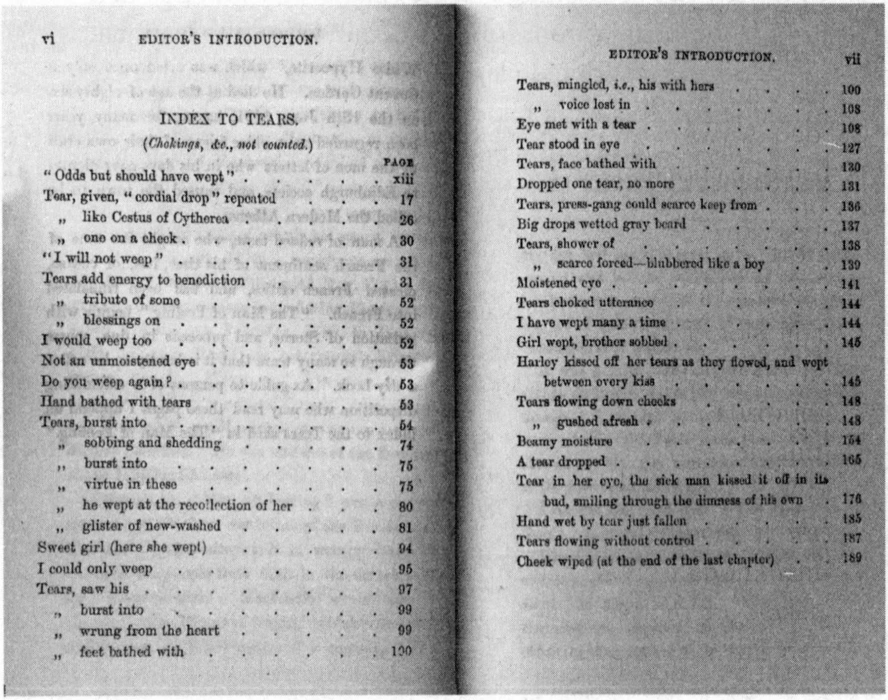

Figure 27: Morley's 'Index to Tears' in Henry Mackenzie's *The Man of Feeling*.

Cytherea, p. 26'), the composed ('Dropped one tear, no more, p. 131') to the unrestrained ('Tears flowing without control, p. 187'), the minimalist ('A tear dropped, p. 165') to the baroque ('Tear in her eye, the sick man kissed it off in its bud, smiling through the dimness of his own, p. 176'). As a performance, it is something like a cross between King's 'Short Account of Dr Bentley' and Oscar Wilde's quip about the *Old Curiosity Shop*, that 'One must have a heart of stone to read the death of Little Nell without laughing.'

The 'Index to Tears' is a highly satisfying take-down, one age sticking the boot in on the manners of another. But there is bluntness too about its operation, about how it works as an index. The 'Index to Tears' is a demolition job on a particular genre, the sentimental novel, but it is not, in fact, an index of sentiments. Its criterion is not emotion, but emotion's physical trace: actual tears. A note at the top of the table even stipulates: 'Chokings, &c., not counted'. This is the index-as-drinking-game, and its rules are clear: that stifled sob or stoical sniff into a balled-up handkerchief will not make the cut. Even so, the 'Index to Tears' still manages to locate forty-six moments of full-blown blubbing in a novel of less than 200 pages.

But *why* do they cry so much? Here, the 'Index' has nothing to say. Morley does not attempt to taxonomize emotions, or to analyse the varied reasons why Mackenzie's characters break down. To do so would be a much trickier endeavour, one riddled with all the complexities of literary criticism: ambiguity, subjectivity, the slipperiness of abstract categories. It risks taking the index into territory where its precision becomes blurry, its usefulness – the reliability of its headwords – blunted by the weight of interpretation that would go into choosing them. The index flounders when it moves from what-is-referred-to to what-is-suggested. But fiction, unlike non-fiction, resists being anatomized into discrete nuggets of information. Morley, in the late nineteenth century, was far too canny to attempt anything more than the barest sketch. Like Carroll, he is able to play facetiously off an established tradition of *not* indexing novels, to draw a puckish energy from the simple act of compiling one, no matter how cock-eyed or useless. A veil of irony covers these gestures. There is nothing at stake: they are successful, in spite of – *because of,* even – being poor indexes. As we return to the eighteenth century and find the greatest literary figures of the age attempting in earnest what their successors attempt only in jest, let us keep in mind that, when it comes to fiction, the measure of an index's success might lie somewhere beyond the ideals of complexity, comprehensiveness, rigour – all the things that Carroll and Morley leave out.

Just as indexes to Addison and Steele's *Spectator* were being compiled, one of that paper's sometime correspondents was embarking on an altogether more serious indexing experiment. Where the single-sheet papers represented print in its most demotic, promiscuous form, designed to be passed from one reader to the next, in Alexander Pope's *Iliad* we see the translator working at the other end of the spectrum, drawing on his audience's desire for books that would stand out in the age of print saturation, their desire to own high-status literature in high-status editions. As we saw before, the *Spectator* indexes are most successful, not as genuine entry-points to the essays, but rather as advertisements for their qualities – their style and lightness. In the manifold indexes to Pope's *Iliad* we will see something similar, where the real meaning is not the tables' ultimate usefulness, but rather the effects they create – of prestige, luxury and abundance.

Pope's translation of Homer's epic appeared in six annual instalments from 1715 to 1720. This commercially pioneering way of bringing out the work allowed the publisher to reduce up-front costs by financing each volume with sales from the previous. Meanwhile, Pope himself would receive 750 deluxe copies of each instalment, and a month's head start to sell them before the publisher brought their own cheaper copies to market. The venture would earn Pope a fortune, enabling him to create the Palladian villa at Twickenham in which he would see out the rest of his days.

When Pope's translation appeared, Richard Bentley, still starting fights almost inadvertently, cavilled at its lack of faithfulness to the original: 'It is a pretty poem, Mr Pope; but you must not call it Homer.'[7] Pope had taken the heroic hexameters of Homer's epic and recast them, squeezing them into the elegant rhyming couplets of the Augustan age. Both the verse and the stately dripfeed of its yearly publication were part of a performance in studied, modern refinement, and naturally the book itself should follow suit. Pope's contract stipulated that a new typeface would be created for it, that Pope's 750 copies would be printed on large-format sheets, that there would be engraved head and tail pieces and ornate initial letters for each volume. The subscriber list for this no-expense-spared edition dripped with earls and dukes, counts and viscounts. At its head was Princess Caroline.

By the time the second instalment had appeared, the success of the venture seemed assured. Pope penned a satirical pamphlet in which another publisher, Edmund Curll, laments that the *Iliad* is putting him out of business, leaving him unable to employ his usual workforce. Summoning all his writers – the historian, the poet, the satirist, the critic, etc. –

from their squalid abodes, Curll declares that it is not his fault that they have gone unpaid:

> Ah, Gentlemen! what have I not done? what have I not suffer'd, rather than the World should be depriv'd of your Lucubrations? I have taken involuntary Purges, I have been vomited, three Times have I been can'd, once I was hunted, twice was my Head broke by a Grenadier, twice was I toss'd in a Blanket; I have had Boxes on the Ear, Slaps on the Chops; I have been frighted, pump'd, kick'd, slander'd, beshitten. – I hope, Gentlemen, you are all convinc'd, that this author of Mr Lintott's [i.e. Pope] could mean nothing else but starving you, by poisoning me. It remains for us to consult the best and speediest Methods of Revenge.[8]

Putting their minds to how to bring down Pope, each suggests something suited to their skills – the historian will write a poisonous biography; the poet an attack in the form of a Pindaric ode. Only the indexer is impotent: 'But the Index-maker said, there was nothing like an Index to his Homer.'

The satire's broader message is straightforward: Pope, triumphant, is crowing at a publisher he has crossed swords with in the past. But the line about the indexer is an odd little moment – difficult to interpret. It comes at the end of a paragraph full of grimy, scatological humour and sly, personal digs, but rather than triumphantly capping the performance, it feels like a punchline that falls flat, closing out the satirical medley not with a bang but a whimper. If anything, it seems to represent a chink of anxiety on Pope's part, an awareness that in an edition where every single detail is on a grand scale – a work that might set its author up for life – there remains one question still to be resolved. Gay's *Trivia*, that same year, had been a poem with an index, but its effect was comical, mock-heroic. Pope's *Iliad* was the real thing, the greatest epic of them all, nothing mock about it. Should Homer have an index? What should it be like?

Four years later, with the final volume complete, Pope would write of exhaustion, and of work brought up short, curtailed due to time constraints: 'having design'd four very laborious and uncommon sort of Indexes to Homer, I'm forc'd, for want of time, to publish two only; the design of which you will own to be pretty, tho' far from fully executed'.[9] For all his frustration, it is hard to imagine how Pope's projected indexes could have been any grander, or more capacious, than the ones that actually appeared. The two indexes are, in fact, subdivided into an explosion of tables, slicing the book in almost any way a reader might imagine: a table of persons and things; of arts and sciences; of 'versification', or the different verbal effects Pope employs to mimic the action being described ('Broken and disorder'd in describing a stormy sea, 13.1005', 'Full of breaks where Disappointment is imag'd, 18.101, 144, 22.378'); there is a table of fables, and another of similes, a table of descriptive passages, of the principal speeches, and an alphabetical index of emotions from Anxiety to Tenderness. It is an extraordinary suite, entirely in keeping with the grandeur of the edition. Like everything else, the indexes imply that this is a book for life, that readers will return to it again and again, using it to consider the greatest epic in the Western canon from every conceivable angle. The indexes turn the poem into an encyclopedia, a work we might mine for military tactics – 'Where to place the worst soldiers, 4.344' – or for classical symbolism; for moral instruction or for aesthetic pleasure; for Homer's poetical effects or for Pope's. In truth, this may not be how readers will ultimately treat the text. But the exhaustiveness and intricacy of the indexes are part and parcel of the edition's experiment in prestige.

When Pope moved on to editing a complete edition of Shakespeare's plays, it was natural that the new venture should include a similarly luxuriant set of indexes. This time, however, Pope would be less than hands-on. He wrote to his publisher with instructions: 'Whoever you set upon the Index, may proceed upon the plan of mine to Homer, & whoever has Sense & Judgment enough to draw up this Index, will find that a Sufficient direction.' Unfortunately, while the Shakespeare indexes are as numerous and varied as those in Pope's Homer, they are also chaotic, poorly realized, and sparsely populated. There is a table of historical characters and a separate one for fictional ones, Macbeth and Lear in the former, Hamlet the latter. An index of the 'Manners, Passions, and their external Effects' across the entire Shakespeare corpus sounds like a wildly ambitious project, but its realization is hopelessly underwhelming: a list running to just three, single-columned pages. If we take the entry for 'Pride', the index directs us to a single instance: Ulysses in *Troilus and Cressida*, Act 3, Scene 7. Might pride, by any chance, feature anywhere else in the thirty-six Shakespeare plays collected here? The index suggests not. Where in Shakespeare might one find a good example of envy? You're thinking *Othello*, perhaps? Wrong. The sole location in Pope's index is Wolsey in *Henry VIII*, Act 3, Scene 5. What could such an index be useful for? It won't help readers to locate a particular incident they have in mind. Perhaps instead its role is to provide paradigmatic examples for a handful of emotions. Fury? Enobarbus in *Antony and Cleopatra* (Act 3, Scene 10). Hope? The Queen in *Richard II* (Act 2, Scene 6). This is not an unreasonable idea – a set of *loci classici*, pre-chosen and ranging across the complete works, something not unlike the anthologies for public reading that began to appear later in the eighteenth century. But that is not quite what we have here. Interspersed with those emotional primary colours – Hope, Envy, Rage – we find other entries – 'French Quack's Airs', 'Pedantry, in Sir Hugh Evans', 'Hostess Quickly' – that don't seem to belong. The table is a mishmash, hurried and unhelpful. The same can be said for the 'Index of Thoughts or Sentiments', while the table of 'Descriptions of Places' is abject, the entirety of Shakespearean drama yielding just fifteen entries, from 'Bank, flow'ry' to 'Vale, a dark and melancholy one'.

The indexes to Pope's Shakespeare are both epic and atrocious. For all the possibilities they suggest, the potential ricÙess and complexity of an index of Shakespearean manners, or passions, or sentiments, the results are slapdash, and sometimes nonsensical. The compilation shows no regard for how the tables might actually be used. Ultimately one is left with the sense that their true purpose is only to bulk out the volume, that the indexes are there as a monument to Shakespeare – a great writer *should* have their work analysed from all these different angles – rather than as an aid for the reader. But the Shakespeare tables also point to a greater problem, the one that Henry Morley will gingerly sidestep a century and a half later: an index is always on firmer ground when its basic unit is the indivisible nugget of facticity: tears, not passions. Where the Homer indexes, on the whole, tabulated categories that are stable – sciences, similes, verbal effects – fields in which the terms can be broadly agreed, the Shakespeare tables turn the focus inwards. Thoughts, sentiments, manners and passions, categories whose objects, like the White Knight's song, will not always sit easily with their names.

*

In the period when Pope's editions – the poetry of Homer, the plays of Shakespeare – were appearing, another literary form was beginning to emerge in English. The new long-form medium of the novel was just as apt to represent the incident and detail of epic as it was the interiority of drama. After early successes like Daniel Defoe's *Robinson Crusoe* (1719) and Swift's *Gulliver's Travels* (1726), the publishing sensation of the 1740s was a printer named Samuel Richardson. His three great novels, *Pamela* (1740), *Clarissa* (1748) and *Charles Grandison* (1753) adopted the epistolary format – pretending to be a collection of private letters that had been discovered and prepared for publication – to narrate the travails of their eponymous heroes. All three works sold in huge quantities, but in the case of *Clarissa*, the masterpiece among them, the novel was not only enormously successful, it was also enormously enormous. When it first appeared, it ran to just under a million words, split over seven volumes; within three years, however, Richardson had brought out an expanded edition, adding several hundred pages to the mass. It remains a milestone of the early novel form, and a millstone for English Literature undergraduates struggling to do their reading ahead of class. Part of its appeal, at least to readers in the mid eighteenth century, was the sense of moral instruction to be gained from the way that its heroine remains incorruptible throughout her suffering at the hands of the wicked rake Lovelace. Like a collection of sermons for trying times, this was a novel that readers would return to – though not, perhaps, in full. How, then, in such an immense work, should they find the passage they wanted?

On 9 March 1751, shortly before *Clarissa*'s expanded edition was to appear, Richardson received a letter from Dr JoÙson urging him not to worry at having made a vast novel even vaster, 'for though the story is long, every letter is short'.[10] But JoÙson's letter ends with a suggestion:

> I wish you would add an *index rerum*, that when the reader recollects any incident, he may easily find it, which at present he cannot do, unless he knows in which volume it is told; for Clarissa is not a performance to be read with eagerness, and laid aside for ever; but will be occasionally consulted by the busy, the aged and the studious; and therefore I beg that this edition, by which I suppose posterity is to abide, may want nothing that can facilitate its use.

Not a one-time fiction to be read then laid aside for ever: JoÙson has hit exactly on the theme of durability and return that we have seen throughout this chapter. An index to *Clarissa* would 'facilitate its use'. In fact, JoÙson need not have worried, for the idea had already occurred to Richardson. In the preface to the new edition, Richardson recounts how 'an ingenious Gentleman' (one of his neighbours, the schoolmaster Solomon Lowe) had presented him with a table of *Clarissa*'s 'instructive sentiments'. Richardson was so pleased with it that he set about enlarging it himself, before having the finished table included with the novel's latest edition.[11]

The *Clarissa* index is a very curious thing indeed. Running to eighty-five pages, it is appropriately voluminous for such a long novel. Even its title is on a Richardsonian scale: 'A Collection of such of the Moral and Instructive Sentiments, Cautions, Aphorisms, Reflections, and Observations, contained in the History of Clarissa, as are presumed to be of General Use and Services, digested under Proper Heads'. Entries are arranged under a series of categories – clusters of related themes such as 'Duty. Obedience', 'Procuress. Profligate Woman', or 'Wit. Talents. Conversation' – and these appear in alphabetical order. In itself, there is nothing too odd about this – it is rather like a vastly more comprehensive version of the 'Index of Thoughts or Sentiments' in Pope's Shakespeare. (So comprehensive, in fact, that there is a supplementary index-to-the-index, giving the pages on which each cluster of entries can be found.) It is only when we look at the entries themselves that we find ourselves in uncharted territory. Here there is nothing of the terse, back-to-front bread-sauce-what-appropriate-for syntax we have come to expect from an index head. Instead, Richardson's entries are elegantly phrased and aphoristic. Rather than brief labels, pointing us off as quickly as possible to the main text, these read like fully formed maxims, ready to be repeated in polite conversation. Under 'Duelling', for example, we find the entry, 'An innocent man ought not to run an equal risk with a guilty one'; under 'Adversity', 'Adversity is the state of trial of every good quality'. These are so polished, so worked-up, one wonders whether they actually send the reader back to the novel at all, or whether the index offers just enough self-contained Richardsonian advice to make the extra effort unnecessary. The index feels less like a jumping-off point than a final destination, with the novel itself acting merely as guarantor, lending its authority like an illustrious parent discreetly underwriting their well-spoken offspring as they make their own way. In one early stand-alone edition, the index even appears with its locators omitted entirely and a note from Richardson explaining that, since two differently paginated versions of the novel were in circulation, it would have been too confusing to supply page numbers. He adds, 'It is humbly presumed, that the Sentiments or Maxims are, generally, of such Importance, as to be found not unworthy of the Observation of the youthful Reader, altho' they were not to have the close Relation which they *have*, to the History of Clarissa'. In other words, even if, dear reader, this index were not linked to a novel – which, I assure you, it is – it would still be worthy of your attention.[12]

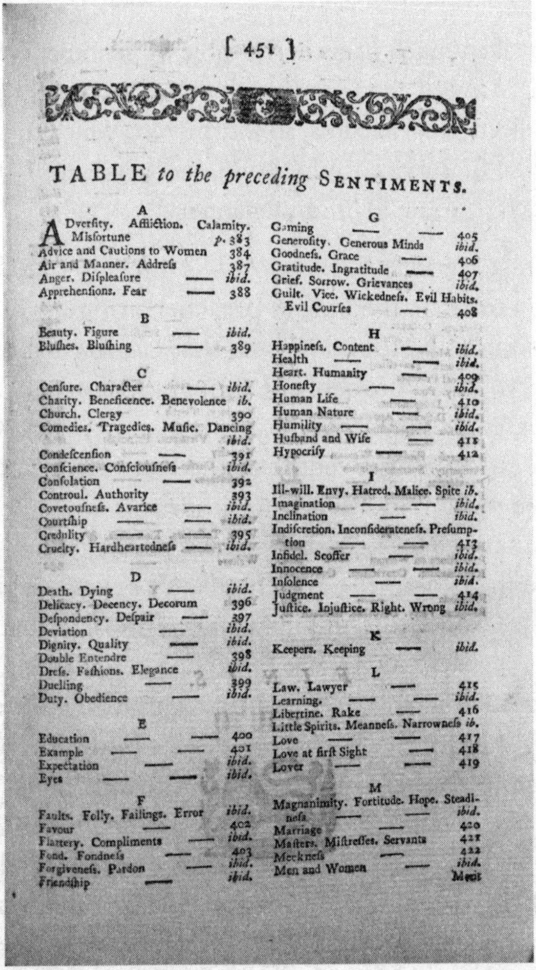

[451]

TABLE *to the preceding* SENTIMENTS.

A

Adversity. Affliction. Calamity. Misfortune — *p.* 383
Advice and Cautions to Women — 384
Air and Manner. Address — 387
Anger. Displeasure — *ibid.*
Apprehensions. Fear — 388

B

Beauty. Figure — *ibid.*
Blushes. Blushing — 389

C

Censure. Character — *ibid.*
Charity. Beneficence. Benevolence — *ib.*
Church. Clergy — 390
Comedies. Tragedies. Music. Dancing — *ibid.*
Condescension — 391
Conscience. Consciousness — *ibid.*
Consolation — 392
Controul. Authority — 393
Covetousness. Avarice — *ibid.*
Courtship — *ibid.*
Credulity — 395
Cruelty. Hardheartedness — *ibid.*

D

Death. Dying — *ibid.*
Delicacy. Decency. Decorum — 396
Despondency. Despair — 397
Deviation — *ibid.*
Dignity. Quality — *ibid.*
Double Entendre — 398
Dress. Fashions. Elegance — *ibid.*
Duelling — 399
Duty. Obedience — *ibid.*

E

Education — 400
Example — 401
Expectation — *ibid.*
Eyes — *ibid.*

F

Faults. Folly. Failings. Error — *ibid.*
Favour — 402
Flattery. Compliments — *ibid.*
Fond. Fondness — 403
Forgiveness. Pardon — *ibid.*
Friendship — *ibid.*

G

Gaming — 405
Generosity. Generous Minds — *ibid.*
Goodness. Grace — 406
Gratitude. Ingratitude — 407
Grief. Sorrow. Grievances — *ibid.*
Guilt. Vice. Wickedness. Evil Habits. Evil Courses — 408

H

Happiness. Content — *ibid.*
Health — *ibid.*
Heart. Humanity — 409
Honesty — *ibid.*
Human Life — 410
Human Nature — *ibid.*
Humility — *ibid.*
Husband and Wife — 411
Hypocrisy — 412

I

Ill-will. Envy. Hatred. Malice. Spite — *ib.*
Imagination — *ibid.*
Inclination — *ibid.*
Indiscretion. Inconsiderateness. Presumption — 413
Infidel. Scoffer — *ibid.*
Innocence — *ibid.*
Insolence — *ibid.*
Judgment — 414
Justice. Injustice. Right. Wrong — *ibid.*

K

Keepers. Keeping — *ibid.*

L

Law. Lawyer — 415
Learning. — *ibid.*
Libertine. Rake — 416
Little Spirits. Meanness. Narrowness — *ib.*
Love — 417
Love at first Sight — 418
Lover — 419

M

Magnanimity. Fortitude. Hope. Steadiness — *ibid.*
Marriage — 420
Masters. Mistresses. Servants — 421
Meekness — 422
Men and Women — *ibid.*

Merit

Figure 28: The index to the index to *Clarissa*. The 'Table to the Preceding Sentiments' shows where each of the different sections of Richardson's great *Collection* begins.

For all his assurance of the table's 'close Relation' to the novel, the necessity, in this instance, of printing it without page references seems to have been suggestive to Richardson. In a letter to his French translator, he began to toy with the idea that the index might be decoupled from the novel entirely:

I have taken much pains in the table of sentiments I mentioned. Many of my friends wish to see it printed by itself, as a collection of maxims, aphorisms, &c. which they think would be of service to the world, independent of the history, as they relate to life and manners.[13]

That phrase 'service to the world' is a telling one. It carries within it a trace of the index's preacherly origins. Elsewhere, Richardson can be found musing that *Clarissa* is more than a mere story: 'It will probably be thought tedious to all such as *dip* into it, expecting a *light Novel*, or *transitory Romance.* '[14] Its purpose, rather, is 'as a vehicle to the Instruction'. Might that vehicle be shrunk to a table of aphorisms and still perform the same service to the world?

As the first volumes of Richardson's next novel began to emerge, JoÙson wrote to him again, proposing that he publish, as a standalone volume, an index to all three novels.[15] Having made the suggestion, JoÙson immediately retracted it, fearing that Richardson might devote his finite energies to such a project *instead of* producing a fourth novel. In fact, both JoÙson's hope and his fear would be realized. For the next two years, Richardson would dedicate himself to the compilation of a unified index for his three fictional works; there would be no fourth novel. The *Collection of the Moral and Instructive Sentiments, Maxims, Cautions and Reflections, Contained in the Histories of Pamela, Clarissa, and Sir Charles Grandison* cost Richardson no little effort, and he would grumble to his friend Lady Echlin about what 'a very painful and laborious task it was'.[16] Nevertheless, he was driven by an altruistic zeal, claiming that the work was carried through 'more with a view to do good, than to profit'. A <u>moral index</u> to the three great novels would be a service to the world.

The preface to the *Collection* reiterates this moralizing intent. But where, a few years earlier, we found Richardson pondering whether a collection of maxims 'independent of the history' – in other words, an index divorced entirely from the novels which gave birth to it – might be a useful thing, now he is more reconciled to the role of the novel itself. Stories, he writes, are effective at sugaring the pill of moral instruction. They can reach an audience that rejects the traditional modes of preaching, 'pursuing to their closets those who fly from the pulpit; and there, under the gay air, and captivating semblance of a Novel, tempting them to the perusal of many a persuasive sermon'.[17] The index, then, exists to draw out the primary improving intent of Richardson's novels. Like the table of sentiments to *Clarissa*, this is not a list of the players, their entrances and their exits, but rather an index to the three novels' sermonizing themes. As Richardson puts it:

> For the use therefore of all such as are desirous of *repeatedly inculcating* on their own minds, and the minds of others, the important Maxims, which those three works contain; and who would *refer* themselves occasionally to the volumes for the illustration of these maxims; this General Index both of Maxims and of References is now offered to the public in one pocket volume.[18]

Entries in the index include '*Children* how to be treated in their Infantile State, with a View to the Cultivation of their

Minds' and '*Marriage* in advanced Years, and with an Inequality as to Age'. In fact, the italicization of the headwords is somewhat misleading. These entries are far too complex and precise for any single word to be adequate – the qualifiers are compound: not just *Marriage*, nor even Marriage late in life, but Marriage late in life to a younger spouse. These are clearly *situations*, specific moral quandaries, where Richardson's novels might offer guidance to the reader, and the index exists so that this guidance might be more efficiently bestowed.

Lady Echlin certainly appreciated the moral point being made here, applauding Richardson for devoting 'time and pains on that choice collection, with no other view but to do good to your fellow creatures'.[19] Not all of Richardson's friends were as enthusiastic, however, and Richardson bemoaned how some were frustrated with him for wasting his energies when he could have been writing a fourth novel. He cavils that these friends 'declared they would not read [the *Collection*]; yet regarded the three pieces I have published [i.e. the novels] more for the sake of instruction, than the story. – So they said'.[20] In other words, could they not see that, where moral improvement was the goal, an index was a more worthwhile project than another novel? That final, suspicious barb, 'So they said', reveals the tension that exists at this point over the role of Richardson's novels: whether they should in fact be for 'mere amusement' or whether they exist primarily as a medium for moral instruction. Richardson's index, pulling in a structure from non-novelistic modes of writing, was an attempt to minimize the distance between fiction and non-fiction, to downplay the story, so that the novel becomes merely another form of treatise. But in his friends' unconvincing assurances and their refusal to read the *Collection*, we can see the pull of the novel away from mere sermonizing.

By the start of the nineteenth century, Richardson's *Collection*, where it was noted at all, was held in derision, a preposterous self-indulgence. Isaac D'Israeli, including it in his *Curiosities of Literature*, decries it as the sign of a 'violent literary vanity', criticizing the aphoristic entries as being essentially banal, and the exercise of indexing one's own novel in the first place narcissistic. 'Literary history', he proposes, 'does not record a more singular example of that self-delight which an author has felt on a revision of his works.'[21] It would be another hundred years, and even then only under the cloak of Morley's irony or Carroll's playfulness, before the indexed novel would risk another appearance.

But what of Dr JoÙson, who had first egged Richardson on in his self-delight? He, at least, made good use of the *Collection*. The White Knight, early on in this chapter, offered a textbook example of just how slippery the business of definition can be. For JoÙson, compiling his *Dictionary of the English Language*, the trick was to draw on the authority of others. 'The solution of all difficulties,' he wrote in the *Dictionary*'s preface, 'and the supply of all defects, must be sought in the examples, subjoined to the various senses of each word.'[22] Only with examples – quotations showing a given word in context – can one tease out the subtle distinctions between the different ways a word can be used. And not just any quotations either. JoÙson's title page announces: 'A DICTIONARY OF THE ENGLISH LANGUAGE in which the WORDS are deduced from their ORIGINALS and ILLUSTRATED in their DIFFERENT SIGNIFICATIONS by EXAMPLES from the BEST WRITERS'.

But in choosing the 'best writers' for his illustrative quotations, JoÙson decided to impose a constraint on himself: no living authors should be included. The reasoning,

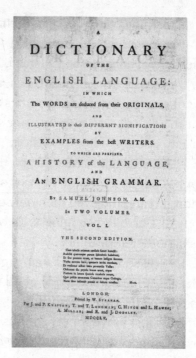

Figure 29: 'Examples from the Best Writers': the title page to JoÙson's *Dictionary*.

essentially, was to avoid any awkwardness among his literary peers: 'that I might not be misled by partiality, and that none of my contemporaries might have reason to complain'.[23] In the case of Richardson, however, the Doctor was prepared to bend his own rule. *Quaggy, bumpkinly, rakish, chuffily*: in each case the *Dictionary* looks to *Clarissa* for clarification. In total, the novel provides JoÙson with no fewer than ninety-six examples. *Craver, devilkin, domesticate, brindle*. No other novel comes close. And yet, more than three-quarters of the time – in seventy-eight instances out of ninety-six – JoÙson is discreetly drawing not on *Clarissa* itself but on its table.[24] Let us, by way of example, turn to romping. The

Dictionary defines the verb *to romp* as 'to play crudely, noisily, and boisterously', backing this up with a quotation which it attributes to *Clarissa*: 'Men presume greatly on the liberties taken in *romping*'. But *Clarissa* contains no such sentence. Rather, it contains Lovelace's defence of himself at the start of Book V: 'All I have done to her, would have been looked upon as a frolick only, a *romping*-bout, and laughed off by nine parts in ten of the sex accordingly.' It is only when this passage is glossed, turned into an axiom in Richardson's curious moral index, that it takes the form, more or less, that the *Dictionary* ascribes to it: 'Men presume greatly on the liberties taken, and laughed off, in romping'. Even for such a professed admirer as Johnson, *Clarissa* is too diffuse a performance to go hunting for particular words in it. The index, instead, would do perfectly.

These days, it is an academic commonplace when considering a word or a topic to turn to the Oxford English Dictionary and find its earliest usage. By affixing illustrative quotations to his definitions, Johnson turned the dictionary into the *par excellence* resource for the index-scholar – the 'apotheosis of index-learning', as Robin Valenza has put it.[25] Nice to know, then, that Johnson was not above a little index-hunting himself. One imagines the ghost of Erasmus cocking an eyebrow archly. Before we get too complacent, however, Johnson has a warning. Boswell's *Life of Johnson* records a conversation between the Doctor and the literary critic Samuel Badcock in which the pair fall into grousing about another writer. Badcock takes up the story:

> I called him an Index scholar; but [Johnson] was not willing to allow him a claim even to that merit. He said, 'that he borrowed from those who had been borrowers themselves,

and did not know that the mistakes he adopted had been answered by others'.[26]

Borrowing from a borrower means missing out on the debate altogether. Anyone, it seems, might fall back on a little index learning now and again; but to take it to the second degree is a dang'rous thing.

7

'A Key to All Knowledge'
The Universal Index

'It's like the index in the back of a book – with an
entry for every word seen on every web page we
index. When we index a web page, we add it to the
entries for all of the words it contains.'

Google, 'How Search Works'

'Kindly look her up in my index, Doctor,' murmured
Holmes, without opening his eyes. For many years he had
adopted a system of docketing all paragraphs concerning
men and things, so that it was difficult to name a subject or
a person on which he could not at once furnish information. In this case I found her biography sandwiched
between that of a Hebrew Rabbi and a staff commander
who had written a monograph upon the deep sea fishes.

The year is 1891, the story 'A Scandal in Bohemia', and the
person Holmes is searching for, sandwiched between the rabbi
and the amateur marine biologist, is Irene Adler, opera singer,
adventuress and lover of the man now standing in Holmes'
drawing room, one Wilhelm Gottsreich Sigismond von Orm-
stein, Grand Duke of Cassel-Felstein and hereditary King of
Bohemia. The tale will find Holmes outsmarted and chastened
by Adler. 'Beaten by a woman's wit,' as Watson puts it. It begins,

however, with Holmes coolly in control, seated in his armchair and not deigning to open his eyes, not even for a grand duke.

It is probably no surprise that Sherlock Holmes should be an indexer. His schtick, after all, his superpower, is his encyclopedic learning, the world's arcana: a human Google, or a walking *Notes and Queries*. But that would be preposterous. Besides, from the very first adventure, *A Study in Scarlet*, we have been informed that, in Watson's appraisal, Holmes' general knowledge is severely limited: 'Knowledge of literature – nil; Philosophy – nil; Astronomy – nil; Politics – feeble . . .' So occasionally Conan Doyle offers us a glimpse behind the curtain, a look at the system which allows Holmes his universal recall. Every now and again we see him pruning and tending his index, 'arranging and indexing some of his recent materials', or 'sat moodily at one side of the fire, cross-indexing his records of crime'. It is, naturally, an alphabetical system, with a 'great index volume' for each letter of the alphabet. When he wants to check something on, say, vampires, he is, characteristically, too lazy to get up himself: 'Make a long arm, Watson, and see what V has to say.' As a line of dialogue, incidentally, isn't this a minor masterpiece of characterization? The asymmetry of the pair's relationship is smoothed over with chummy slang: *make a long arm*. Watson, the gopher, will take the book down from the shelf, but he will not be the one to see what V has to say; Holmes, of course, will do the reading, balancing the book on his knee and gazing 'slowly and lovingly over the record of old cases, mixed with the accumulated information of a lifetime':

'Voyage of the Gloria Scott', he read. 'That was a bad business. I have some recollection that you made a record of it, Watson, though I was unable to congratulate you upon the result. Victor Lynch, the forger. Venomous lizard or gila. Remarkable case, that! Vittoria, the circus belle. Vanderbilt and the Yeggman. Vipers. Vigor, the Hammersmith wonder.'

'Good old index,' he purrs. 'You can't beat it.' The index – *his* index, with its smattering of everything – is the source of his mastery.

Holmes' alphabetical volumes represent the index unbound, not confined to a single work but looking outwards, docketing anything that might be noteworthy. It is by no means a new idea; Robert Grosseteste was practising something similar six-and-a-half centuries previously. In the Victorian period, however, it is taken up with a new intensity. Coordinated, resource heavy: the universal index is becoming industrialized. Looking closely at Holmes' index, there is something charmingly, inescapably homespun about it. Victor Lynch, venomous lizard, Vittoria the circus belle: this is a rattlebag of headers: patchy, piecemeal. Like Grosseteste's *Tabula*, Holmes' index brings together the collected readings and experiences of a single, albeit extraordinary, figure – the index as personal history. But Holmes, in his way, represents the last of a kind. Not long after 'A Scandal in Bohemia' first appeared in the *Strand Magazine*, Holmes would come to be indexed himself, a recurring entry in the annual *Index to Periodicals*, which trawled the year's papers, magazines and journals, keeping a record of every article. The efforts of even a Holmes or a Grosseteste appear paltry alongside a venture of this scale, available to anyone with access to a subscribing library. But how to bring such a thing into existence? That will be a three-pipe problem.

What do we mean when we characterize the nineteenth century and the decades leading up to it as the Age of Industry? A way of producing things that was new, certainly: new materials, cast iron and steel; the harnessing of steam power and the mechanization of manufacturing processes; a reorganization of labour in the factories into specialist and menial tasks. But also, perhaps, a new conception of scale: engineering projects – Brunel's railway, Bazalgette's sewer system – that are still held up today as examples of the confidence and ambition of the time. It would betray, surely, a hopeless lack of self-awareness, a lack of proportion, to place any book index alongside these achievements. But that, in 1865, is precisely what the priest and publisher Jacques-Paul Migne did. To be fair to Migne, his achievement *was* an extraordinary one, and one which – like those large-scale engineering projects – involved overseeing a whole army of workers. Appearing between 1841 and 1855, his *Patrologia Latina* offered a comprehensive collection of the writings of the Church Fathers. The main texts fill 217 volumes, beginning with Tertullian in the third century and running through St Augustine, Bede and hundreds of others, until it concludes with Pope Innocent III at the beginning of the thirteenth. It remains the standard source for many of those writings today. But Migne knew that such an encyclopedic collection brought with it a Big Data problem. Readers, he noted, would take fright at enormity of the *Patrologia*. 'Who will sound this abyss?' he imagines them asking. 'Who could ever find the time to study all these Fathers, and read their writings in any way?'[1] The solution, of course, is to make the work navigable: the *Patrologia* needs an index. But Migne, publishing's Isambard Kingdom Brunel, knows that it will need to be an index on a massive scale.

In producing the *Patrologia*, Migne's aim had been to keep costs down so that the volumes would be accessibly cheap. It was printed on low-quality paper, and where possible Migne chose to reprint the best available existing text of each work, rather than commission new editions. When it came to the index, however, Migne did not skimp. The *Patrologia*'s index – or rather indexes – occupy the final four books of the great series, volumes 218 to 221. These four tomes are filled with an enormous series of tables, 231 of them in all, including a lengthy index of indexes. The material in the preceding 217 volumes is broken down by author, by title, by country of origin, by century, by rank (popes first, then cardinals, archbishops, and so on), by genre (didactic works, interpretations of the scriptures, moral philosophy, canon law); there is a vast subject index that treats a huge swathe of subjects with a middling degree of detail, and a series of individual indexes that treat certain subjects – death, heaven, hell – with a fine-tooth comb.

The four index volumes even come with their own lengthy preface, in which Migne sounds a suitably grand note. Working himself up, he first describes the process by which the indexes have been produced. It is a passage no doubt intended to evoke the industrialization of labour, but which also recalls the friars at St Jacques compiling the original Bible concordance. Migne describes 'more than fifty men working on the indexes for more than ten years for the feeble recompense of 1,000 francs a year each'.[2] It may be feeble recompense for the hard-pressed indexer, but for the publisher of course it all adds up, with Migne bragging that the total comes to 'more than half a million francs, not even counting all the printing costs'.[3] He is moving through the gears now, using the figures to build himself up to a state of rapture as he contemplates his achievement:

> After all that, have we not the right to cry out: What are the twelve tasks of Hercules next to our two hundred and

thirty-one Indexes! What are all other literary endeavours! What are the encyclopedias of the eighteenth and nine-teenth centuries! What is any other work of typography! Child's play, the greatest of which is nothing next to our achievement. We can say, without fear of contradiction, that never before has any large publication gone to such lengths for the convenience of the subscribers . . . Our *Patrologia* has been squeezed like a grape in a winepress so that not even the tiniest drop of precious juice has been allowed to escape.[4]

It's a lovely image – the indexing process as a winepress, extracting the 'précieuse liqueur' from the plump, ripe text. But Migne hasn't finished. If creating an index is like wine-making, using one is more like going on a journey:

Our Indexes have cleared the way; they have levelled moun-tains and straightened the most tortuous paths . . . With the help of our Indexes, this vast subject has become small; dis-tances have become shorter, the first and last volume come together . . . What a timesaver! More than the railway, more even than the balloon, this is electricity![5]

This is the index as modernity itself, shrinking time, making vast distances small. The images of levelling and straighten-ing come straight from the railways: this could be Brunel speaking. But this is not enough, and Migne's final rhetorical flourish – that it is the index, not the railway, that is short-changed in this comparison – is a glorious one. Migne's indexes do not merely save time, they eliminate it with the lightning instantaneity of electricity. We have entered an age that can think, in flashes, of our own twenty-first-century electronic searching.

And yet, do we really find ourselves awestruck by the *Patrologia* indexes today? From the distance of a century and a half, there is certainly a charm to Migne's bombast. It is delightful – vivid, elegant – but it is hard to take entirely seriously. For one thing, navigating a work that fills up an entire bookcase will *never* feel electric, no matter how good the index. This is rather like the problem of the English Concordance in the thirteenth century: it was so detailed that it made the physical book that contained it cumbersome to use. Moreover, the *Patrologia*'s obscurity has increased exponentially over the intervening years. We still use the railway lines – not to mention the sewers – that the Victorians bequeathed us, but the Church Fathers have retreated to an extent Migne could not have imagined. Even if, by some miracle (which would be apt), the *Patrologia* indexes made finding what one wanted as easy as tapping the screen on a tablet, they would surely strike us today as so particular, so niche as to be little more than quaint. For most of us, at least, they have lost the wonder of scale. But how would something less specialist, something with a wider, more modern application, look? An index with the fine-grained focus of the *Patrologia* but covering a broader field, or covering *every* field: a universal index?

On 2 October 1877, the library world descended on London. Representatives from 140 of the world's great collections arrived for the second Conference of Librarians. The first had taken place in Philadelphia the year before, but the distance had meant that few European libraries were represented. This time, there were delegations from Italy, France, Denmark, Belgium and Australia – some on behalf of their national libraries, others private ones; the Greek and German governments sent special representatives; the keepers of seventeen libraries from the United States – among them the great universities of Harvard, Wellesley and Brown – made the trip across the Atlantic; and, of course, more than anywhere else, the United Kingdom swelled the roster. In attendance were the heads of the British Museum, the libraries of Oxford and Cambridge and their constituent colleges, of the great cathedrals: Salisbury, St Paul's, Canterbury, Exeter; of the learned societies: the College of Surgeons, the Statistical, Asiatic and Historical Societies, the Society of Biblical Archaeology, of Telegraph Engineers, the Queckett Microscopical Club. And most of all, delegates were sent from the new free municipal libraries that, following the Public Libraries Act of 1850, had opened their doors across the country – from Plymouth to Dundee, South Shields to Sunderland, and across the industrial belt of Liverpool, Manchester, Bolton, Bradford, Leeds – providing books, providing knowledge, for anyone who sought it. Within the grand porticoes of the London Institution in Finsbury Circus, just behind the newly built Moorgate Street Station, some 216 attendees came together to discuss how best to preserve and disseminate the heady proportion of the world's written knowledge that had been entrusted to their care.

The event made *The Times* that morning – their reporter was particularly taken with a revolving bookcase exhibited by one of the American delegates: 'an attractive contrivance to any student who is furnishing his own library'.[6] (This enthusiasm was only half misplaced: revolving bookcases may be found today in every bookshop, though not so often in student digs.) Along with this type of hardware demonstration, the four-day conference addressed all the matters that are so important for a long-lasting, smooth-running library – for the survival of knowledge, effectively – but which, nonetheless, non-specialists do not always rank among the most riveting of subjects: cataloguing methods, durable bookbindings, how to select books for acquisition or disposal. On the evening of the second day, however, a paper was delivered on a more eye-catching theme. The speaker was J. Ashton Cross, former librarian of the Oxford Union Society, and the lecture was entitled, 'A Universal Index of Subjects'. In it, Cross would propose a vast, international project for a grand, joined-up index to every branch of knowledge. In case this should sound hopelessly quixotic, Cross reminded his audience that the work for such an index was already being carried out: it was happening every time a student indexed a textbook for their own use. But this effort was being wasted, lost or duplicated, because there was no system to collect and publish the results: 'Hundreds of librarians and students are now ... indexing over and over again the very same books.'[7] Besides, in many fields valuable general indexes had already been made available, albeit in piecemeal fashion:

> The literature ... of many miscellaneous subjects, such as Printing, Shorthand, Chess, Wine, Tobacco, Angling, the Gypsies, Slang, Mountains, Cyclones, Earthquakes and Volcanos, the Drama, Romanticism, Mesmerism, Darwinism, the Devil, the Doctrine of a Future Life, has been indexed by individual effort.[8]

What was needed now, asserted Cross, was a regulated drive – different libraries with their own specialisms, indexing the major works in that field, and feeding up to a clearing-house that could join these myriad sub-indexes together, along with an international committee to oversee where fresh efforts

INDEX, A HISTORY OF THE

should be directed. There would need to be money. In the discussion after Cross had concluded his paper, the head of the London Library apologized for throwing 'a damper on the project' but declared that he had 'no great faith in the plan of employing gratuitous labour'.[9] Of course, responded Cross, nobody wanted librarians to work for nothing, but the division of labour between libraries might free up time that was currently being wasted by inadvertently duplicating each other's catalogues.

Whatever the financial arrangements, Cross's idea caught the imagination. When the literary journal the *Athenaeum* reported on the conference the following week, it was Cross's suggestion that received the most attention. Financing, surely, could be found; after all, other projects of less obvious value – a swipe at the Palestine Exploration Fund – were being funded:

> Find the labourers, or the money that will pay a competent staff of labourers for a series of years, and the thing may be done. If funds were found for the execution of a task so remote from most men's business as the exploration of Palestine, a purse ought soon to be made for the erection of so mighty an instrument of education as a Universal Index of Knowledge.[10]

Cross's lecture had ended with a prediction in the form of a challenge to the assembled delegates: 'The question for this Conference ought to be, not whether a Universal Index shall be made, but only in what way it can best be made.'[11] The Universal Index had the zeitgeist behind it. The question now was how to make it happen.

Imagine a challenge: your task is to build a steampunk search engine, a kind of Wile E. Coyote internet-in-a-box. What is the best way to 'teach' it, to pre-load it with all the information it will need to be useful? Do you (a) decide on all the fields of knowledge that the machine ought to be expert in? First the major areas – let's say, Science, Literature, Art – then their sub-divisions: meteorology, French poetry, classical sculpture . . . If you like, you can keep dividing into narrower and narrower specialisms. After all, how granular you go at this stage will determine how sophisticated – how detailed, how appropriate – the engine's responses will be. Once you have mapped out our topics, you can establish the central texts for each – the key works, the most respected textbooks – compiling a bibliography capable of painting a representative picture of the field. These are the books that will be fed into your contraption (a rectangular slot at the front giving onto a whirring conveyor belt behind). Choose carefully: everything your machine knows, every answer it will give to future users, is fixed at this point, determined by this blueprint, this gigantic syllabus for its electronic self-improvement. Or do you (b) teach the engine to read the papers, buying it subscriptions not just to the dailies but to the specialist periodicals too: *New Scientist*, the *Economist*, the *Times Literary Supplement* . . . ? Then simply leave it to its own devices, assuming that, after a long-enough period of immersion, your robotic autodidact will have become expert enough to answer anything a user might throw at it?

Each approach has its advantages. The top-down method offers control, the chance to fix each field, to make sure that it is properly – authoritatively, comprehensively – covered: these are the answers, as determined at the outset by a team of experts. But it is a static system – inflexible and siloed by discipline. The second method, by contrast, is dynamic and interdisciplinary, a version of knowledge that is layered, built up over time and open-ended. But there is no outside agent to ensure that the machine knows the basics in any given subject. The plan is that information, to begin with, will be dispersed, unconstellated like the first few grey pocks on a paving stone when rain starts to fall; if it keeps on raining, eventually the dots will join up, the whole slab will be wet: the coverage will have become general. But how long will that take?

Three weeks after the Conference of Librarians, a meeting was held at the London Library in St James's Square. Advertisements had been placed in the literary press, and anyone interested in rising to Cross's challenge was encouraged to attend. That evening, barely three weeks after the librarians' conference, the Index Society came into being. Its Secretary

Figure 30: JoÙ Fenton's insignia for the Index Society. It first appears on the title page to Henry Wheatley's *What Is an Index?* (1878).

would be one Henry B. Wheatley, and membership – subject
to approval by the Society's committee – could be had for a
guinea a year.

The Society's insignia, designed by the printer and engraver
JoÙ Fenton, depicts 'a student seeking for information at
the index post, which points to the three roads of Science,
Literature, and Art'.[12] There are numerous things to note
here. First of all, the good old physical metaphor of the fingerpost, the index literally pointing the way. The idea of
study as a journey is a rich one, and the image chimes visually
with Migne's rhapsodies of mountains levelled and paths
straightened by the power of a good index. Then there is the
ouroboros – the snake eating its own tail – a curious alchem-
ical detail, and one which goes unmentioned in the Society's
description of the image. In its earliest incarnations, carved
on the walls of Egyptian tombs, the circular snake represents the formless disorder that surrounds the orderly world,
and perhaps it plays the same role here: outside the index is
only chaos. Lastly, touchingly, is the detail that the traveller is
a student. Students, it has to be said, have come in for a rough
time in our narrative so far, the subjects of a lingering suspicion that they might be workshy, disinclined to read *properly*,
grasping lazily after the elusive eel of Science. Now, the keen,
stockinged student is pictured standing attentively at the start
of his quest. In the Index Society, he will be met, not with
scorn, but with sympathy and assistance from the eminent
scholars of the generation before.

The week after the Society's formation, an announcement
in the *Athenaeum* described its aims as follows:

> the compiling of indexes to well-known books that are def-
> icient in that respect, and also the formation of subject

indexes . . . The Society will at the same time proceed with the work of making a General Index of Universal Literature, which should be accessible to members at the office during compilation. A Library of Indexes will be commenced, and will include whatever can contribute to the formation of a comprehensive key to all knowledge.[13]

Cross's Universal Index, woven into the society's statutes from the outset, finds a deliciously bold – or ominously hubristic – expression in that phrase, 'a comprehensive key to all knowledge'. Did nobody think of *Middlemarch*, published five years earlier, and the Reverend Casaubon's doomed obsession for his unfinishable *Key to All Mythologies*? But the announcement shows, too, how the Society's founders, from the outset, had broken this central task down into a hierarchy of three tiers. The most straightforward, achievable goal would concern the humble book index. A list was to be drawn up of 'standard works' that lacked indexes. Histories, biographies, classics of heraldry, of archaeology, of antiquarianism; Moore's *Life of Sheridan*, Mill's *Principles of Political Economy*, D'Israeli's *Life of Charles I* . . . Members, it was hoped, would adopt items from the list, taking it upon themselves to index them and send their work back to the Society for publication. The second task would be to take this new material, along with other existing indexes, and use it to produce 'subject indexes', miniature versions of the General Index, restricted to single disciplines – Anthropology, Astronomy, Botany, etc. – breaking the universe of knowledge down into categories, like the shelves in a university bookshop. The final stage, of course, would be to consolidate everything that had gone before and feed it up into the all-knowing vastness of a single Universal Index.

Things moved swiftly for the new Society. Early interest was promising. Within a month, seventy members had paid their guinea. By the time of their first annual general meeting at the Royal Asiatic Society in Mayfair, individual membership stood at 170, along with a smattering of libraries and learned societies. A couple of large donations had almost doubled the funds at the Society's disposal. Work was already afoot on several of the indexes to individual books that the committee had deemed important, while the Society's first publication – Wheatley's *What Is an Index?* – was already available in print. (The rush to publication had originally led to a significant omission: *What Is an Index?* had no index. Happily, by the time of the first annual general meeting the matter had been rectified.) As the Society's early achievements were enumerated in the meeting's opening remarks, a sense of optimism, of purpose, is palpable from the minutes. This was about to be compounded by a sense of nobility as the Society's figurehead, the Earl of Carnarvon, rose to deliver his Presidential Address.

Carnarvon's speech was lofty, it was literary, it drew on both biblical imagery and the orientalist surroundings of the Asiatic Society in which it was read out. But it comes down to us in a curious format, not as Carnarvon composed it, but as it was reported by the minute-taker in the room, all past tenses and indirect speech, flattening the sonorous oratory, squeezing it into the syntax of a witness statement. It begins modestly: '[The President's was] an animated address, full of valuable suggestions. He thought that in a literary point of view this was an important meeting. They [i.e. the Society] had to make their way, but he was satisfied the object they had in view, when once understood by the public, would be quite sufficient to recommend its usefulness.'[14] So far, so bland. We can hear Carnarvon's voice beneath the reportage, and it suggests nothing more than a mid-ranking industrialist defending a failing widget in front of a sceptical board. But Carnarvon is only clearing his throat, working up to something grander. Soon the address becomes more florid:

> The field of knowledge was a very large one. Like the Garden of Eden, the tree of knowledge of good and evil grew within its precincts; the fruits of the tree were many and various – some growing on the top, some on the boughs, some close to the ground, some very accessible, and some very difficult to obtain; and every student knew that it was not enough to have knowledge within sight, but it was necessary also that it should be within reach. It was important that the knowledge men possessed should be accessible, docketed, pigeon-holed – in fact, ready for use.

Bringing the highest fruits of the tree of knowledge within reach? The comparison suffers a little if we remember how things turned out in the Garden of Eden thanks to its accessible fruit. But the tree is still a compelling metaphor for the Society's project. Do we balk slightly at Carnarvon's phrasing when *accessible* gives onto *docketed* and *pigeon-holed*? A moment of bathos as we tumble from the tree of knowledge – tall and ancient – into the world of modern bureaucracy? Maybe Carnarvon noticed it himself. He seems, at least, to have recognized where his best imagery lies, and, after running through the story of the Society's formation and its early successes, he concludes with a return to nature, one which moved even the assiduous minute-taker to report the Earl's words directly:

> I may venture to hope that the young Society which we have this evening inaugurated – I may say planted – will, like a

young sapling, spread, and grow, and flourish, and hereafter, like the Banyan-tree of the East, throw down new stems, and put forth new branches, till it forms a grove and a very forest of leaves, flowers, and fruit, under the shelter of which the literary men of all countries, and of every occupation, may come together for mutual information and assistance.

It is a rich and complex image, with a grandeur worthy of Migne. It suggests the universality of the Society's greatest aim, but also that this monumental project can only be achieved by the flourishing of many shoots. It confers on the Society a sense of generosity, of working in a spirit of all-embracing humanity, taking the work of its members and making it into the act of an idyllic, worldwide brotherhood: something noble, something timeless, a return to Eden.

Unfortunately, for all its apparent dynamism, the fledgling Society was already beginning to fall short of Carnarvon's ideal. The General Index project – without which Carnarvon's words amount to little more than high-flown bluster – had been discreetly placed on the back burner, and there it would remain. The problem, in the Society's reasoning, was one of space, the lack of a fixed office to store and arrange all the slips that would make up the giant brain of the Universal Index. When finally, after six years, premises were found, the move was too late: the Society was already in decline. Despite the diligence and energy of its core members, it had failed to ignite a wider public interest in its work. Completed indexes were being held back from publication for want of funds, while those that made it into print were met with a lukewarm response in the literary press. Membership had long plateaued. In 1887, a decade after its first appearance, the Society effectively ended its existence. Wheatley, considering its demise from a decade-and-a-half's distance, would wonder if it had been its universal aspect that had made it unsustainable: '[The Society's] want of permanent success was probably owing to its aim being too general. Those who were interested in one class of index cared little for indexes which were quite different in subject.' Quite possibly, but Wheatley's next thought seems closer to the mark: 'I fear that the interest of the public in the production of indexes (which is considerable) does not go to the length of willingness to pay for these indexes.'[15]

As for the key to all knowledge, Wheatley remained sanguine:

> Some think this to be an impossibility, and that to attempt its preparation is a waste of time. Those who hold this opinion have not sufficient faith in the simplicity and usefulness of the alphabet. Every one has notes and references of some kind, which are useless if kept unarranged, but, if sorted into alphabetical order become valuable. The object of the general index is just this, that anything, however disconnected, can be placed there, and much that would otherwise be lost will there find a resting-place. Always growing and never pretending to be complete, the index will be useful to all, and its consulters will be sure to find something worth their trouble, if not all they may require.

The irony was that the resource that Wheatley describes here – a single, alphabetical index, 'always growing but never pretending to be complete' – was already available. It had been discussed at the very conference at which Cross had delivered his call to arms, its first edition appearing five years later, while the Society was still casting about for a home. And it had been designed by a sophomore undergraduate to help his classmates with their essays.

Among the delegates listening to Cross's lectures at the Conference of Librarians is William Poole. Where Cross has made the train journey from Oxford – little more than an hour away – to attend, Poole has travelled from much further afield. One of the most distinguished librarians in America, Poole is head of the Chicago Public Library, founded in the wake of the Great Chicago Fire six years previously. Prior to this, he has overseen the private libraries of the Boston Athenaeum, the Naval Academy at Annapolis and the public libraries at Newton and Northampton in Massachusetts. Most significantly, he ran the Cincinnati Public Library, swelling its collection by 300 per cent, and shepherding the move to its new, exquisite, unreal premises on Vine Street, with four-storey-high shelves, vertiginous spiral staircases and fluted cast-iron columns as spindly as the legs on Dalí's elephants.

An excursion has been arranged for Poole during his time at the conference. A visit to the British Museum Library, forerunner to today's British Library, its collection second in size only to France's Bibliothèque Nationale. In the company of the principal librarian, Poole is taken on a guided tour. Now, in the great domed reading room, his eye falls on a little book, 'its leaves discolored and nearly worn through by constant handling'.[16] It is twenty years since he has last seen a copy. The work is his own: *An Alphabetical Index to Subjects Treated in the Reviews, and Other Periodicals.* Published while he was still a student, Poole's *Alphabetical Index* already contained, in miniature, the project he is orchestrating now, the one he has travelled to London to unveil.

William Frederick Poole was not born into money. His father was a wool merchant in Salem, Massachusetts, and Poole, a gifted and diligent child, attended the local school

wow!

Figure 31: Shelves and ladders in the old Cincinnati Public Library, which was open to the public from 1870 to 1953.

there, stretching himself by teaching himself Latin at home. Noticing his gifts, his mother determined that Poole should attend university. Financially, however, this was beyond the family's immediate means. After finishing school, Poole spent three years working as a teacher, putting money aside and preparing himself for a college education. At twenty-one, he entered Yale, but a lack of funds forced him to drop out after his first year. Poole went back to teaching, saving up for another three years before returning in his mid-twenties.

This time he was able to find work to support himself through his studies by becoming assistant librarian for one of the university's societies, the Brothers in Unity.

In those days, students' essay topics would be announced in the college chapel, and each time they were Poole, as librarian, would be inundated with requests from his classmates, asking him to suggest reading material – sources, authorities, references – for them to consult. Poole took to posting up lists – ready-made bibliographies on the latest topic – each time a new essay was announced, and these would include both books and articles in the learned journals. In the case of the latter – articles rather than books – Poole was aware that, were it not for his interventions, these would probably be overlooked by his peers: 'I had noticed that the sets of standard periodicals with which the library was well supplied were not used, although they were rich in the treatment of subjects about which inquiries were made in vain every day.'[17] Who, apart from the poor assistant librarian, had the time to browse through hundreds of volumes of periodical literature on the off-chance of finding something useful? Ever the conscientious public servant, Poole's response was to do the heavy lifting himself. For a year, he worked his way through 560 volumes of the most important journals in the Brothers' collection. The latest criticism and research from his own nation – the *New York Review*, the *American Library of Useful Knowledge* – and from the other side of the Atlantic – *Blackwood's Magazine*, the *Edinburgh Review*, the *Dublin University Review*. Politics, history, literary criticism: Poole scanned every article, every issue, noting down the topics they treated and arranging the whole into a single, handwritten list, a subject index 154 pages long, running alphabetically from 'Abd-el-Kader, Memoir of' through to 'Zuinglius, the Swiss Reformer'.

Needless to say, Poole's index, like his reading lists, was a success with his fellow students. So much so that before long its sheets were ragged from overuse, and Poole decided to have the document printed. Although the *Alphabetical Index* included only those journals that could be found in the Brothers in Unity's relatively limited collection, it attracted attention far beyond Yale. The print run was for 500 copies, but Poole records that 'no sooner was the preparation of this work announced, than orders from abroad exceeded the whole edition'.[18] The student librarian had hit on a resource that the whole scholarly community was crying out for.

But why should an index to periodicals be such hot property, sought after on both sides of the Atlantic? For Poole, the answer lay in the rise of the serious journal, which he dated to the establishment of the *Edinburgh Review* in 1802. Since then, he wrote,

> The best writers and the greatest statesmen of the world, where they formerly wrote a book or pamphlet, now contribute an article to a leading review or magazine, and it is read before the month is ended in every country in Europe, in America, in India, Australia, and New Zealand. Every question in literature, religion, politics, social science, political economy, and in many other lines of human progress, finds its latest and freshest interpretation in the current periodicals. No one can thoroughly investigate any of these questions without knowing what the periodicals have said and are saying concerning them.[19]

For the serious scholar in the mid nineteenth century the learned journals were the principal forums for debate and the cutting edge of discourse in every field. But how does one mine them retrospectively? The vast intellectual reserves of periodical literature lay untapped since, as Poole went on, 'their contents are not available, for the want of a clue to the labyrinth of topics dispersed through the leaves of many hundred volumes'. Index the periodicals and one creates a map of the labyrinth, a switchboard of contemporary learning. Little wonder, then, that Poole's project, accomplished in his spare time while still an undergraduate, should have attracted so fervid a following. A second edition followed five years later, expanding the index both in terms of range and in terms of granularity – twice as many journals, six times as many entries – and moving beyond the constraint of the Brothers' collection.

But the problem with periodical literature that sits at the forefront of its discipline, however, is that it is forever in motion – a progression of knowledge that will always, by definition, surpass itself. Poole's second *Index* had brought its references down to January 1852, but the stream of new material flowed inexorably on. Poole found himself assailed, on an almost daily basis, by requests for an updated version of his index, but as his skill as a librarian had begun to be recognized, his accelerating career left him little time for what had always been, effectively, a side project. He looked to recruit a successor – someone, as he put it, 'with the zeal, experience, and staying qualities needed' – but no such character presented themselves. In the meantime, libraries, whose readers had become accustomed to using Poole's *Index*, were forced to produce their own supplements, duplicating each others' work – and compounding their expenses – many times over.

And so it was that in 1876, nearly a quarter of a century after the second edition of the *Index*, a special committee was set up by the American Library Association to address the problem. It was too much, it was agreed, to imagine that a new index could be the work of an individual, as it had been when Poole had first taken up the challenge. Periodical literature had only become more abundant in the intervening decades. Besides, there were no funds to pay a dedicated indexer. Instead, the general subject index would be a collaborative effort, the work of as many libraries as could be persuaded to sign up. Poole, still, would oversee the project. He would draft a list of the major publications to be included, and a set of rules for how the sub-indexes should be prepared. Participating libraries would be assigned one or more periodicals to work through, and would send their completed indexes back for collation. When Poole attended the London Conference in 1877, he was there to expand the enterprise, drumming up support from libraries on the other side of the Atlantic. Copies of the proposal, including Poole's rules and his periodical list, had been printed and brought over, ready to be circulated among the delegates. But when Cross gave his paper on the Universal Index, the discussion that followed was the perfect setting for Poole to give a spoken outline of the plan. Cross's response was enthusiastic, earnestly advocating the adoption of Poole's scheme and suggesting that it constituted a part of exactly what he himself was proposing. British libraries pledged their support, and were duly allotted publications to work through.

The new edition of Poole's *Index* appeared in 1882, with supplements appearing every five years up until 1908. As a collaborative project, the work was a triumph. As Poole put it,

> That fifty libraries different in organisation and objects – Nation, State, stock, subscription, college, and free public institutions – scattered over this broad country from San

Francisco to Boston, and across the ocean in England and Scotland, should have joined hands and worked in harmony for a common object, each receiving the full benefit of the work of all the others, is an incident in bibliography and literature which has no parallel.[20]

As a general subject index to the knowledge and concerns of the nineteenth century, Poole's *Index* had come a very long way from its first dog-eared, handwritten incarnation. It is a monumental work. Two hundred and thirty-two journals are analysed, with every issue broken down to the contents of its individual articles. It takes in everything from Dickens' *Household Words* to *Kitto's Journal of Sacred Literature*, from the *American Journal of Science* to the *English Woman's Domestic Magazine*. Double-columned and just short of 1,500 pages long, it is a breeze block of information. It can be consulted on tecÙical subjects – *Dynamo-Electric Machines* or *Friction Clutches for Rolling-Mills* – and historical ones, from *Etruscan Jewellery* to the *South Sea Bubble*; there is a full column of entries on Edgar Allen Poe, five pages on Shakespeare; in an instant one can find out where to learn about *Card-sharping* or *Forged Bank-Notes*, *Piracy* or *Pilchards*, *Opium*, *Opossums*, *Optical Illusions*. To run a finger down one of its columns is to be reminded of the wild, seductive miscellaneousness of Sherlock Holmes' home-made indexes: Vanderbilt and the Yeggman. Vipers. Vigor, the Hammersmith wonder . . .

There are, however, a few deficiencies. Certain key journals – among them, the *Athenaeum*, the *Literary Gazette* and the *Economist* – are not represented, and here the blame can be laid at the feet of the librarians courted at the London conference. Among the British, enthusiasm for the project had not been matched by vigour in carrying it through. While the American libraries had been prompt in returning their sub-indexes, only eight of the twenty-five periodicals allotted to the British had been indexed in time to be included in the 1882 edition. In that work's introduction, Poole attempts half-heartedly to find excuses for this continental discrepancy, concluding archly, 'Perhaps the climate and social customs of England are not so favourable as they are in America for night work.' (A cynic might translate this as: 'Perhaps you're all drunks on your cold little island.') For all this, however, the 1882 *Index* really is a step towards the comprehensiveness of the search engines we now take for granted. Its method, concentrating on periodicals, is necessarily limited, but if the journals – with a few unfortunate, British exceptions – discussed it, *Poole's* would have it.

Poole lived until 1894, long enough to oversee the first two of the supplements to the *Index*. These would continue until 1907, by which time the *Index* had variants and imitators that would carry its model far into the twentieth century. In London, W. T. Stead's annual *Index to Periodicals*, produced from 1891 to 1903, cast its net wider than Poole – some 300 journals – but catalogued only the previous year's contents, while the *Reader's Guide to Periodical Literature*, still running today, has performed the same function for US publications since 1901. The dawn of the twentieth century might not yet have brought about Migne's vision of instantaneous information, the electric index, but the industrious age had come a long way in its goal of squeezing the whole of knowledge, like a grape in a winepress, to its essence. On the title page of every edition of Poole's *Index* the same epigraph appears, given to Poole by his Latin professor back when he was a hard-pressed student at Yale: 'Qui scit ubi sit scientia habenti est proximus': 'He who knows where knowledge may be had is close to having it.' The perfect motto, perhaps, for the superhero of the age, seated under the boughs of his own, carefully tended tree of knowledge but too imperious to pluck the low fruit himself. Make a long arm, Watson, there's a good chap.

8

Ludmilla and Lotaria
The Book Index in the Age of Search

'Where is the knowledge we have lost in
information?'
T. S. Eliot, 'Choruses from The Rock'

Among the glitching, self-conscious narratives of Calvino's
If on a Winter's Night a Traveller – that novel of factory slips
and misbound gatherings – is the story of Silas Flannery, a
novelist who has become obsessed with his beautiful, idealized reader, Ludmilla. One day, Flannery is visited, not by
Ludmilla, but by her twin, Lotaria, instead. This presents a
problem for the lovelorn Flannery. Ludmilla, the undisputed
heroine of *If on a Winter's Night*, thinks of the creative process via a series of fruity, organic metaphors – an author, for
example, is a pumpkin vine swelling forth the ripe, juicy
pumpkins of his work – and Flannery's vegetable love for
her, naturally, grows. But where Ludmilla is voluptuous, her
twin is spiky, and the way Lotaria consumes literature seems
to short-circuit the erotics of the relationship between author
and reader. Where Flannery sees writing as something like a
seduction or an act of courtly devotion directed at the reader,
Lotaria is immune to such overtures. This is because she
doesn't *read* books, she *analyses* them. Or, rather, she gives
them to a machine to 'read' for her, and this generates an

output that tells her all she needs to know. When Flannery asks Lotaria whether she has read the novels – *his* novels – that he lent her, she apologizes, saying that she hasn't had the chance: she has been away from her computer.

Lotaria goes on to explain her method. A suitably pro-grammed computer can read a novel in a few minutes and regurgitate it as a table of all the words it contains, in order of how often each appears: 'I only have to glance at [this] to form an idea of the problems the book suggests to my critical study.' The most common words – articles, pronouns, particles – are not worth her attention. Rather, she explains, 'In a novel of fifty to a hundred thousand words . . . I advise you to observe immediately the words that are repeated about twenty times.' An example:

> 'Look here. Words that appear nineteen times: *blood, cartridge belt, commander, do, have, immediately, it, life, seen, sentry, shots, spider, teeth, together, your* . . .
>
> 'Words that appear eighteen times: *boys, cap, come, dead, eat, enough, evening, French, go, handsome, new, passes, period, potatoes, those, until* . . .
>
> 'Don't you already have a clear idea what it's about?' Lotaria says. 'There's no question: it's a war novel, all action, brisk writing, with a certain underlying violence. The narra-tion is entirely on the surface.'

Typically for what is a dazzlingly playful novel, this is a trickier scene to parse than it first looks. We know – we can tell, if only from the way she is contrasted with the lovely Ludmilla – that our sympathies are *not* supposed to be with Lotaria and her analytical unreading. And yet, Calvino is far too clever a writer to make our resistance an unconflicted one. When we first read through Lotaria's example – the computer's output: *blood, cartridge belt, commander* – we surely found ourselves forming exactly the judgements she predicts. When she asks 'Don't you already have a clear idea what it's about?', we do. Of course we do. A war novel. Action. Surface description rather than emotional depth. We don't *want* to approve of Lotaria's methods, but Calvino makes it hard not to suspect that she might be onto something. If we wish to maintain our disapproval, we'll need to try a different tack. It's not that a machine – or an alphabetical wordlist – can't tell us anything about a book's contents; rather, it must be that this isn't the *whole* experience of reading. We are right back with the cynics of the early modern period, with Erasmus and Gessner griping that, in the age of the index, students no longer bother to read books, or with Caxton warning his readers not to confuse the map for the territory.

If on a Winter's Night appeared at the end of the 1970s, at a moment when machine-generated concordances and word frequency tables were hovering on the fringes of literary criticism, and when slips of paper, the tools of the professional indexer's trade for seven centuries, were about to dematerialize into bytes of data. It speaks to its specific tecÙological context, reflecting anxieties about the encroachment of late twentieth-century computing on the literary domain. But these anxieties are only iterations of an older set of misgivings. They have everything in common with the Christ Church classicists who howled execrations at Dr Bentley and his 'alphabetical learning', or even with Socrates warning Phaedrus that writing brings about inattentiveness and 'the appearance of wisdom, not true wisdom'. Our discomfort about reading machines is also a version of an old anxiety about mediation. Contemporary concerns about the black box of Google's algorithm – that the results of our searches might not be ideologically untainted, that they might exhibit biases that we are not comfortable with, boosting some voices, silencing others – echo the eighteenth-century pamphleteer who discovered JoÙ Oldmixon serving up anti-Tory propaganda in the back pages of Echard's Tory history. When Donald Trump tweets that 'Google & others are suppressing voices of Conservatives . . . They are controlling what we can & cannot see', he is only – inadvertently – dragging an ancient paranoia into the digital arena, the twenty-first-century Republican version of Macaulay's 'Let no damned Tory index my History!'[1] The search engine, it should be noted, was soon exonerated.[2] But as we move into the present, tracking the entry of computing into the practice of indexing, it seems that a complex of old doubts – about reading and attention, effort and convenience, direct and mediated experience – are closer to the surface now than they have been for centuries. It is good for the nerves, I think, to have some historical perspective.

This is not to say that nothing has changed. Look under the bonnet of the string-searching we use to navigate digital documents and you will find something not unlike Lotaria's reading machine, where the basic units are not concepts but letters. The subject index has dominated all but the earliest chapters of this history; by contrast, our twenty-first-century Age of Search is, in effect, an age of the automated concordance. Still, just as the internet has not killed off the physical book, so subject indexes and their compilers still have roles to play in our reading lives. The indexing professional has been around for a good century longer than the printing press – papal records show payments being made for the compilation of indexes since the 1320s – and the emergence of the home computer, far from sounding a death knell for the trade, has brought about a welcome change in practice.[3] It has eliminated menial tasks, freed up intellectual resources. But above all, for the ever-humble subject indexer, it has ushered in an altogether tidier way of doing things.

'If you had come in yesterday you would have seen me with the floor all strewn with little squares of paper, like the learned pig.'[4] Virginia Woolf is writing to her friend – and, for the last three months, her lover – Vita Sackville-West. The yesterday in question was a Sunday, but Woolf had nevertheless been hard at work. She had been compiling an index. A decade earlier, she and her husband had bought themselves a small, hand-operated printing press. With Virginia setting the type and Leonard operating the machine, the Woolfs had founded the Hogarth Press with the intention of publishing short literary works by themselves and their friends. But the press had exceeded the couple's early ambitions. It had grown into a substantial publishing operation, producing dozens of books a year. Now, alongside the fiction and poetry of their Bloomsbury circle, the Woolfs were bringing out non-fiction – histories, essays, works on politics, economics, psychoanalysis: the kind of books where readers would expect an index. And so it came to pass that one weekend in the early spring of 1926, Virginia found herself stranded in a sea of her own making, a mess of indexing slips, each one bearing a fragment of *Castles in the Air*, the effervescent memoir of the actress and socialite Viola Tree.

The index that Woolf would create was not a remarkable one. It confines itself to proper names, the great and the good of Edwardian life. Lord and Lady Asquith are there, as is Winston Churchill. One entry – 'Crippen, Hawley Harvey, murder by, 41, 42' – stands out, a blunt interloper amongst so much landed gentry. Tree herself is treated to a volley of subheadings that tell her life story in miniature:

> Tree, Viola, leaves stage, 11; studies music, 12; engaged to A. P. 13; goes to Milan, 15; at Milan, 18 ff., sings to Ricordi, 23; life at Milan, 27 ff.; in her own house at Milan, 53–90; visit to Strauss, 115 ff.; returns to England, 138; summer in England, 159; returns to Italy, 181; Christmas in England, 224; returns to Italy, 233; engagement to A. P. announced, 257; marriage, 290.

The most interesting thing about the *Castles in the Air* index is that it would provide the model for another index that Woolf would compile a year later, this time for a work of her own. *Orlando*, or *Orlando: A Biography* to give it its full title, is a novel that plays at being life-writing – fiction dressed up as non-fiction – and including an index would be part of that cross-dressing. Despite a jealous threat to Vita – 'Look in the Index to Orlando – after Pippin and see what comes next – Promiscuity *passim*!' – the *Orlando* index has nothing to say about its subject's errant libido.[5] Rather it follows *Castles in the Air* in restricting itself to the novel's *dramatis personae*, an index of proper names. And once again subheadings are more or less reserved for the work's main character, at which point they effloresce into a potted biography. This time, however, Woolf introduces a tiny innovation – the word *and* – which she deploys at the start of several subheadings, linking them to the one before and ensuring that the breathless forward movement of *Orlando*'s narrative carries through to its index in sprees like 'entertains the wits, 129; and Mr Pope, 132; and Nell, 135'.

But in spite of these moments of playfulness, for Woolf there was no getting away from the fact that compiling an index was hard work. In 1940, a year before her death, we find her putting the finishing touches to her biography of the art critic Roger Fry and grumbling in her diary of 'working till eyes blind at Index'. Two days later she writes, 'My Index sent off – so thats the very final full stop to all that drudgery.'[6] Drudgery. We have seen this word before – 'the Drudgery of compiling an Index', sneered the anonymous pamphleteer in Chapter 5, hoping to put JoÙ Oldmixon in his place. But as we picture Woolf, on a Sunday afternoon, sat on a floor strewn with paper scraps, let us pause to consider the indexer's toil more carefully.

Intellectually, the indexer atomizes the book's contents, identifying its personalities and tracking them through the course of the work. She sifts the ideas at play and mulls over the best labels for them, whether a concept needs to be ramified or subdivided, or whether two related themes might reasonably be rolled up under one head. A challenge, certainly, an exercise in concentration, in deep reading; but not drudgery by any definition. Physically, however, the process involves preparing and marshalling a paper tide. Sorting, switching between orders – page order to alphabetical order – and recopying. Woolf's method of 'little squares of paper' was no different – except a little more chaotic, perhaps – than the wall full of pigeonholes in the Index Society's office, or, paging back further through our history, than Conrad Gessner's minutely detailed advice four centuries before:

One method for compiling a well-ordered index in a very short time is as follows. Whatever references one wants to include in the index are written down, as they present themselves, in no particular order on a sheet of paper on one side only, leaving the other blank . . . Finally, having cut up every-thing you have written with scissors, divide the slips into the desired order, first into larger parts, then subdividing again and again, however many times are needed. Some people cut up all the slips before arranging them; others put them into a preliminary order immediately while cutting them up. Finally, the individual slips that have been divided up by the scissor blade are laid out in different places on the table or arranged into small boxes on the table. If there are a large number of slips, I recommend subdividing them fur-ther, for this will make them much easier and less confusing to sort . . . When the slips have been arranged in the desired order, if need be you can copy them out at once; or, if the original writing was clear enough – which is preferable – mount them using glue made from flour.[7]

Plenty has been written over the centuries on how to dissect the argument of a book, how to choose one's headwords, to imagine the way that readers will use the index. But as Gess-ner's detailed instructions remind us, indexing is also a material activity. Slips of parchment or paper (*cedules* in Middle English, whence our modern word *schedule*); cutting and pasting; scissors and glue. It can be done badly – too many top-level heads will make the slips confusing to arrange; the wrong type of glue makes it hard to correct sorting errors – but it has to be done somehow. The finished index can only come into being as the result of earlier physical stages, of drafts cut, reorganized and copied. It was ever thus, since the friars of St Jacques.

At the start of the eighteenth century, two scholars produc-ing a massive history of the Dominican order turned their attention to Hugh of St Cher and his Bible concordance.

Running through early surviving copies of the work, they remarked ruefully,

> There once existed, in our convent of St Jacques in Paris, leaves from a volume on fine vellum, but a reckless keeper of the chest of books gave them to bookbinders to use in binding books; still today, some leaves of it can be seen in the same library at the start and end of a manuscript volume in which are contained St Bernard of Clairvaux's sermons, bound together roughly a hundred and fifty years ago.[8]

In other words, thanks to the negligence of the librarian at St Jacques, one of these early concordances was allowed to be broken up into its individual sheets and used as binding waste – that is, spare sheets that would be squashed tight and wrapped with leather to form the hard cover for another book – in this case, a book of sermons. This was a common practice, and many medieval texts come down to us now as fragments, preserved only as padding inside the covers of other works. Our eighteenth-century scholars are hard on the librarian, calling him *imprudens* – reckless – for having allowed this concordance to be handed over to the bookbinder. To be fair to him, however, this version of the concordance was never meant to survive. These sheets – now preserved at the Bibliothèque Mazarine in Paris – are fragile, marked by folds and stained from the glue that would have held the leather cover in place. But they are imperfect in other ways too. There are crossings-out and extra entries missed out in the first pass and now squeezed in alongside the text column. The handwriting changes from one entry to the next, and gaps riddle the page, in anticipation that more material – more headwords, more locators – might be written in later. These are not leaves from a copy of the first concordance; they are sheets from a draft, a rough version put together while the work was still in preparation. No wonder the librarian let them go to the binding shop. These are merely 'Notes Towards', and parchment – unlike paper – doesn't grow on trees. To recycle these sheets is only imprudent from a modern perspective, when the distance of centuries has given them a historical interest, and when the experiment that they testify to has proved so dizzyingly successful that its processes have become a matter of speculation. The leaves in the Mazarine are fascinating to us; to the medieval librarian, however, they were simply the scaffolding from a building that had already, magnificently, gone up.

What these worm-eaten ancient scraps remind us is that, for 700 years, from St Hugh to Virginia Woolf, a <u>final index</u> was *necessarily* a second version. The indexer passes through

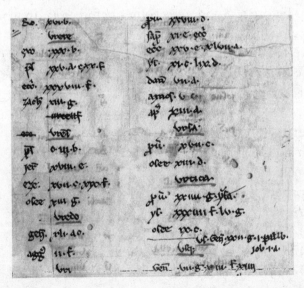

Figure 32: Detail from a draft sheet for the St Jacques Concordance, showing crossings-out, added entries and wormholes.

the work producing a series of entries and locators in the order in which they occur. But this then has to be rearranged – rewritten or retyped – into alphabetical order. The intellectual labour is frontloaded in the indexing process; the drudgery comes later.

Even putting things in alphabetical order is not as straightforward as it seems. One wonders if Callimachus, compiling his catalogue to the Library of Alexandria, ever pondered the problem of word-by-word versus letter-by-letter alphabetization. This issue arises when index heads run on for longer than a single word: *printing press*, say, or *New York*, or *detective fiction*. How should we treat the space? Should *Oldman, Gary* come before or after *Old Possum's Book of Practical Cats*? Should *Newman, Paul* come before or after *New York Trilogy*? In the letter-by-letter system spaces between words are ignored – the actors come before the books because *oldm* comes before *oldp* and *newm* comes before *newy*. In word-by-word alphabetization, however, those spaces count: words are treated individually, one at a time, so that *Old* comes before *Oldman*. Consider this example derived from the index of this book:

Letter-by-letter
Newman, Cardinal (JoÙ Henry)
Newman, Paul
newspapers and news-sheets
New Tenures
New York Review of Books, The
New York Times, The
New York Trilogy, The (Auster)
nitpickers, and windbags
Notes and Queries

Old Curiosity Shop, The (Dickens)
Oldenburg, Henry
Oldman, Gary
Oldmixon, JoÙ
Old Possum's Book of Practical Cats (Eliot)

Word-by-word
New Tenures
New York Review of Books, The
New York Times, The
New York Trilogy, The (Auster)
Newman, Cardinal (JoÙ Henry)
Newman, Paul
newspapers and news-sheets
nitpickers, and windbags
Notes and Queries
Old Curiosity Shop, The (Dickens)
Old Possum's Book of Practical Cats (Eliot)
Oldenburg, Henry
Oldman, Gary
Oldmixon, JoÙ

It is more than a little confusing, and different publishers will have different preferences, maybe even preferring one system for certain genres and the other for others. Physically reordering a card index from word-by-word to letter-by-letter alphabetization is a laborious task, and one prone to error. It may even involve rewriting or retyping the whole index into fine copy for the publisher. If only these mechanical, material tasks – the *filing* aspect of indexing; the copying – could magically take care of themselves.

*

This is the first page of Guy Montgomery's *Concordance to the Poetical Works of JoÙ Dryden* (1957). By this point in our history, we should be fairly comfortable with how to read it. With its headwords and locators and its multi-column format to save space on the page, there is little difference between this and the St Jacques Concordance. Instead of abbreviations for books of the Bible – *Je* for *Jeremiah*, *Eze* for *Ezekiel* – here we have shortcodes for Dryden's works: *AA* for *Absalom and Achitophel*, *AE* (plus the book number) for the *Aeneid*, and so on. But if we look a little closer at the table, some of the details might strike us as unusual. For a start, it looks a little *too* much like that first Bible concordance. Thinking back to the friars of St Jacques, within a couple of decades of the first concordance they had discovered the usefulness of a little contextual quotation, a few words to embed each reference. Otherwise users are forced to trawl blindly through long strings of undifferentiated locators before they find the passage they need. This Dryden concordance, then, is a step in the wrong direction, offering no context for any of its instances. Imagine needing to find a particular line from Dryden, and remembering that it

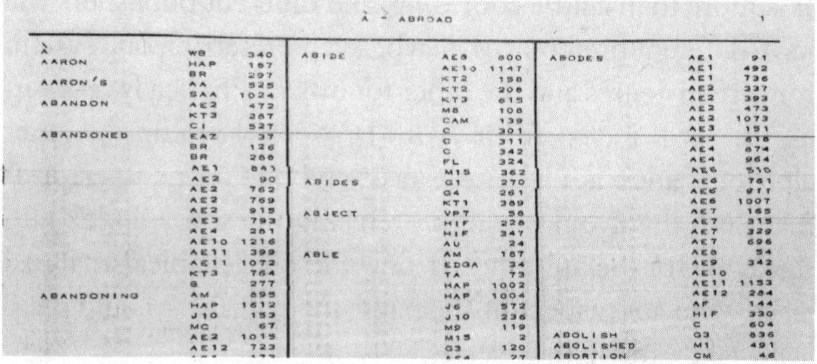

Figure 33: First page of the *Concordance to the Poetical Words of JoÙ Dryden*.

contains the word *abodes*. Imagine one's heart sinking as the concordance reveals twenty-seven different instances of the word. Pretty sure it's from the *Aeneid*? Hard luck – they're *all* from the *Aeneid*! What happened to the idea – first introduced by the friars of St Jacques – of including a brief quotation from the main text, situating the search term within the phrase in which it appears? Why has an innovation that has served readers helpfully for more than half a millennium been jettisoned? And what about that curious typeface: blocky, sans-serif, and – the giveaway – monospaced? This page hasn't been typeset: this is *output*.

The title page of the Dryden concordance tells a curious half-story. The work is credited to Montgomery and one of his grad students, Lester A. Hubbard. Below their names, a line in smaller type notes that the editors were 'assisted' by two others, Mary Jackman and Helen S. Agoa. Finally, a line in even smaller, italic letters states, 'Preface by Josephine Miles'. But the credits here are topsy-turvy. Jackman and Agoa were Miles' grad students, not Montgomery's, and, by the time they gave their assistance to the project, Montgomery was dead and Hubbard had washed his hands of it. And Miles' involvement goes far, far deeper than simply writing the preface. Without her, the Dryden concordance – the original electronic index – would never have seen the light of day.

A poet and literary critic, in 1951, Miles had been teaching in the English Department at Berkeley when Montgomery, her colleague, died. In his office were quarter of a million index cards: every word of Dryden's poetry along with a locator – poem and line number – indicating where it appeared. It was Montgomery's life's work, packed into sixty-three shoeboxes. Not wishing to see such a vast amount of effort wasted, the head of department approached Miles, asking if she would see the concordance through to publication. But the cards were in a disastrous state – fragile, incomplete, badly arranged.[9] After a year of struggling with Montgomery's shoeboxes, Miles decided to try something radically different.

In Berkeley's Electrical Engineering department were a number of large IBM machines that could take in a series of punch cards and sort them according to a given field. Not only that, but information stored as holes or 'chads' in the cards could be printed out in human-readable form. If Montgomery's index cards could be converted into punch cards, then some of the tasks involved in preparing the concordance for publication could be automated. To check the data, for example, the cards could be sorted by poem and line number and printed out, in which case proofing would be simply a matter of reading the output against the poems themselves – each word should be present and in the right order. Once any corrections had been made, the machine could re-order the cards into alphabetical order by headword and print the results a second time to produce the finished concordance. All that was needed was to create 240,000 punch cards . . .[10] Five years later, the Dryden concordance was ready. Aside from the small matter of how, economically, to turn a book into punch cards, we have reached the era of Lotaria's reading machine, when literature can be carved up and shuffled, regurgitated in different orders, *analysed* by a computer.

The initial entry of computing into the indexing process could hardly be said to have dematerialized the task. It merely swapped one type of paper card for another. But the difference in potential is immense. Once our indexing information – heads, locators – can be 'read' by machines, then it doesn't much matter whether it is stored on punch cards, magnetic tape or integrated circuits. We have opened up the possibility of reordering without rewriting. The indexer's job has been distilled to its analytical essence; the drudgery – the shuffling and copying – has been delegated to the machine.

But why stop there? 'Reading', for Calvino's Lotaria, means feeding novels into a computer and perusing the output. Could an indexing machine do more than simply shuffle cards? Could it analyse a text and choose an appropriate set of headwords for it? In 1963, a student named Susan Artandi submitted her PhD thesis at Rutgers University, New Jersey. Artandi's doctorate had been supported by a grant from the US Air Force. Its title was 'Book Indexing by Computer'. The military's interest in Artandi's project was, in a way, a tangential one. Artandi's work was part of a broader effort whose roots can be found in the universal indexing projects of the nineteenth century. The problem, as ever, was of information overload: how to manage the vast tide of research published by the international scientific community. To be on top of the research is to be ahead of one's rivals. Indexing and abstracting scientific papers is necessary but labour-intensive work. Artandi's objective, then, was 'to do the job of indexing directly from the unedited text of the document and thus eliminate the human intellectual effort'.[11]

The system she devised depended on a pre-existing dictionary of search terms. The machine's job was to work through the given document looking out for any of the words on its list, and noting the locations of those that occurred. The index it produced, then, would be limited in advance, its headwords a subset of the terms in its dictionary. In order to be effective, this dictionary had to be relatively small – a subject-specific list of specialized vocabulary. Artandi gives a worked example in which Rutgers's IBM 1620 machine was fed a chapter of work on organic chemistry and a dictionary of appropriate terms: *bromine, calcium fluoride, chloric acid*, etc. The results, in this case, were satisfactory. Artandi's programme identified the chemicals that appeared in the document, logged their locations and arranged its output alphabetically. There was, however, one obvious drawback. 'The only major limitation,' admitted Artandi, 'is . . . that terms must be known to be indexed.'[12] Artandi's system was essentially an electronic Spotter's Guide, a tool for picking out the things one already anticipated might be found. 'Terms which appear for the first time in primary sources are missed,' she conceded, 'because they are not yet included in the dictionary.'

Artandi's approach worked by inclusion – given a list of potential keywords, the programme analysed documents to see which ones they included. Seven years later, Harold Borko set out to evaluate the opposite approach. As Borko put it,

> Indexing by exclusion avoids the difficult problem of defining a good index term and instead tries to specify and define those words and classes of words that are not good index terms. Thus by a process of exclusion, all words that have not been eliminated are treated as good index terms.[13]

This time, the programme would be fed a dictionary of 'function' words – *and, but, the, with, this*, and about 500 others. Borko's programme could then 'read' through a document eliminating all instances of these terms. Any words left standing after this purge would be deemed index-worthy. The results, conceded Borko, were not altogether inspiring. In practice, the blacklist would need to be immense, weeding out whole categories of words: pronouns, verbs, adverbs, conjunctions. Even then, Borko's programme could only parse single words: *press* and *conference*, but not *press conference*; *cat* and *food*, but not *cat food*. 'After months of effort,' he wrote, 'I came to the reluctant conclusion that there was no reasonable way to prepare a machine index based solely on the principle of exclusion.'[14] Nevertheless, Borko was loath to write his experiments off as entirely fruitless. Instead, he argued, computer-generated output could be used as a starting point for 'machine-aided indexing' – in other words the indexer would run their book through Borko's programme before tidying up and pruning back the results.

Ultimately, however, what both inclusion and exclusion methods produce is a scaled-back concordance. The terms of the index are taken directly from the text: nothing appears in the former except in the precise form in which it appears in the latter. By contrast, if we consider what a true subject index actually looks like, it is often rather different. 'Falling house, life in a', 'Jewsbury, Miss, cheats time with stuffed owl', 'Zembla, a distant, northern land': we expect our back-of-book indexes to be more than mere word lists. We expect them to provide context, interpretation, to recognize when the same concept appears in different guises.

A still greater drawback to the methods trialled by Miles, Artandi and Borko was cost. 'Machine indexing,' wrote Borko, 'is . . . expensive and thus not a substitute for human indexing.'[15] Thus, for a quarter of a century after Miles' Dryden concordance, professional indexers would continue to work as Guy Montgomery had. Those of a certain age can still recall their despair on accidentally spilling a shoebox full of cards – the pre-digital equivalent of the laptop crashing at the end of a day's work – or their exasperation at the family cat, jealous of attention, jumping up on the table and bringing chaos to the carefully ordered piles laid out there.

In 1981, however, MACREX arrived. Designed by the husband-and-wife team of Hilary and Drusilla Calvert – she an indexer, he a doctor and amateur programmer – and aimed at the newly burgeoning home computer market, MACREX offered professional indexers the same functionality Berkeley's mainframes had offered Miles decades before. Once installed – via floppy disk: the internet is still a good decade away at this stage – users could key in individual entries and locators, abstracting the index card, morphing it into its digital equivalent, the database row. MACREX allowed indexers to switch, on screen, between orderings – by headword or by locator – allowing them to see the alphabetical table being built up or to zone in on entries for a particular section of the book. It would soon be joined by rival applications – CINDEX (1986) and SKY Index (1995) – but all would provide similar functionality, taking care of the drudgework, keeping things in order. Indexing programmes can draw attention to hanging cross-references (for example, '*see* orphan' where no entry for 'orphan' has been created), or to entries where a snarl of undifferentiated locators might benefit from being broken down with subheadings. They can rejig the finished output to match publishers' style guides, and flip with ease between word-by-word and letter-by-letter alphabetization.

The arrival of computing into the indexing process, then, has been a huge timesaver. Now professional indexers, like City traders, work with two or even three screens arcing around them, one displaying the text to be indexed, another for the

COMPUTER-ASSISTED INDEXING

Thoroughly tested and documented
programs to run on microcomputers using the
CP/M operating system

AVAILABLE NOW

Capable

Close co-operation between the programmer and an indexer with ten years' experience of manual indexing has produced a package which takes account of the specialised needs of the professional indexer. Layout follows BS3700:1976.

Easy to use

No technical knowledge is needed. Clear and simple instructions guide the user at all stages; there are no disasters if the 'wrong' key is pressed; upper-case and lower-case letters and all punctuation marks can be used in entries without any special codes.

Fast

Sorting time is negligible; corrections, additions and deletions are made in seconds; typing time can be reduced substantially; merging of identical entries with different page numbers is accomplished automatically; temporary page numbers are quickly transformed to the correct final page numbers when they are known.

For more details contact

Hilary and Drusilla Calvert 01-267 3793
or
Transam Microsystems 01-405 5240
9/61 Theobalds Road, London WC1

Figure 34: No disasters if the 'wrong' key is pressed. A 1982 advertisement for MACREX in *The Indexer*.

indexing software, and perhaps a browser in the third ready to check any details the indexer is unclear on. But machines can only speed up the tasks that can be sped up – sorting, layout, error checking. The work of compiling a subject index is still, principally, a subjective, humanistic one. It is a job of deep reading, of working to understand a text in order to make the most judicious selection of its key elements. Professional indexers have subject specialisms – chemistry, cookery, law or literature – and they expend their time reading carefully, expertly, the whole way through, so that we don't have to. (Remember Pliny describing his table of contents to the Emperor: 'I have appended to this letter a table of contents of the several books, and have taken very careful precautions to prevent your having to read them.') The indexer will want a feel, before they begin, for the concepts that will need to be flagged, or taxonomized with subheadings. They might skim the book – reading it in full but at a canter – before tackling it properly with the software open. Or they may spend a while, as a preliminary, with the book's introduction, paying attention to its chapter outline – if it has one – to gain a sense of what to look out for. Often, having reached the end of the book, the indexer will return to the first few chapters, going over them again now that they have gained a conceptual mapping of the work as a whole. When we buy a non-fiction book, the index is priced into the amount we pay at the till, and what we are paying for is the indexer's time as a reader. Indexing software has removed the need for cards and shoeboxes, scissors and wood glue, but reading – patient, active reading for the preparation of an index; alert and attentive like Calvino's Ludmilla – is the same task it was in the days of Woolf, or Pope, or Gessner.

*

But what of Lotaria? Surely this is her chapter? Isn't this the Age of Search, the Age of Distraction, of compulsive detail-checking? Of *What was he in again? Isn't she dead?* Of *Let me Google that for you.* Isn't our current information culture one that is defined by machines that read the world for us, 'crawling and indexing' as Google's documentation puts it, gathering data on an almost inconceivable scale and arranging it so that we can pick up the results downstream and do the things that humans are good at: browsing, synthesizing, interpreting. 'An electronic reading supplies me with the frequencies, which I only have to glance at,' says Lotaria. The most prescient thing about Josephine Miles' work on the Berkeley mainframes was not that she produced an electronic index *per se*, but that the kind of index she built was the most basic type. Its cards comprised the text itself – Dryden's poems – in atomized form, stored and accessible as individual words. The subject index – expertly made, Kitemark compliant – is not, perhaps, the symbol for our times. Instead, that would be the concordance.

This digital 'searchability' – concordance searchability, the ability to find and count instances of specific words – of literary works has meant that Lotaria's critical methods have become a reality. 'Distant reading' uses the algorithms of database engineers to query large bodies of literature – hundreds of novels, say – in a single instant. As an approach, it has been used, for example, by Matthew Jockers in 'sentiment analysis' – a kind of Big Data version of Morley's 'Index to Tears' – mapping the use of positive or negative emotion words as they occur throughout a novel.[16] Do they correlate with what we think of as that novel's plot – its moments of crisis, its happy (or unhappy) ending? When the algorithm is run across many, many novels (41,383 of them, to be precise), are there any basic emotional patterns that appear as novelistic archetypes, a finite number of narrative arcs? As with Boyle's attacks on Bentley, distant reading has not been without its critics. Does this type of alphabetical learning produce results of any validity? How accurate is its parsing of emotion? How can we evaluate this? Meanwhile, Google's nGram application can tell me, for instance, that, based on its vast corpus of historical texts, the word *detective* had a marked usage spike in the middle of the 1920s, or that *unconscious* showed only a small uptick after Freud, having become steadily more common throughout the nineteenth century. What to do with this information? How to interpret it, turn it into narrative? That is the job of the literary historian. But to produce the initial observation, to dredge it from the measureless indexes of digital corpora is now the work of an instant. The electronic reading supplies me with the frequencies. I only have to glance.

Older analyses, however, do not easily make the jump to digital. The patient interpretations contained in subject indexes originally compiled for physical books do not translate well when those books are remediated as reflowable electronic editions. Sometimes indexes are unceremoniously dumped in the conversion; sometimes they are retained but useless in a format that eschews page numbers, their spectral locators gazing wanly after features of a terrain that is no longer visible. Even when an eBook retains information about how the pages in its print edition were divided up, navigation is clumsy. Working onscreen through a string of locators, using the Go To function to switch back and forth between the index and a sequence of other places in the text, is off-puttingly laborious compared to holding one page open with your thumb and flipping the pages physically.

Thanks to the recent tecÙological revolution in our reading, the functionality of the concordance has become ubiquitous; the subject index, however – careful, conscientious, expert – has not been well served.

And yet this need not be the case. Since the invention of the printing press, an index that uses page numbers as locators can only be compiled once the book has been typeset and its pagination fixed. But the arrival of digital mark-up – the ability to insert invisible codes within an electronic document – has allowed for 'embedded indexing', a different take on the software-based approaches described above. With embedded indexing, as the name implies, the index – or the *potential* index: it need not have actually been produced in its final form yet – is 'embedded' within the text itself as a collection of tags – like this one: {XE 'index, embedded, example of'} – each indicating a keyword and a position in the text. Once the text has been fully marked up in this way, the index can be generated automatically by extracting all the tags, assigning locators to them and putting them into alphabetical order. If the book's layout should subsequently change – if an extra image is inserted, or a page break, or a chapter is scaled back further down the line – the index can simply be regenerated, its locators refreshing themselves to reflect the new pagination. Developed in the 1990s, embedded indexing is more labour intensive than other software-based approaches, but it allows indexers to start their work at an earlier stage in a book's production cycle, working from the author's Word document rather than from the final PDF proofs. Designed as a time-saver for print indexes, then, embedded indexing nevertheless opens up the possibility of fully-functioning subject indexes in eBooks. The digital mark-up that drives an embedded index is the same tecÙology that underlies the hyperlink, the navigational putty that binds a billion discrete pages into the World Wide Web. An indexer who tags a document has already done the work needed to produce an 'active index', where each locator is a clickable link that will bring up its target page immediately.

Active indexes, however, are, at time of writing, not common. In an age where searchability is something we take for granted, the Society of Indexers, ironically, is a somewhat embattled institution. The reasons are financial. If readers on digital platforms feel adequately, if not luxuriantly, served by the built-in search function on their devices, then publishers will save money by not providing anything more. Meanwhile, where Borko once noted that the associated costs of working with computers meant that machine-generated indexes would be prohibitively expensive in all but a few situations, the tables have now been turned so that automated indexing offers a much cheaper alternative to hiring the services of a qualified indexer. Much like Borko's experiments in automated indexing fifty years ago, modern automatic index generators filter out function words before applying rudimentary AI to determine which terms should be retained as important. The results, at this stage, are not impressive, but given the savings in time and in cost some publishers will use this software before – as Borko suggested – sprucing up the results by hand. For comparison, at the back of this book are two indexes, the first produced using automatic index-generating software, the second compiled by Paula Clarke Bain and (mostly) compliant with the International Standards Organization's ISO 999:1996: 'Guidelines for the content, organization and presentation of indexes'. The difference in quality, in usefulness, is stark.

But it is not just machines that are making inroads into the world of indexing. In our electronic lives we have all become not only consummate searchers, but enthusiastic sorters too. Consider the hashtag. On 23 August 2007, a web developer named Chris Messina posted a message on the fledgling social media network, Twitter:

> how do you feel about using pound (#) for groups. As in #barcamp [msg]?

In Messina's example, a user tweeting about the programming conference, BarCamp, might begin with the label #barcamp, before typing the rest of their message. The hash sign (#) – also known as 'pound' – would indicate that the word following it was a tag, identifying the tweet's contents and making it easier to find for potentially interested parties.

In a blogpost a couple of days later, Messina expanded on this suggestion. The hashtag, he suggested, might serve as an 'ad hoc verbal guidepost', a phrase which recalls the insignia of the Index Society, with its fingerpost pointing the way for the seeker after knowledge.[17] As for 'ad hoc', Messina explained that existing social media sites were already well set up to cater to special interest groups, as long as these were formally defined. In other words, if you wanted to be part of a group, you had to opt in by actively joining, which may require approval from a group administrator. But what about looser, more instantaneous groupings? Do I have to sign up just to see what people are saying, right now, about the test match or the news? As Messina put it, 'I'm more interested in simply having a better eavesdropping experience on Twitter.'

From the outset, Messina described his suggestion as *folksonomic* – that is, a taxonomy, a classification system, but one whose terms are not determined in advance. Instead they are created, on the fly, by anyone – by *folk*. A hashtag that hasn't been used before comes into being instantly at the point the message containing it is sent. What's more, no higher authority owns or controls it. This latter characteristic routinely throws up a special kind of public relations gaffe when brands invite customers to endorse them online. When the publicity team for the singer Susan Boyle decided to promote the launch of her 2012 album *Standing Ovation* under the hashtag #susanalbumparty, there was no registration panel to point out that this sequence of letters could be read in different ways, and no mechanism to separate out supportive messages from Boyle's fans from amused responses from the wider twittersphere. The same year, McDonald's invited customers to tweet their 'good news stories' about the restaurant under the hashtag #McDStories. Pulling up the hashtag now makes for grim reading – from gross-out tales of the things people found in their burgers to condemnations of the company's questionable environmental and employment record.

The success of the hashtag, its ubiquity, is to do with its arrival into a search-savvy culture. It belongs to the age of the search bar, to a global online community who, over the previous decade, had become expert Googlers, and for whom the next step was not merely to look things up but to categorize them: to link new material – a tweet, a photograph, a sound file – to an existing tag, or to create – seriously or ironically – a new label for others to adopt or reject. The tagger emulates the indexer, sifting ideas, choosing the best head for a concept: #WeAreAllSubjectIndexersNow maybe, but the hashtag is a truly demotic form, governed by conventions that are unpredictable, ironic, carnivalesque. In the form of the tagger, our patient, bookish indexer has acquired a younger sibling, one who is capricious, sarcastic and fluent in the ever-shifting inflections of the new media.

As for Google, on 2 October 2015, the company underwent a transfiguration. An announcement a couple of months earlier by one of its founders, Larry Page, explained that Google had grown baggy. Through acquisitions and its own developments the company's interests had come to include a mapping agency (Google Maps), a media organization (YouTube) and a major operating system (Android), not to mention a vast number of smaller businesses. A restructuring was necessary, unbundling each of these different interests. Google itself would be slimmed down – it would become a sibling rather than a parent, a wholly owned subsidiary of a newly created umbrella company. Page's briefing reassured investors that the change would be minimally disruptive. All shares in Google would automatically be converted into shares in the new holding company, and to make matters simple the stock market codes would continue to be GOOGL and GOOG. But these codes were only a matter of convenience. The umbrella company would have a new name, something more basic, less of a tech student in-joke than Google, but something which would reference the searching and indexing that had been the company's cornerstone. Google would become Alphabet.

The name implies universality, the alpha and the omega for an organization with its finger in every pie. It implies order too, the basic tool of information management, from the Library of Alexandria to Silicon Valley. Page would make the indexing connection explicitly in that first announcement: 'We liked the name Alphabet because it . . . is the core of how we index with Google search.'[18] But to me Alphabet is also a reminder of the gap – the uncanny valley – that has still not been decisively bridged between concordance and subject index, matching letters versus identifying concepts, Hugh's vision versus Grosseteste's.

Google itself, to be fair, is at the cutting edge of intelligent search tecÙology. Give it the phrase 'how to catch a cow fishing' and it will deduce – noting the other search terms: *catch*, *fishing* – that *cow* is probably being used here in one of its slang senses, an angling term for striped bass. Results for bass fishing are promoted; livestock results are relegated to the outer pages.[19] But few of our other search-bar interactions – in our word processors, our social media pages, our eReaders, our file managers – go beyond simple letter-to-letter matching. The alphabet will only get us so far – this is why Borko's algorithm was disappointing and SuBo's hashtag calamitous. Just as distant reading will not make close reading redundant (as long as we instinctively prefer Ludmilla to Lotaria), the search bar will not replace the subject index any time soon.

For this we should be grateful. A good index can be a pleasure of its own; but a good index can only be the product of a good indexer. At the Society of Indexers' first international conference in 1978, the art historian William Heckscher delivered an address in praise of the kind of index that might 'pride itself on being the child of imagination'. Such a work, he went on, 'should enable us to spend a peaceful evening in bed, reading [it], as if we were reading a good novel'.[20] This feels like a tall order, an inappropriate request, perhaps, for a device whose very role, after all, is to break up the linear flow of the text it serves. And yet, looking at an entry like the following, from Robert Latham's index to Pepys' diaries, it is easy to see what Heckscher means:

BAGWELL, ——, wife of William: her good looks, 4/222; P plans to seduce, 4/222, 266; visits, 4/233–4; finds her virtuous, 4/234; and modest, 5/163; asks P for place for husband, 5/65–6, 163; P kisses, 5/287; she grows affectionate, 5/301–2; he caresses, 5/313; she visits him, 5/316, 339; her resistance collapses in alehouse, 5/322; amorous encounters with: at her house, 5/350–1; 6/40, 162, 189, 201, 253, 294; 7/166, 284, 285; 8/39, 95; 9/211; Navy Office, 6/186; 7/351, 380; tavern, 6/20; assignations frustrated, 9/25, 217; P's valentine, 6/35, 226, 294; asks for promotion for husband, 6/39–40; P strains a finger, 6/40; she returns from Portsmouth, 7/96; has sore face, 7/191; returns from Harwich, 9/12, 25; also, 6/158; 7/96, 210, 339; 8/99; ~ servant dies of plague, 7/166.[21]

It is, indeed, a masterpiece of compressed storytelling and characterization: the intrigue of the tacit transaction between Pepys and the Bagwells, the comedy of Pepys' sexual incontinence told through seventeen unspooling locators, amorous encounters that end in frustration; Pepys's farcically strained finger and Mrs Bagwell's ominously sore face; the rug pulled out from underneath the whole saucy tale in that final detail of the servant's death from plague. This is indexing that really sings. To borrow another of Heckscher's phrases, it 'has a life of its own'.

Not every subject index can or should tell stories in this way, and even in Latham's Pepys index not every entry has a heroine like Mrs Bagwell. And yet, every subject index worth its salt must, in an important sense, be a work of the imagination. A good subject index can only be the product of a good indexer, an expert reader who knows something about the topic in hand before tackling the work. A specialist indexer knows that it can be helpful to tag a concept even if it is not explicitly named, that a passage on Jean-Paul Sartre might warrant an entry under *existentialism*, or that a gardener might use either the common or the botanical name when looking up a particular plant; they can tell the difference – even without first names – between *Marx, Karl, Marx, Groucho*, and *Marx, Richard*; they know that, thanks to metonymy, sometimes a reference to 'Number Ten' or to 'Downing Street' belongs under *JoÙson, Boris*, and sometimes it doesn't. The limitations of *unimaginative* indexing, of the simple string search, become starkly apparent if one tries to locate the parable of the prodigal son, that famous tale of mercy and forgiveness, using a Bible concordance. The parable does not contain the words *forgiveness* or *mercy*, or, for that matter, *prodigal*. Neither Artandi nor Borko can help us here.

The professional indexer, learned, vigilant, goes before us, levelling mountains and beating paths so that we, time-poor students at the fingerpost, can arrive swiftly but unruffled at the passage – the quotation, the datum, the *knowledge* – we need. For the last century, since the emergence of the secretarial agencies in the 1890s, these indexers have been increasingly – now overwhelmingly – women.[22] And like the generations of indexers before them, these women have been, for the most part, anonymous, their work uncredited. If nothing else, I hope this book may serve as a wreath laid at the tomb of these unknown readers.

Looking to the future, we find that the book, the old-fashioned paper-and-ink book, its pages unreflowable, bound at the spine, has proved an enduring tecÙology in the face of its electronic offspring. For the time being, at least, it retains its place as the dominant symbol of our intellectual endeavours, displayed on our shelves and on the crests of the great universities. As long as we navigate the waters of print, the book index, child of the imagination but as old as those universities themselves, will continue to serve as our compass.

Coda: Archives of Reading

'The composition of vast books is a laborious and
impoverishing extravagance . . . A better course of
procedure is to pretend that these books already
exist, and then to offer a resumé.'

Jorge Luis Borges, *Ficciones*

Late autumn, 2019: upstairs at the Witte de With Centre for
Contemporary Art in Rotterdam. Under white strip-lighting
the white walls are hung with white frames, each containing

Figure 35: Alejandro Cesarco's *Index*.

a sheet of text, black on white. It is a minimalist, even austere show. Visitors are leaning in, raising their spectacles, squinting to read the narrow lines of small black print. This is the *Index* series, by the Uruguayan artist Alejandro Cesarco. These, like the Ballard story which began our first chapter, are indexes to imaginary books.

The indexes on the walls of the gallery offer up several types of pleasure, which come through in different stages like the courses of a meal. Most immediately, we can enjoy the juxtapositions. Like Zembla in Nabokov's *Pale Fire* index, the arrangement of these indexes is design posing as arbitrariness. Belle and Sebastian next to *Being and Time*, punk next to Proust, these are discreet rebellions, cultural levelling on a microscopic scale. Or, with a little more effort, we can read against the alphabet, matching entries that have the same locator, triangulating concepts to picture the hypothetical page on which they are all united. *Bossanova, chocolate, dates, desperateness*: how we read *dates* here – as fruit or as hook-ups – will determine how we read *desperateness*. Or *crying, endings, fragility, holding-hands*, all on an imaginary page 2. What sequence do they play out in when alphabetical order is removed?[1]

Then there are the general impressions that the indexes leave us with. A preponderance of twentieth-century thinkers – just trawling through the *L*s in one frame throws up Lacan, Laclau, Le Corbusier, Lefebvre, Lenin, Levinas, Lukács, Lyotard ... – but also a concern with emotion, sometimes but not always framed in the language of therapy. One run of entries yields up:

direction: and decisions, 5–8
discipline, 16

Cesarco's indexes track his own interests, the culture – books, films, art – that he consumes over time: 'an archive of my reading', as he puts it.[2] But the focus on affect is similarly reflexive. Cesarco calls his indexes 'a form of self-portraiture that unfolds over time'. The phoney locators, pointing offstage to the pages of non-existent texts, might be dissimulations but that is not to say that the indexes do not ultimately have a real referent. Like the Christ Church attack on Richard Bentley, these are the indexes not to a book but a personality, A Short Account of the Artist by Way of Index. Naturally, then, a recurrent figure is Freud. One entry runs:

> Freud, Sigmund, 62; *A Special Type of Choice of Object Made by Men*, 10; on delusion, 7; on ego, 9; on fetishism, 26; and identity and identification, 34; on narcissism, 29; on sexuality, 5, 28, 73.

It is hard not to read this as a reflection on Cesarco's curious process, a mode of autobiography that makes a fetish of the index, filtering identity – observations, memories – through headwords, backwards syntax, alphabetical order.

I want to end this history by proposing that Cesarco's indexes are not, in that way, remarkable. That, just as every translation bears the trace of the translator, every index is inevitably haunted by its indexer. I am speaking only of the subject index; the concordance – man- or machine-made – is a different matter. But when J. Horace Round demolishes his medievalist rival in the back pages of *Feudal England*, he reveals something of his character – his tenaciousness, certainly, but also pedantry, professional frustration, a capacity for unremitting contempt. There is personality in an index; in a concordance, or a search bar, there is not.

In 2015, I spent the summer as a Visiting Fellow at the Folger Shakespeare Library in Washington, DC. I was working my way through their catalogue looking for early printed books with indexes on their flyleaves. How did early modern readers mark their books up to make to make them navigable for referencing? In the time I was there I saw hundreds upon hundreds of reader indexes, in satires and polemics, religious texts and profane ones, even poetry books and fiction. Some were long, detailed, fully alphabetical – written, presumably, on draft paper then copied neatly into the book they serviced; others were nothing more than a few scribbled lines, a brief list of keywords and page numbers. Sometimes the compiler had drawn a grid – a table, like we would today in Microsoft Word – to keep their entries evenly spaced; sometimes the gridlines were uninked, a blind scoring that would leave a ghostly impression several pages deep.

For all their variety, however, every one of these tables was the archive of a reading, the record of a particular response to a particular book. From the most elaborate to the merest sketch, every one carried the mark of an indexer: of what they thought was important, the details they expected to return to, a map for a future visit. One of them, a six-line table in an early seventeenth-century tract against alcohol, runs simply: 'Filthy talk, 2; Fornication, 4; Wrath, 8; Murther,

Figure 36: A blind impression, several leaves deep, for compiling an index in the back pages of Hierocles of Alexandria, *Hierocles upon the golden verses of Pythagoras, teaching a vertuous and worthy life* (1656).

13; Swearing; Cursing'. A catalogue of ills, and yet it trails off, its last two entries missing their locators, nothing at all noted beyond the first quarter of the book. As an index, it raises more questions than it answers. What was it for? How did the compiler expect to return to this text? Was it to sermonize some errant and bibulous family member, browbeating them with passages from Young? Or can we imagine our anonymous indexer taking a certain vicarious pleasure in these descriptions of sin, bookmarking their appearance for future, secret trysts with the text? Why does the list end so abruptly? Did the reader lose interest, putting the book aside once

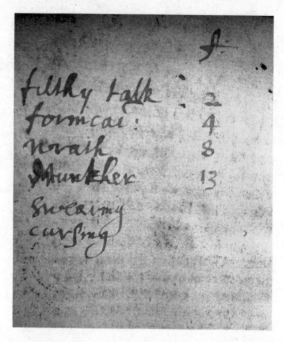

Figure 37: An aborted attempt to list the highlights – or lowlights – of Thomas Young, *Englands Bane, or the Description of Drunkennesse.*

Young's lurid opening had begun to drift into tedious biblical examples? As historians we are at a loss, unable to move beyond speculation. But the index still stands as an inerasable testament to one reader's now-irretrievable intention, as much the archive of someone's reading as Cesarco's framed and mounted tables.

The midpoint of this history considered a visual, or rather mixed-media, index: the woodcuts and doggerel verse that serve as the table to Peter Frarin's *Oration*. Like Frarin's text itself, these graphical index entries were unrelentingly violent, full of death, scorn and mutilation. Let's end with another blend of poetry and image, but in a different, mellower key:

playful, light, domestic, an index that celebrates life – a life – rather than disdaining it. The book is *The Gorgeous Nothings*, Marta Werner and Jen Bervin's edition of Emily Dickinson's 'envelope poems'. These are a trove of scraps – envelopes and parts of envelopes – on which Dickinson composed brief verses. The poems themselves are fragmentary, seemingly ephemeral, crossed with other types of writing, or unfinished, with undecided variants included. They are fleeting, impressionistic, they break off, often with a dash, mid-sentence. For an editor, they pose an unusual problem. The envelope poems were never prepared for publication, never stabilized by being written out in the author's final fine hand. Are they drafts, like the concordance scraps in the Mazarine Library? A draft, surely, implies *becoming*: the intention, at the very least, of a return, a working-up, a fair copy. With these poems we have no evidence of such an intention. How, then, should one present them in a way that preserves their delicacy and tentativeness? Werner and Bervin transcribe the poems, using a system of glyphs and codes to indicate the idiosyncrasies of the text: where the writing changes direction, or is crossed out, or divided into columns. But on the facing page, across from these transcriptions, the editors have included full-colour images of the envelopes themselves. The physical form, scratched on ejecta, on torn corners of used envelopes, is treated as a part of each poem, reminding us how provisional, how momentary, these singular jottings were.

The norm for poetry books, of course, is to provide an index of first lines. Here, however, to treat the poems in such a way would be to flush out their material aspect, to turn them into pure text, exactly what the rest of the presentation militates against. *The Gorgeous Nothings*, then, is served better by Bervin's 'Visual Index', really a suite of indexes, that divide the poems up in a range of ways. There is an index of envelopes by page shape, another by addressee, one for those where the text is in columns, or with pencilled divisions, for those with multidirectional text, or where the envelope is turned diagonally, an index of envelopes with cancelled or erased text, another for variants. Like the indexes to Pope's Homer, the material is considered from a dazzling variety of angles. Many envelopes appear in several different tables, but each index is explicitly concerned with the envelopes – their shape, their orientation, who they are addressed to – rather than the poetry on them. If you are trying to locate that poem about *hair* or *mushrooms*, then you're on your own. Bervin's index won't help you. But if you're looking for the poem written diagonally on an arrow-shaped envelope, that will be A364 ('Summer laid her simple Hat').

Whether this is actually useful, even for the most visual thinker, I'm not sure. One of Bervin's categories of envelope shape is 'pointless arrows', and this might be a good name for the locators in these indexes. But that seems to be missing the point. The 'Visual Index' is an impish way to make a serious argument about what these poems really are, not mere texts but *things*. The envelope poems remind us of Dickinson the eccentric, the recluse, but also Dickinson the inveterate correspondent; the poet who would never leave her house, who spoke from behind closed doors, but who sent herself into the world through gifts, flowers, letters. The index is a wry gesture, imbued with the character of its compiler, the artist sorting shapes, dreaming up an order – a new alphabet – where columns come before arrows, diagonal text before crossings-out. It is warm and witty, respectful but not slavish towards this most idiosyncratic of poets, alive to her

Index of Envelopes by Page Shape

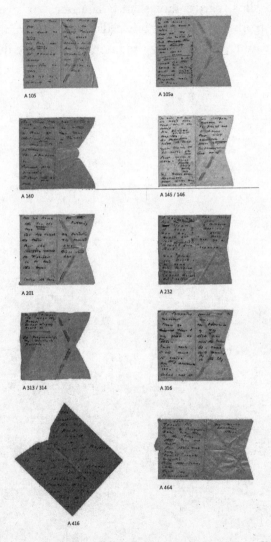

Figure 38: 'Pointless arrows' in the 'Index of Envelopes by Page Shape' in Emily Dickinson's *The Gorgeous Nothings*.

peculiar domesticity. Whether or not it helps us to navigate the poetry, Bervin's index nevertheless joins Cesarco's art-works, Woolf's little paper squares, Holmes' great volumes and the slips, cards, tables and databases of every other indexer from Grosseteste onwards, each the archive of an earlier reading, still wearing the faint, ineradicable flush of its creator.

Notes

Introduction

1 Its topic, fittingly, is the WorldWideWeb project. The page can be viewed at http://info.cern.ch/hypertext/WWW/TheProject. html. It was Simon Rowberry, at the Society of Indexers conference in 2014, who observed that the page was an index.

2 Matt Cutts, 'How Search Works', embedded video at https://www.google.com/intl/en_uk/search/howsearchworks/crawling-indexing/.

3 Thomas Babington Macaulay, *Macaulay's Life of Samuel JoÙson*, ed. by Charles Lane Hanson (Boston, MA: Ginn & Company, 1903), p. 13.

4 Robert L. Collison, *Indexes and Indexing*, 4th edn (London: Ernest Benn, 1972), p. 12.

5 See Joseph A. Howley, 'Tables of Contents', in Dennis Duncan and Adam Smyth (eds.), *Book Parts* (Oxford: Oxford University Press, 2019), pp. 65–79 (pp. 68–9).

6 Pliny the Elder, *Natural History*, trans. by H. Rackham (Cambridge, MA: Harvard University Press, 2014), 1.33.

7 Will Self, 'The Novel is Dead (This Time It's for Real)', *Guardian* (2 May 2014): https://www.theguardian.com/books/2014/may/02/will-self-novel-deal-literary-fiction.

8 Nicholas Carr, 'Is Google Making Us Stupid?: What the Internet is Doing to Our Brains', *Atlantic* (July/August 2008). Carr expands on this argument at book length in *The Shallows: How the Internet is Changing the Way We Think, Read and Remember* (London: Atlantic, 2011).

9 Galileo Galilei, *Dialogue Concerning the Two Chief World Systems*, trans. by Stillman Drake (Berkeley, CA: University of California Press, 1967), p. 185.

10 Campbell writes, 'So essential did I consider an Index to be to every book, that I proposed to bring a Bill to parliament to deprive an author who publishes a book without an Index of the privilege of copyright; and, moreover, to subject him, for his offence, to a pecuniary penalty.' One wonders whether we should take Campbell entirely at his word. Hansard has no record of Campbell ever mentioning such a bill in parliament. (If he did, and it has gone unrecorded, it was most likely in the context of the Copyright Bill introduced repeatedly by Thomas Taulford in the late 1830s). But in fact Campbell's whole bold claim takes place in the context of an admission of guilt. The above quotation goes on: 'from difficulties started by my printers, my own books have hitherto been without an Index.' Were his bill to have come into being, Campbell, the shrewdest of legal minds, would have fallen foul of his own legislation. John Lord Campbell, *The Lives of the Chief Justices of England*, 4 vols. (London: John Murray, 1874), III, p. x.

11 John Marbeck, *A Concordance, that is to saie, a worke wherein by the ordre of the letters of the A. B. C. ye maie redely finde any worde conteigned in the whole Bible, so often as it is there expressed or mencioned* (London, 1550), sig. A3r.

12 John Foxe, *Actes and Monuments* (London, 1570), p. 1391.

13 For the best account of Marbeck's trial and the heretical implications of his concordance, see David Cram, 'John Marbeck's Concordance to the English Bible', in Nicola McLelland and Andrew R. Linn (eds.), *Flores grammaticae: Essays in Memory of Vivien Law* (Münster: Nodus, 2005), pp. 155–70.

14 J. Horace Round, *Feudal England: Historical Studies on the XIth and XIIth Centuries* (London: Swann Sonnenschein, 1895).

Chapter 1: Point of Order

1 J. G. Ballard, 'The Index', *Bananas*, 8 (1977), pp. 24–5 (p. 24).
The story is also anthologized in *War Fever* (London: Collins,
1990), pp. 171–6 and *Complete Short Stories* (London: Flamingo,
2001), pp. 940–45.

2 Henri-Pierre Roché, 'The Blind Man', *The Blind Man* 1 (1917):
3–6 (3).

3 *Catalogue of the First Annual Exhibition of The Society of Independent Artists (Incorporated)* (New York: Society of Independent
Artists, 1917).

4 Beatrice Wood, 'Work of a Picture Hanger', *The Blind Man* 1
(1917): 6 (6).

5 [Le Moyen Âge n'aimait pas l'ordre alphabétique qu'il considérait comme une antithèse de la raison. Dieu avait créé un
univers harmonieux, aux parties liées entre elles; il revenait à
l'érudit de discerner ces rapports rationnels – ceux de la hiérarchie, de la chronologie, des similarités et différences, etc. – et
de les refléter dans la structure de ses écrits. L'ordre alphabétique impliquait l'abdication de cette responsabilité ...
Employer délibérément l'ordre alphabétique revenait à reconnaître tacitement que chaque utilisateur d'un ouvrage pouvait
recourir à un ordre personnel, différent de celui d'autres utilisateurs et de l'auteur lui-même.] Mary A. Rouse and Richard
H. Rouse, 'La Naissance des index', in Henri-Jean Martin and
Roger Chartier (eds.), *Histoire de l'édition française*, 4 vols. (Paris:
Promodis, 1983), I, pp. 77–85 (p. 80).

6 Robert Cawdrey, *A Table Alphabeticall* (London: I. Roberts for
Edmund Weaver, 1604), sig. A4v.

7 Both of these are quoted and translated in Lloyd W. Daly, *Contributions to a History of Alphabetization in Antiquity and the Middle Ages* (Brussels: Collection Latomus, 1967), pp. 71–3.

8 See David Diringer, *The Alphabet: A Key to the History of Mankind*, 3rd edn, 2 vols. (London: Hutchinson, 1968), I, pp. 169–70.

9 For a representation of the inscription as well as a longer discussion of it, see Olga Tufnell, *Lachish III (Tell Ed-Duweir): The Iron Age* (London: Oxford University Press, 1953), pp. 118, 357.

10 C. H. Inge, 'Excavations at Tell Ed-Duweir: The Wellcome Marston Archaeological Research Expedition to the Near East', *Palestine Exploration Quarterly* 70.4 (1938): 240–56 (256).

11 Joseph Addison, *Spectator* 58 (7 May 1711): 1.

12 For estimates of the collection's size see Rudolf Blum, *Kallimachos: The Alexandrian Library and the Origins of Bibliography*, trans. by Hans H. Wellisch (Madison, WI: University of Wisconsin Press, 1991), pp. 106–7.

13 The papyrus, known as P. Oxy. X 1241, was first published in B. P. Grenfell and A. S. Hunt, *The Oxyrhynchus Papyri* 10 (London, 1914), pp. 99–100.

14 The argument, based on the Oxyrhynchus parchment, that Callimachus was passed over for the head job at the library is not accepted by all scholars. See, for example, Blum, pp. 127–33, and Jackie Murray, 'Burned After Reading: The So-called List of Alexandrian Librarians in *P. Oxy.* X 1241', *Aitia* 2 (2012), online.

15 Athenaeus, *The Learned Banqueters*, trans. by S. Douglas Olson, 8 vols (Cambridge, MA: Harvard University Press, 2007), VII, p. 263 (xiv 643e).

16 See Blum, *Kallimachos*, pp. 152–5.

17 Cicero, *Letters to Atticus*, ed. and trans. by D. R. Shackleton Bailey (Cambridge, MA: Harvard University Press, 2014), p. 78 (IV.4a).

18 Daly, *Contributions*, p. 25.

19 (Pseudo-)Plutarch, 'On Homer (II)', in *Homeric Hymns, Homeric Apocrypha, Lives of Homer*, ed. and trans. by Martin L. West (Cambridge, MA: Harvard University Press, 2003), p. 417 (II.4).

20 See Daly, *Contributions*, pp. 18–20; William Roger Paton and Edward Lee Hicks, *The Inscriptions of Cos* (Oxford: Clarendon, 1891), pp. 236–60.

21 Ephraim Lytle, 'Fish Lists in the Wilderness: The Social and Economic History of a Boiotian Price Decree', *Hesperia: The Journal of the American School of Classical Studies at Athens* 79.2 (2010): 253–303.

22 Now at Columbia University. P. Columbia 1 recto 1a-b. See William Linn Westermann and Clinton Walker Keyes (eds.), *Tax Lists and Transportation Receipts from Theadelphia* (New York: Columbia University Press, 1932), pp. 3–36.

23 Pliny the Elder, *Natural History*, trans. by D. E. Eichholz, 10 vols. (Cambridge, MA: Harvard University Press, 2014) X, XXXVII.53.

24 See Daly, *Contributions*, p. 59.

25 Plautus, *Amphitryon, The Comedy of Asses, The Pot of Gold, The Two Bacchises, The Captives*, trans. by Wolfgang de Melo (Cambridge, MA: Harvard University Press, 2014), V.ii. 864–6.

26 See A. M. Cook, 'Virgil, *Aen.* VII.7.641 ff', *Classical Review* 33.5/6 (1919): 103–4.

27 The Corpus Glossary – Cambridge, Corpus Christi College MS 144 – dates from either the eighth or early ninth century and provides glosses, mostly in Latin but many in Old English, for thousands of terms.

28 M. Dolbier, 'Books and Authors: Nabokov's Plums', *New York Herald Tribune*, 17 June 1962, Books section, p. 2.

29 Another index entry – 'Botkin, V., American scholar of Russian descent' – discreetly reveals the extent of the narrator's delusion.

30 See Simon Rowberry, 'Translating Zembla; or, How to Finish *Pale Fire*', *The Indexer*, 31 April 2013: 142.

Chapter 2: The Births of the Index

1 Amelia Carolina Sparavigna, 'On the Rainbow, Robert Grosse-teste's Treatise on Optics', *International Journal of Sciences* 2.9 (2013): 108–13 (109).

2 *The Booke of the Common Prayer and Administration of the Sacraments* (London: 1549), sig. Biiv.

3 St Augustine, *Letters*, trans. by Wilfrid Parsons, 5 vols. (Baltimore, MD: Catholic University of America Press, 1956), V, Letter 211, 'To a Convent of Consecrated Virgins', p. 43.

4 *St. Benedict's Rule for Monasteries*, trans. by Leonard J. Doyle (Collegeville, MN: Liturgical Press, 1948), p. 67.

5 *The Rule for Nuns of St Caesarius of Arles*, trans. by Maria McCarthy (Washington, DC: Catholic University of America Press, 1960), p. 175.

6 [au moyen âge, on lit généralement en pronançant avec les lèvres, au moins à voix basse, par conséquent en entendant les phrases que les yeux voient.] Jean Leclercq, *Initiation aux auteurs monastiques du Moyen Âge*, 2nd edn (Paris: Cerf, 1963), p. 72.

7 St Augustine, *Confessions*, trans. by Carolyn J. B. Hammond, 2 vols. (Cambridge, MA: Harvard University Press, 2014), I, p. 243 (VI 3.3).

8 JoÙ of St Arnulf, 'Vita Joannis abbatis Gorziensis', *Patrologia Latina*, 137.280D.

9 See Hastings Rashdall, *The Universities of Europe in the Middle Ages*, 2 vols. (Oxford: Clarendon, 1895), I, pp. 6–7.

10 See Otto Schmid, *Über Verschiedene Eintheilungen der Heiligen Schrift: insbesondere über die Capitel-Eintheilung Stephan Langtons im XIII. Jahrhunderte* (Graz: LeuscÙer & Lubensky, 1892), p. 95.

11 For example, Bibliothèque municipale de Lyon MS 340, a Bible produced in England, includes a note at the start of

both Genesis and Proverbs, stating 'This book is divided into chapters according to master S[tephen], archbishop of Canterbury' (f. 33r).

12 For more on the Paris Bible and its influence, see Laura Light, 'The Thirteenth Century and the Paris Bible', in Richard Marsden and E. Ann Matter, *The New Cambridge History of the Bible*, 4 vols. (Cambridge: Cambridge University Press, 2012), II, pp. 380–91.

13 Translation from R. W. Hunt, 'English Learning in the Late Twelfth Century', *Transactions of the Royal Historical Society* 19 (1936): pp. 19-42 (pp. 33-4).

14 Understanding the *distinctio*-collection as merely a set of pre-cooked sermons for lazy preachers is slightly underselling the genre. Joseph Goering stresses their variety, noting that users might be 'the preacher, the teacher, the student, and the pastor [each of whom might] find something suitable for their diverse needs'. Goering, *William de Montibus: The Schools and the Literature of Pastoral Care* (Toronto: Pontifical Institute of Medieval Studies, 1992), p. 264.

15 Mary Carruthers, 'Mental Images, Memory Storage, and Composition in the High Middle Ages', *Das Mittelalter* 13.1 (2008): 63–79.

16 Goering, *William de Montibus*, p. 264.

17 Thomas Fuller, *The Church History of Britain, from the Birth of Jesus Christ until the Year MDCXLVIII*, 6 vols. (Oxford: Oxford University Press, 1845), II, p. 181.

18 Giraldus Cambrensis, *Opera*, ed. J. S. Brewer, J. F. Dimock and G. F. Warned, 8 vols. (Rolls Series, 1861–91), I; translated in R. W. Southern, *Robert Grosseteste: The Growth of an English Mind in Medieval Europe* (Oxford: Clarendon, 1986), p. 65.

19 S. Harrison Thomson, 'Grosseteste's Topical Concordance of the Bible and the Fathers', *Speculum* 9.2 (1934): 139–44 (140).

20 This expanded section is taken from Philipp Rosemann's superb edition of the *Tabula*: Robert Grosseteste, *Tabula*, ed. by Philipp Rosemann, *Corpus Christianorum: Continuatio Mediaevalis* 130 (1995): 233–320 (265).

21 P. W. Rosemann, 'Robert Grosseteste's *Tabula'*, in *Robert Grosseteste: New Perspectives on His Thought and Scholarship*, ed. by James McEvoy (Turnhout: Brepols, 1995), pp. 321–55 (pp. 335–6).

22 As Rouse and Rouse have shown, much of the detail surrounding the composition of the first concordances is based on assertions from much later which have circulated without corroboration. One such detail is the dating for the completion of the St Jacques Concordance, commonly given as 1230, although this is almost certainly too early. All that can be stated with certainty is that it was begun during Hugh's time at St Jacques (i.e. by 1235) and completed by 1247, by which date a copy had been made at Jumièges in Normandy. See Richard H. Rouse and Mary A. Rouse, 'The Verbal Concordance to the Scriptures', *Archivum Fratrum Praedicatorum* 44 (1974): 5–30 (6–8).

23 Oxford, Bodleian Library, MS Canon Pat. lat. 7.

24 Ian Ker, *JoÙ Henry Newman: A Biography* (Oxford: Clarendon, 1988), p. 762.

25 Bernard Levin, 'Don't Come to Me for a Reference', *The Times*, 10 November 1989, p. 16; reprinted as 'The Index Finger Points', *Now Read On* (London: Jonathan Cape, 1990), p. 159.

26 Although these three are traditionally associated with the English Concordance, Rouse and Rouse point out that only Richard can be verified by contemporary textual evidence. Rouse and Rouse, 'Verbal Concordance', p. 13.

27 Oxford, Bodleian Library MS Lat. misc. b. 18 f.61. Translations are from the corresponding passages in the Douay-Rheims

version as it hews especially close to the Latin, making it easy to spot the keyword.

28 [iste modus praedicandi, scilicet per colligationes auctoritatum, est multum facilis, quia facile est auctoritates habere, ex eo quod factae sunt Concordantiae super Bibliam ... secundum ordinem alphabeti, ut auctoritates possint faciliter inveniri.] Thomas Waleys, 'De modo componendi sermones', in Thomas Marie Charland, *Artes praedicandi: contribution à l'histoire de la rhétorique au moyen âge*, Publications de l'Institut d'études médiévales d'Ottawa; 7 (Paris: Vrin, 1936), p. 390.

29 Troyes, Bibliothèque municipale, MSS 186 and 497.

30 Another of the four surviving manuscript copies of the *Moralia* – Oxford, Trinity College MS 50 – ascribes the work to Grosseteste. This ascription has been disputed by E. J. Dobson, *Moralities on the Gospels: A New Source of the 'Ancrene Wisse'* (Oxford: Clarendon, 1975), but Richard Rouse and Siegfried Wenzel, reviewing Dobson's book, convincingly demolish his redating of the text and his reattribution of its authorship (*Speculum* 52.3 (1977): 648–52).

Chapter 3: Where Would We Be Without It?

1 In fact, Rolevinck's first edition of the *Fasciculus* went to press in 1474, before Mehmet's demise. Later editions, however, kept the work current. The detail of the Ottoman Sultan can be found in the edition printed in Venice by Erhard Ratdolt in 1485.

2 Daniel Sawyer notes how an early fifteenth-century manuscript draws attention to its foliation by means of a note in the text stating that the leaves have 'ben markid ... on the right side of the leef, in the higher part of the margyn'. 'No one today',

remarks Sawyer, 'would feel compelled to highlight, in such explicit terms, the exact positioning of numbering on the page.' Daniel Sawyer, 'Page Numbers, Signatures, and Catchwords', in Dennis Duncan and Adam Smyth (eds.), *Book Parts* (Oxford: Oxford University Press, 2019), pp. 135–49 (p. 135).

3 See Nicholas Dames, *A Literary History of the Chapter* (Princeton, NJ: Princeton University Press, forthcoming).

4 [Considerentur primo numeri foliorum in angulo superiori versus manum dextram scriptorum, singulorum foliorum numerum representantes. Deinde inspiciatur tabula ubicumque placuerit, ut verbi gratia. 'Alexander tirum destruxit excepto genere stratonis . 72 . 2 . 3'. Per istum numerum . 72 . denotatur quod in folio ubi scribuntur . 72 . in angulo superiori reperietur in tabula intitulatum. Et immediate ubi habetur iste numerus . 72 . inferitur eciam talis numerus . 2 . 3 . per quem innuitur quod in secunda colundella et tercia de dictis tractat Alexandro et stratone.] Cambridge, St JoÙ's College MS A.12, f. 218r.

5 I am grateful to Dr James Freeman of Cambridge University Library for drawing my attention to the broken index in St JoÙ's College MS A.12. He mentions it in his unpublished PhD dissertation, 'The Manuscript Dissemination and Readership of the "Polychronicon" of Ranulf Higden, *c.* 1330–*c.* 1500' (University of Cambridge, Trinity Hall, 2013), p. 190.

6 Letter of 12 March 1455 from Enea Silvius Piccolomini to Juan de Carvajal, quoted and translated in Martin Davies, 'Juan de Carvajal and Early Printing: The 42-line Bible and the Sweynheym and Pannartz Aquinas', *The Library* 18.3 (1996): 193–215 (196).

7 Raoul Lefèvre, *The Recuyell of the Historyes of Troye*, trans. by William Caxton (Bruges, *c.* 1473), f. L6r.

8 Margaret M. Smith, 'Printed Foliation: Forerunner to Printed Page-Numbers?', *Gutenberg-Jahrbuch* 63 (1988): 54–70.

9 The idea that early printing represents the cradle days of the press endures in the term *incunabla* used by historians to refer to any book printed before the beginning of the sixteenth century. In Latin the word means *swaddling-clothes*, so these are printed books in their cradle dress.

10 There is some controversy about this claim since, within a year or so of Schöffer's text, an almost identical edition of the work, with the same preface and the same index, was issued from the press of Johann Mentelin of Strasbourg. Since neither book is dated, there is no definitive way of knowing which is the original and which the pirate. Fred Householder, however, comes down convincingly on the side of Schöffer. Fred. W. Householder, 'The First Pirate', *The Library*, 4.24 (1943–4): 30–46.

11 See Hans H. Wellisch, 'The Oldest Printed Indexes', *The Indexer* 15.2 (1986): 73–82 (78).

12 [amplissimam eius tabulam alphabeticam magno cum studio elaboratam . . . Que quidem tabula et figura, toto ipsius libri precio, digne sunt habende, quia reddunt ipsum, ad sui usum expediciorem.] St Augustine, *De arte praedicandi* (Mainz, *c.* 1464), sig. 1v.

13 [nota tibi in extremitate libri arithmeticis numeris singulas chartas.] Giovanni Craston, *Dictionarium graecum copiosissimum secundum ordinem alphabeti cum interpretatione latina* (Venice: Aldus Manutius, 1497), sig. O4v. I am grateful to Maria Tavoni for identifying this text. Maria Gioia Tavoni, *Circumnavigare il testo: Gli indici in età moderna* (Napoli: Liguori, 2009), p. 28.

14 See Ann Blair, *Too Much to Know: Managing Scholarly Information Before the Modern Age* (New Haven, CT: Yale University Press, 2010), pp. 137–40.

15 The text is from Gessner's *Pandectae* (1548). The translation is that of Hans H. Wellisch, 'How to Make an Index – 16th

Century Style: Conrad Gessner on Indexes and Catalogs', *International Classification* 8 (1981): 10–15 (11).

Chapter 4: The Map or the Territory

1 J. Michael Lennon, 'The Naked and the Read', *Times Literary Supplement*, 7 March 2018.

2 [eos plerique solos legunt.] Erasmus, *In Elenchum Alberti Pii brevissima scholia per eundem Erasmum Roterodamum* (Basel: Froben, 1532), sig. m2r.

3 [Perlege, quae sequitur tabulam mi candide lector, / Qua duce mox totum mente tenebis opus. / Primus scriptus habet numerus caput: inde libellum / Accipe: particulam tercia cifra notat.] *Lucii Flori Bellorum Romanorum libri quattuor* (Vienna, 1511). I am grateful to Kyle Conrau-Lewis at Yale for bringing this passage to my attention.

4 Peter Frarin, *An Oration against the Unlawfull Insurrections of the Protestantes of our Time*, trans. by JoÙ Fowler (Antwerp, 1567), sig. Kiiv.

5 James Howell, *Proedria Basilike: A Discourse Concerning the Precedency of Kings* (London, 1664), p. 219.

6 It sounds even worse in the Latin edition that followed later in the same year. Here the bookseller's note lands finally on a Greek term – '& hac ratione Posticum esset aedificio ἀσύμμετρον' – just in case anyone failed to catch the high-handedness. (James Howell, *Proedria basilike: dissertatio de præcedentia regum* (London, 1664), p. 359.)

7 Jorge Luis Borges, 'On Exactitude in Science', in *Collected Fictions*, trans. by Andrew Hurley (London: Penguin, 1998), p. 325.

8 *Grub Street Journal* 318 (29 January 1736).

9 Henry Billingsley's 1570 translation of Euclid uses manicules for the page signatures of its front matter (☞i, ☞ii, ☞iii, etc.), which makes citing specific pages from Billingsley's preface in a modern footnote look bizarre!

10 Christopher Marlowe – one of Shakespeare's great influences and a possible early collaborator – also uses the image of the index in this sense in his long poem *Hero and Leander*: 'Therefore even as an index to a book, / So to his mind was young Leander's look' (II.129–30). In other words, Leander's thoughts were written all over his face, but the precedence – the face is in front – is already there.

11 Olga Weijers discusses this looseness of terminology in her monograph *Dictionnaires et répertoires: Une étude de vocabulaire* (Turnhout: Brepols, 1991), pp. 100–110.

12 Plato, *Euthyphro, Apology, Crito, Phaedo, Phaedrus*, trans. by Harold North Fowler (Cambridge, MA: Harvard University Press, 2014).

Chapter 5: 'Let No Damned Tory Index My History!'

1 D. B. Wyndham Lewis and Charles Lee (eds.), *The Stuffed Owl: An Anthology of Bad Verse* (London: J. M. Dent, 1930), p. 256; Francis Wheen, *How Mumbo-Jumbo Conquered the World* (London: Harper, 2004); Hugh Trevor-Roper, *Catholics, Anglicans and Puritans: 17th Century Essays* (London: Secker & Warburg, 1987), p. 302. For more examples of index humour in contemporary books, Paula Clarke Bain's indexing blog – http:// baindex.org – is a wonderfully funny resource.

2 Jonathan Swift, *A Tale of a Tub* (London, 1704), pp. 138–9.

3 Jonathan Swift, 'A Discourse Concerning the Mechanical Operation of the Spirit', in *A Tale of a Tub* (London, 1704), pp. 283–325 (p. 315).

4 Alexander Pope, *The Dunciad in Four Books* (1743), p. 69 (I. 279–80).

5 Charles Boyle, *Dr Bentley's Dissertations on the Epistles of Phalaris, Examin'd* (London: T. Bennet, 1698) (Oxford, Bodleian Library, Vet. A3 e.1743). Macaulay, incidentally, was an inveterate marker-upper of his books. On every page – whether he had something to say or not – he would trace a vertical pencil line down the margin to show how far he had read.

6 ['Richardum quendam Bentleium Virum in volvendis Lexicis satis diligentem'.] *Fabularum Aesopicarum Delectus*, ed. by Anthony Alsop (Oxford: Sheldonian Theatre, 1698), sig. a4r.

7 Interestingly, the *OED* dates the phrase *to look something up* as emerging at around this time, giving the first instance as 1692.

8 William Temple, 'An Essay upon the Ancient and Modern Learning', in *Miscellanea, the Second Part. In Four Essays* (London: Ri. and Ra. Simpson, 1690), pp. 1–72 (p. 59).

9 Richard Bentley, *A Dissertation upon the Epistles of Phalaris, Themistocles, Socrates, Euripides, and Others, and the Fables of Aesop* (London: Peter Buck, 1697), p. 16.

10 Atterbury, in a letter to Boyle, speaks of 'laying the design of the book [and] writing above half of it', while William Warburton, half a century later, gives the names of the other conspirators, having learned them from Pope who had been 'let into the secret'. (Francis Atterbury, *The Epistolary Correspondence, Visitation Charges, Speeches, and Miscellanies, of the Right Reverend Francis Atterbury, D.D., Lord Bishop of Rochester*, vol. 2 (London: J. Nichols, 1783), pp. 21–2.) The other two conspirators were exposed many years later by William Warburton. (Letter to Richard Hurd (19 August, 1749), William Warburton, *Letters from a Late Eminent Prelate to One of His Friends* (London: T. Cadell and W. Davies, 1793), p. 9.)

11 Solomon Whateley, *An Answer to a Late Book Written against the Learned and Reverend Dr. Bentley Relating to Some Manuscript Notes on Callimachus, Together with an Examination of Mr. Bennet's Appendix to the Said Book* (London, 1699).

12 Thomas Macaulay, 'Life and Writings of William Temple', *Edinburgh Review* 68 (1838): 113–87 (184).

13 This claim has been repeated enough – everywhere from Isaac D'Israeli to the *Encyclopedia Britannica* – for us to let it stand as true. Earlier claimants, however, exist in Joseph Hall's *Mundus alter et idem* (1605) – which King certainly had read – and Annibale Caro's *Apologia contra Lodovico Castelvetro* (1558) – which Bentley knew of but speculates that his tormentors did not.

14 King's text is a pseudo-translation, appearing not under his own name but as the work of one Martin Sorbiere, a combination of Lister's first name and the surname of Samuel de Sorbière, whose unflattering portrayal of London in *Relation d'un voyage en Angleterre* (1664) earned him four months in prison.

15 William King, *A Journey to London in the Year 1698 after the Ingenuous Method of That Made by Dr. Martin Lyster to Paris in the Same Year, &c.* (London: A. Baldwin, 1699).

16 Letter from Henry Oldenburg to René Sluse, 2 April 1669. *The Correspondence of Henry Oldenburg*, ed. by A. Rupert Hall and Marie Boas Hall, vol. 5 (Madison, WI: University of Wisconsin Press, 1965), pp. 469–70.

17 William King, *The Transactioneer, with Some of His Philosophical Fancies: In Two Dialogues* (London, 1700), sig. a3r.

18 Ja. Newton, 'An Account of Some Effects of Papaver Corniculatum Luteum, Etc.', *Philosophical Transactions* 20 (1698): 263–4.

19 King, *Transactioneer*, pp. 39–41.

20 By the early nineteenth century, Bromley's copy had come into the possession of the Whig writer and schoolmaster Samuel Parr. The transcription of Bromley's annotation comes from Henry G. Bohn, *Bibliotheca Parriana: A Catalogue of the Library of the Late Reverend and Learned Samuel Parr, LL.D., Curate of Hatton, Prebendary of St. Paul's, &c. &c.* (London: John Bohn and Joseph Mawman, 1827), pp. 702–3.

21 John Oldmixon, *History of England, during the Reigns of King William and Queen Mary, Queen Anne, King George I., Being the Sequel to the Reigns of the Stuarts* (London: Thomas Cox, 1735), p. 345.

22 *A Table of the Principal Matters Contained in Mr. Addison's Remarks on Several Parts of Italy, &c in the Years 1701, 1702, 1703* (London, 1705).

23 *A Table of All the Accurate Remarks and Surprising Discoveries of the Most Learned and Ingenious Mr. Addison in his Book of Travels thro Several Parts of Italy, &c.* (London, 1706).

24 C. E. Doble et al. (eds.), *Remarks and Collections of Thomas Hearne*, 11 vols. (Oxford: Oxford Historical Society, 1885), IV, p. 45.

25 Samuel Johnson, *Lives of the English Poets*, 10 vols. (London: J. Nichols, 1779), IV, sig. b1r–v.

26 John Gay, 'The Present State of Wit, in a Letter to a Friend in the Country', in John Gay, *Poetry and Prose*, ed. by V. A. Dearing, 2 vols. (Oxford: Oxford University Press, 1975), II, p. 449.

27 John Gay, *The Shepherd's Week. In Six Pastorals* (London: R. Burleigh, 1714), sig. E7v. The fact that the model for *The Shepherd's Week* is Edmund Spenser's *The Shepheardes Calender* (1579), which was published with often ironic glosses by 'E. K.' (possibly Spenser himself), gives licence to Gay's paratextual play.

28 John Gay, *Trivia: Or, the Art of Walking the Streets of London* (London: Bernard Lintott, 1716), pp. 35–6.

29 Alexander Pope, *Dunciad Variorum* (London, 1735), pp. 158–60 (II.271–78).

30 Letter to Jacob Tonson, Sr, 30 December 1719. London, British Library, Add. MS 28275 f. 78.

31 Letter to Jacob Tonson, Jr, 9 November 1717. *The Letters, Life, and Works of JoÙ Oldmixon: Politics and Professional Authorship in Early Hanoverian England*, ed. by Pat Rogers (Lampeter: Edwin Mellen, 2004), pp. 48–9.

32 *The Index-Writer* (London: J. Wilford, 1729), p. 2.

33 Laurence Echard, *The History of England*, 3 vols. (London: Jacob Tonson, 1707–18) III, p. 779.

34 *The Index-Writer*, p. 5.

35 Echard, *History of England*, III, pp. 863–4.

36 *The Index-Writer*, pp. 19–20.

37 JoÙ Oldmixon, *Memoirs of the Press, Historical and Political, for Thirty Years Past, from 1710 to 1740* (London: T. Cox, 1742), p. 35.

38 *The Mathematician, Containing many Curious Dissertations on the Rise, Progress, and Improvement of Geometry* (London: JoÙ Wilcox, 1751), p. iv. The original observation of how this work inverts Pope's intention comes from Robin Valenza, 'How Literature Becomes Knowledge: A Case Study', *ELH* 76.1 (2009): 215–45.

Chapter 6: Indexing Fictions

1 'Adventures of a Quire of Paper', *London Magazine, or Gentleman's Monthly Intelligencer* 48.8 (August 1779): 355–8 (355).

2 Joseph Addison, *Spectator* 10 (12 March 1711).

3 The Multigraph Collective, *Interactions with Print: Elements of Reading in the Era of Print Saturation* (Chicago, IL: University of Chicago Press, 2018).

4 Benjamin Franklin, *The Private Life of Benjamin Franklin LL.D* (London: J. Parsons, 1793), p. 19.

5 Leigh Hunt, 'Upon Indexes', *The Indicator* 52 (4 October 1820).

6 Henry Wheatley, *What Is an Index?* (London: Index Society, 1878), p. 42.

7 The remark is recorded by JoÙ Hawkins in an editorial footnote to JoÙson's 'Life of Pope'. In Hawkins' telling, Pope and Bentley run into each other at a dinner where Pope attempts to solicit praise for his translation from Bentley, who tries in vain to change the subject before awkwardly giving his verdict. *The Works of Samuel JoÙson, LL.D.*, 11 vols. (London, 1787), XI, p. 184n.

8 Alexander Pope, *A further account of the most deplorable condition of Mr. Edmund Curll, Bookseller* (London, 1716), pp. 14–15.

9 Letter to Robert Digby, 1 May 1720, *Letters of Mr. Alexander Pope, and Several of his Friends* (London: J. Wright, 1737) pp. 179–80.

10 Anna Laetitia Barbauld (ed.), *The Correspondence of Samuel Richardson*, 6 vols. (Cambridge: Cambridge University Press, 2011), V, pp. 281–2.

11 Samuel Richardson, *Letters and Passages Restored from the Original Manuscripts of the History of Clarissa, to which is subjoined A Collection of such of the Moral and Instructive Sentiments, Cautions, Aphorisms, Reflections and Observations contained in the History as are presumed to be of General Use and Service, Digested under Proper Heads* (London, 1751), p. vi.

12 Richardson, *Letters and Passages*, p. vi.

13 Letter to Mr de Freval, 21 January 1751, in Barbauld, *Correspondence of Samuel Richardson*, V, pp. 271–2.

14 Samuel Richardson, 'Preface', in *Clarissa, or The History of a Young Lady*, 3rd edn, 8 vols. (London, 1751), I, p. ix.

15 Letter from Dr JoÙson, 26 September 1753, in Barbauld, *Correspondence of Samuel Richardson*, V, p. 284.

16 Letter to Lady Echlin, 7 July 1755, in Barbauld, *Correspondence of Samuel Richardson*, V, p. 48.

17 Samuel Richardson, *A Collection of the Moral and Instructive Sentiments, Maxims, Cautions and Reflections, Contained in the Histories*

of Pamela, Clarissa, and Sir Charles Grandison (London, 1755), pp. vi–vii.

18 Richardson, *Collection of the Moral and Instructive Sentiments*, p. ix, Richardson's italics.

19 Letter from Lady Echlin, 2 September 1755, in Barbauld, *Correspondence of Samuel Richardson*, V, p. 53.

20 Letter to Lady Echlin, 7 July 1755, in Barbauld, *Correspondence of Samuel Richardson*, V, p. 48. Johnson, who certainly did use the *Collection*, decidedly preferred the instruction to the story, declaring to Thomas Erskine, 'Why, Sir, if you were to read Richardson for the story, your impatience would be so much fretted that you would hang yourself. But you must read him for the sentiment, and consider the story as only giving occasion to the sentiment.' (James Boswell, *Life of Johnson* (Oxford: Oxford University Press, 1998), p. 480.)

21 Isaac D'Israeli, *Curiosities of Literature*, 5th edn, 2 vols. (London: JoÙ Murray, 1807), II, p. 406, D'Israeli's italics.

22 Samuel JoÙson, 'Preface', in *A Dictionary of the English Language* (London, 1755), p. 7.

23 JoÙson, 'Preface', p. 7.

24 See William R. Keast, 'The Two *Clarissa*s in JoÙson's *Dictionary*', *Studies in Philology* 54.3 (1957): 429–39.

25 Robin Valenza, 'How Literature Becomes Knowledge: A Case Study', *ELH* 76.1 (2009): 215–45 (222).

26 Boswell, *Life of JoÙson*, p. 1368n.

Chapter 7: 'A Key to All Knowledge'

1 [Qui sondera cet abîme? qui pourra jamais trouver le temps d'étudier tous ces Pères, et de lire leurs écrits de toute sorte?]

Jacques-Paul Migne, 'Avis important', *Patrologia Latina*, CCXVIII, sig. a1v.

2 [plus de cinquante hommes travaillant aux Tables pendant plus de dix ans, quoique avec la faible retribution de 1000 francs par homme et par an.] Migne, 'Avis important', sig. a1v.

3 [donnent plus de 500,000 francs, sans compter tous les frais d'impression.] Migne, 'Avis important', sig. a1r.

4 [Après tout cela, n'avons-nous pas le droit de nous écrier: Que sont les douze Travaux d'Hercule auprès de nos 231 Tables; Que sont tous les autres travaux littéraires! Que sont les Encyclopédies du XVIIIe et XIXe siècle! Que sont tous les autres oeuvres typographiques! Des jeux d'enfant, dont le plus grand n'est rien auprès de nôtre. Nous pouvons dire, sans crainte d'être démenti, que jamais aucune grande Publication n'aura été ainsi remuée pour la commodité du Souscripteur. En effet, parmi les Ouvrages qui, jusqu'à ce jour, ont offert le plus grand nombre de Tables, nous ne connaissons que la *Bibliotheca Maxima Patrum* de Marguerin de la Bigne, et la *Summa Theologica* de Saint Thomas par Nicolaï, lesquelles toutefois n'en comptent chacune que dix. Notre *Patrologie* au contraire a été en quelque sorte pressurée et tourmentée comme le raisin sous le pressoir pour que la moindre goutte de la précieuse liqueur ne pût échapper.] Migne, 'Avis important', sigs. a1r–a1v.

5 [Nos Tables ont frayé le chemin; elles aplanissent les montagnes et rendent droits les sentiers les plus tortueux . . . A l'aide de nos Tables, ce grand Cours devient petit; les distances se rapprochent, le premier et le dernier volume se touchent . . . Quelle économie de temps! c'est plus que le chemin de fer, et même que le ballon, c'est l'électricité!] Migne, 'Avis important', sig. a1v.

6 'The Librarians' Conference', *The Times*, 2 October 1877, p. 4.

7 J. Ashton Cross, 'A Universal Index of Subjects', in *Transactions and Proceedings of the Conference of Librarians Held in London, October 1877*, eds. Edward B. Nicholson and Henry R. Tedder (London: Chiswick, 1878), pp. 104–7 (p. 107).

8 Cross, 'Universal Index', p. 105.

9 'Proceedings of the Conference of Librarians, Fourth Sitting', in Nicholson and Tedder, pp. 159–64 (p. 163).

10 'The Conference of Librarians', *Athenaeum* 2607 (13 October 1877): 467–8 (467).

11 Cross, 'Universal Index', p. 107.

12 Index Society, *First Annual Report of the Committee* (London: Index Society), p. 3.

13 'Literary Gossip', *Athenaeum* 2610 (3 November 1877): 566–7 (567).

14 Index Society, *First Annual Report*, p. 16.

15 Henry Wheatley, *How to Make an Index* (London: Eliot Stock, 1902), p. 210.

16 William Poole, 'Preface', in *An Index to Periodical Literature* (Boston, MA: James R. Osgood, 1882), p. iii.

17 Poole, 'Preface' (1882), p. iii.

18 William Poole, 'Preface' in *An Alphabetical Index to Subjects Treated in the Reviews, and Other Periodicals, to which No Indexes have been Published; Prepared for the Library of the Brothers in Unity, Yale College* (New York: George P. Putnam, 1848), p. iv.

19 Poole, 'Preface' (1848), p. iv.

20 Poole, 'Preface' (1882), p. v.

Chapter 8: Ludmilla and Lotaria

1 On 28 August 2018, @realDonaldTrump tweeted, 'Google search results for "Trump News" shows only the viewing/

reporting of Fake News Media. In other words, they have it RIGGED, for me & others, so that almost all stories & news is BAD. Fake CNN is prominent. Republican/Conservative & Fair Media is shut out. Illegal? 96% of results on "Trump News" are from National Left-Wing Media, very dangerous. Google & others are suppressing voices of Conservatives and hiding information and news that is good. They are controlling what we can & cannot see. This is a very serious situation – will be addressed!'

2 A statistical study by *The Economist* the year after Trump's tweet found 'no evidence of ideological bias in the search engine's news tab'. ('Seek and You Shall Find', *The Economist* (8 June 2019).)

3 Rouse and Rouse, 'La Naissance des index', p. 85. In the same article, the Rouses also outline the career of an early named indexer, Jean Hautfuney, who, around 1320, advanced his career by compiling a vast index to the *Speculum historiale* of Vincent of Beauvais. A fuller treatment of Hautfuney's index can be found in Anna-Dorothee von den Brincken, 'Tabula Alphabetica von den Alfängen alphabetischer Registerarbeiten zu Geschichtswerken', *Festschrift für Hermann Heimpel* (Göttingen: Vandenhoeck & Ruprecht, 1972), 900–923.

4 Letter to Vita Sackville-West, 29 March 1926, *The Letters of Virginia Woolf*, ed. by Nigel Nicolson and Joanne Trautmann, 6 vols. (London: Hogarth, 1977), III, p. 251.

5 Letter to Vita Sackville-West, 25 July 1928, Woolf, *Letters*, III, p. 514.

6 Entry for 13 June 1940, *The Diary of Virginia Woolf*, ed. by Anne Olivier Bell and Andrew McNeillie, 6 vols. (London: Hogarth, 1977), V, p. 295.

7 [Porro methodus qua quis brevissimo tempore et ordine optimo indices conficiat, huiusmodi est. Quaecumque in

indicem referre libuerit, omnia ut primum se obtulerint, nulla ordinis ratione habita in charta describantur, ab altera tantum facie, ut altera nuda relinquatur ... Tandem omnia descripta forfice dissecabis, dissecta quo volueris ordine divides, primum in maiores partes, deinde subdivides semel aut iterum, vel quotiescunque opus fuerit. Aliqui dissectis omnibus, demum disponunt: alij inter dissecandum statim primam divisionem perficiunt, dum singulas schedulas in fine singularum dissectionis mucrone forficis apprehensas digerunt per diversa mensae loca, aut vascula per mensam disposita. Ubi plurimae schedulae fuerint, saepius subdividere suaserim: sic enim omnia facilius et minori confusione peragentur ... atque ita partem primam subdividendo in ordinem quem volveris reducito: ordinatam vel statim describito si opus sit: vel si prima descriptio satis bene habeat, quod potius fuerit, agglutinato tantum, glutine ex farina: cui si ullam xylocollam aut fabrile glutinum miscueris.] Conrad Gessner, *Pandectae* (Zurich, 1548), ff. 19v–20r.

8 [Extabant etiam alias apud nostros Sanjacobeos Parisienses cod. fol. par. memb. eleganti, sed arcae librorum custos imprudens bibliopegis tradidit quo ad concinnandos libros uterentur: ejusque adhuc quaedam folia in eadem bibliotheca videri possunt ad initium & finem codicis MS quo sermones S. Bernardi de B. Virgine continentur a 150 annis circiter compacti.] Jacob Quétif and Jacob Echard, *Scriptores ordinis praedicatorum recensiti*, 2 vols. (Paris, 1719), I, p. 203.

9 See Josephine Miles, *Poetry, Teaching, and Scholarship* (Berkeley, CA: University of California Press, 1980), p. 124.

10 For more on Miles and the creation of the Dryden concordance, see Rachel Sagner Buurma and Laura Heffernan, 'Search and Replace: Josephine Miles and the Origins of Distant Reading', *Modernism/Modernity Print Plus* 3.1 (April 2018).

11 Susan Artandi, 'Automatic Book Indexing by Computer', *American Documentation* 15.4 (1964): 250–57 (250).

12 Artandi, 'Automatic Book Indexing': 251.

13 Harold Borko, 'Experiments in Book Indexing by Computer', *Information Storage and Retrieval* 6.1 (1970): 5–16 (6).

14 Borko, 'Experiments in Book Indexing': 12.

15 Borko, 'Experiments in Book Indexing': 15.

16 Matthew L. Jockers, 'The Rest of the Story' (25 February 2015):http://www.matthewjockers.net/2015/02/25/the-rest-of-the-story/.

17 Chris Messina, 'Groups for Twitter; or A Proposal for Twitter Tag Channels' (25 August 2007): https://factoryjoe.com/2007/08/25/groups-for-twitter-or-a-proposal-for-twitter-tag-channels/.

18 Larry Page, 'G is for Google' (10 August 2015): https://abc.xyz.

19 Roger Montti, 'Google BERT Update – What it Means', *Search Engine Journal* (25 October 2019): https://www.searchenginejournal.com/google-bert-update/332161/#close.

20 William S. Heckscher, 'The Unconventional Index and Its Merits', *The Indexer* 13.1 (1982): 6–25 (25).

21 Robert Latham and William Mathews (eds.), *The Diary of Samuel Pepys*, 11 vols. (London: Bell & Hyman, 1983), XI, p. 8.

22 Of the indexers advertising their services on the Society's website as at August 2019, women outnumber men by four to one (134 to 31). Meanwhile, a 2016 survey by the American Society for Indexing reported that 90 per cent of respondents were women (https://www.asindexing.org/professional-activities-salary-survey/). For an excellent biographical treatment of Nancy Bailey, founder in 1892 of the first indexing agency for women, see David A. Green, 'The Wonderful Woman Indexer of England: Nancy Bailey', *The Indexer* 32.4 (2014): 155–60.

Another agency was opened shortly afterwards by Mary Petherbridge, author of *The TecÙique of Indexing* (London: Secretarial Bureau, 1904).

Coda

1 It is sometimes fun to play the same game with real books. The index to Ralph Walker's introduction to Immanuel Kant includes 'happiness, 137, 151, 152, 156–8', 'masturbation, 158, 190' and 'wig-making, 158'. Walker's text is exemplary, but page 158 will always be more delightful in the mind than it is in real life. (Ralph C. S. Walker, *Kant: The Arguments of the Philosophers* (London: Routledge & Kegan Paul, 1982).)
2 Witte de With Centre for Contemporary Art, 'Alejandro Cesarco: A Solo Exhibition': https://www.fkawdw.nl/en/our_program/exhibitions/alejandro_cesarco_a_solo_exhibition.

List of Figures

Acknowledgements

The similarities between publishing a book and cycling the Tour de France have so far, I think, gone unremarked. The long procession broken into stages or chapters, some with significant peaks, others flat-out time trials before the teaching term begins; the gruelling, *hors catégorie* uphill of the last push before submission, followed by the thrilling, breakneck run-in towards publication. I'm surprised more hasn't been made of this. Most of all, though, both events manage to pull off a slightly shifty apportionment of acclaim: both are team pursuits in which one person seems to take all the credit at the end. It is no exaggeration to say that this book simply wouldn't have been written without the generosity, support and expertise of a great many people. The following acknowledgements are really just the tip of the ice bath.

The research that went into this book was made possible thanks to fellowships from the British Academy, the Bodleian Library, Cambridge University Library, and the Folger Shakespeare Library. As well as funding me and giving me a space to work in, not to mention housing and conserving the manuscripts and printed books on which this research is principally based, these libraries were also vital in subtler ways. Through seminars and printing workshops and coffee mornings (not to mention the Folger's famous three o'clock tea) they have provided a limitless resource in the form of useful leads offered genially, over a biscuit, by librarians or by other researchers. I suspect that most of the material in this book comes via those conversations. Long may the library tradition of communal coffee continue.

As for individuals, I should thank first of all Alexandra Franklin of the Bodleian Centre for the Study of the Book, who rescued this project when it seemed unlikely to survive infancy, and whose support has been a constant throughout. Also at the Bodleian, Richard Ovenden for having me back for a second stint. Jill Whitelock, Suzanne Paul and Emily Dourish were all instrumental in making my time in Cambridge a joyful and productive one, helping me to find my way around backstage in the UL's stacks, while the Electors of the Munby Fellowship were responsible for making it happen at all. Meanwhile, I am grateful to the staff and Fellows of Jesus and St Peter's Colleges, Oxford and Darwin College, Cambridge for sharing their food, their wine and their expertise with me during my spells with them.

Thanks are due to Anna Webber and Seren Adams at United Agents, for their belief – astonishing to me – that a history of indexes might be of interest to more than a handful of academics. Without their vision and encouragement this would be a *very* different book. To Cecilia Stein at Penguin for first taking the work on, for her careful reading and judicious excisions, and for her patience when suddenly the deadline slipped. And to the fantastic Chloe Currens for picking things up where Cecilia left off. I couldn't have wished for a kinder, wiser or more tactful editor as we worked through the last drafts together and moved through the gears in the final downhill to publication. Also at Penguin I'm grateful to Aniké Wildman, to Ania Gordon and Fiona Livesey, to David Watson, Richard Duguid and Chris Shaw, to Francisca Monteiro, to Emma Brown and to Katy Banyard.

In these late stages it becomes more clear than ever just how many people are involved in bringing a book out.

On the off-chance that you are reading these acknowledgements before starting on the rest of the book, a spoiler alert: Chapter 4 tackles an underdiscussed truism, namely that reading a book is a significant investment of one's precious time. Real thanks are due, then, to my brilliant friends – Jacqueline Norton, Adam Smyth, Gill Partington, Olivia Smith and Tom Templeton – who read the whole book in its early drafts and whose thoughtful and expert suggestions improved it immeasurably. Similarly, to Isabel Davis, Paulina Kewes, Heather Tilley, Joseph Hone, Laura Salisbury and Abigail Williams, all of whom read and commented on sections of the work during its long gestation.

The Society of Indexers have been infinitely patient with me as I've trespassed on their professional patch. If the work you are holding can be distilled to a single piece of advice, let it be this: if you've written a non-fiction book, you should hire an SoI indexer. The Society are represented in the back pages here by the estimable Paula Clarke Bain, who manages to combine all the erudition and punctiliousness one would expect from a professional indexer with a wicked sense of humour.

Finally, my family, who, through every crisis – domestic or global – of the last few years, have been an inexhaustible well of humour, kindness and wisdom. Mum, Dad, Mia, Molly, Pete and Shruti, Paul and Soph and Glynis: they're the team you want behind you when you're pedalling up the Mont Ventoux of writing a book. Gratitude, boundless and love, endless, *passim*.

Appendix:
A Computer-generated Index

These are the first few pages of an index compiled automatically using commercial indexing software. The whole table runs to several thousand entries, the intention being that the software supplies an overabundance which a human editor can easily prune back to an appropriate level of detail. Some human tidying would also be necessary – for example, merging the entries for *acrostics*, *Acrosticks* and *acrostic form*, or placing *ABC Murders, The* under *Christie, Agatha*. Some obvious – and surely forgivable – errors jump out: mistaking signature marks (Aii, Aiii, Aiv) for words, for example, or breaking up different forms of the Latin *abyssus*. And when the software tries to pick out phrases rather than single words, the results are generally more amusing than useful: *absolutely necessary*, *age sticking*, *all the letters*. Meanwhile, the squall of entries around the topic of alphabets would take some serious work to tease out. More seriously, some subjects are notable by their absence. The 'Adventures of a Quire of Paper' has gone missing. (In fact it has been rolled up under the word *adventure* which I used, once, to describe the first Sherlock Holmes novel.) The emergence of indexing agencies in the 1890s is only glancingly referenced towards the end of Chapter 8, but this is an important topic with supplementary reading supplied in the endnotes. *Agencies, indexing* should be in the index. And so on.

As an indexing aid, then, the software is a mixed bag. On

the one hand, by casting its net so widely, it successfully manages to pull together a considerable swathe of the book's genuine subject matter. On the other hand – and partly because of the hyper-exhaustiveness of its method – it is still reliant on a lot of human labour downstream. What's more, the items that slip through the net put one in mind of Caxton's proviso from over half a millennium ago:

> And over and above these that be conteyned in this sayd table is many a notable commaundement / lernynge and counceylle moche prouffitable whiche is not sette in the sayd regystre or rubrysshe.

American School, 277
American Society, 139
amour, 48–49

amused responses, 256
amusement, 180
    mere, 198

That will do. Let *amusement, mere* serve as a reminder that this is not our real index. The time has come, at last, to hand the stage over to Paula Clarke Bain, our human indexer, to bring an end to the proceedings, and to show how things should be done.

Index

Note to the gentle Reader: Page numbers in *italic* indicate figures. Page numbers in the form 273n1 indicate endnotes. Entries are sorted in letter-by-letter order, except where noted. This index was created by Paula Clarke Bain, who is a professional indexer and a human being. [PCB]